DYNAMITE ENTERTAINMENT PRESENTS

JIM STARLIN'S
ID KOSMO
COSMIC GUARD

DYNAMITE ENTERTAINMENT PRESENTS

JIM STARLIN'S
KID KOSMOS
— COSMIC GUARD —

Writer/Artist
JIM STARLIN

Colorist
JUNE CHUNG

Letterer
RICH WENZKE

For more on Kid Kosmos, visit WWW.DYNAMITEENTERTAINMENT.COM.

DYNAMITE ENTERTAINMENT

NICK BARRUCCI — PRESIDENT
JUAN COLLADO — CHIEF OPERATING OFFICER
JOSEPH RYBANDT — DIRECTOR OF MARKETING
JOSH JOHNSON — CREATIVE DIRECTOR
JASON ULLMEYER — GRAPHIC DESIGNER

To find a comic shop in your area, call the
comic shop locator service toll-free at
1-888-266-4226

First Printing
ISBN-10: 1-933305-02-9   ISBN-13: 9-781933-305028
10 9 8 7 6 5 4 3 2 1

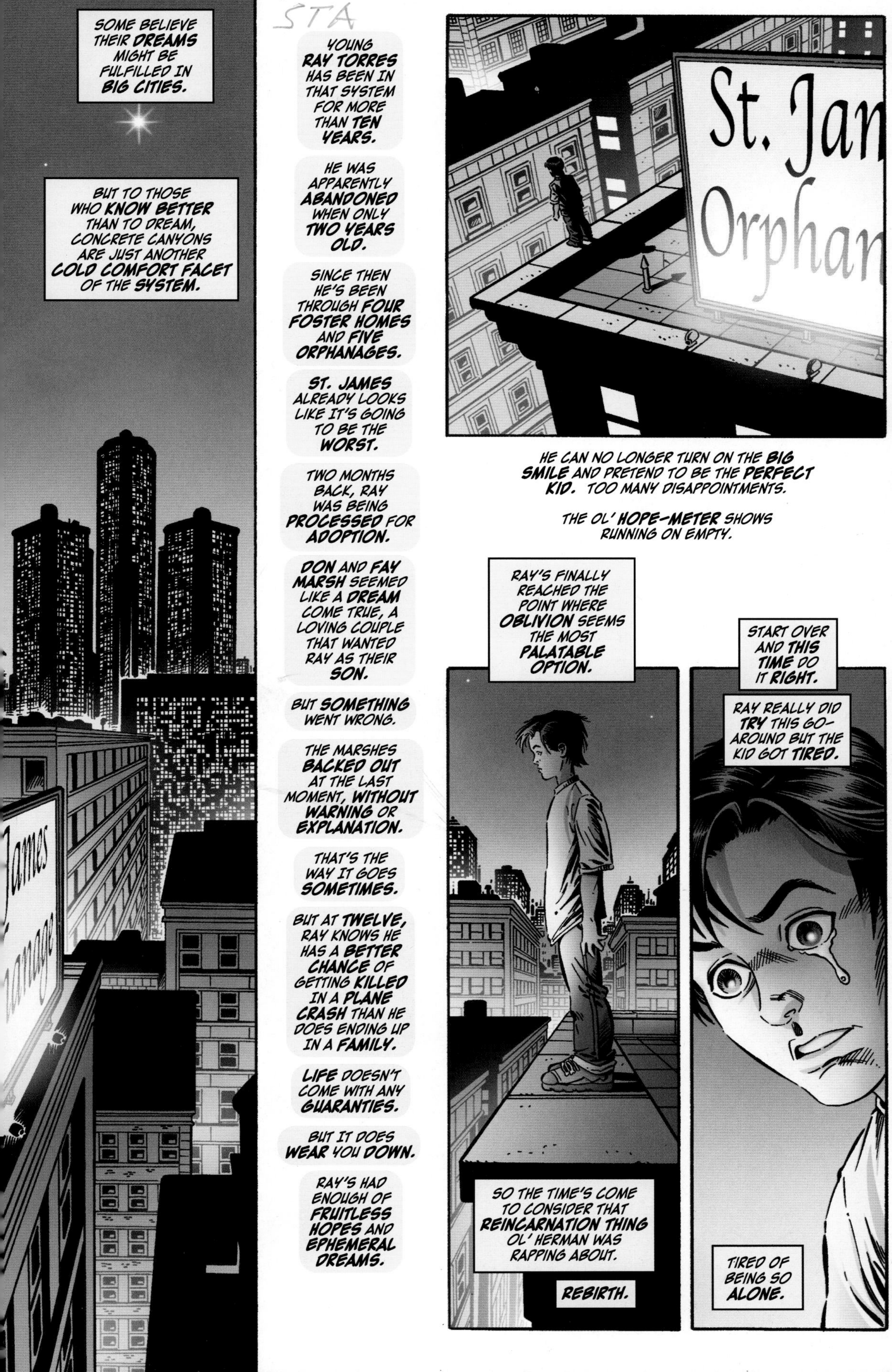
SOME BELIEVE THEIR DREAMS MIGHT BE FULFILLED IN BIG CITIES.
BUT TO THOSE WHO KNOW BETTER THAN TO DREAM, CONCRETE CANYONS ARE JUST ANOTHER COLD COMFORT FACET OF THE SYSTEM.
James
anage
YOUNG RAY TORRES HAS BEEN IN THAT SYSTEM FOR MORE THAN TEN YEARS.
HE WAS APPARENTLY ABANDONED WHEN ONLY TWO YEARS OLD.
SINCE THEN HE'S BEEN THROUGH FOUR FOSTER HOMES AND FIVE ORPHANAGES.
ST. JAMES ALREADY LOOKS LIKE IT'S GOING TO BE THE WORST.
TWO MONTHS BACK, RAY WAS BEING PROCESSED FOR ADOPTION.
DON AND FAY MARSH SEEMED LIKE A DREAM COME TRUE, A LOVING COUPLE THAT WANTED RAY AS THEIR SON.
BUT SOMETHING WENT WRONG.
THE MARSHES BACKED OUT AT THE LAST MOMENT, WITHOUT WARNING OR EXPLANATION.
THAT'S THE WAY IT GOES SOMETIMES.
BUT AT TWELVE, RAY KNOWS HE HAS A BETTER CHANCE OF GETTING KILLED IN A PLANE CRASH THAN HE DOES ENDING UP IN A FAMILY.
LIFE DOESN'T COME WITH ANY GUARANTIES.
BUT IT DOES WEAR YOU DOWN.
RAY'S HAD ENOUGH OF FRUITLESS HOPES AND EPHEMERAL DREAMS.
St. Jan
Orphan
HE CAN NO LONGER TURN ON THE BIG SMILE AND PRETEND TO BE THE PERFECT KID. TOO MANY DISAPPOINTMENTS.
THE OL' HOPE-METER SHOWS RUNNING ON EMPTY.
RAY'S FINALLY REACHED THE POINT WHERE OBLIVION SEEMS THE MOST PALATABLE OPTION.
SO THE TIME'S COME TO CONSIDER THAT REINCARNATION THING OL' HERMAN WAS RAPPING ABOUT.
REBIRTH.
START OVER AND THIS TIME DO IT RIGHT.
RAY REALLY DID TRY THIS GO-AROUND BUT THE KID GOT TIRED.
TIRED OF BEING SO ALONE.

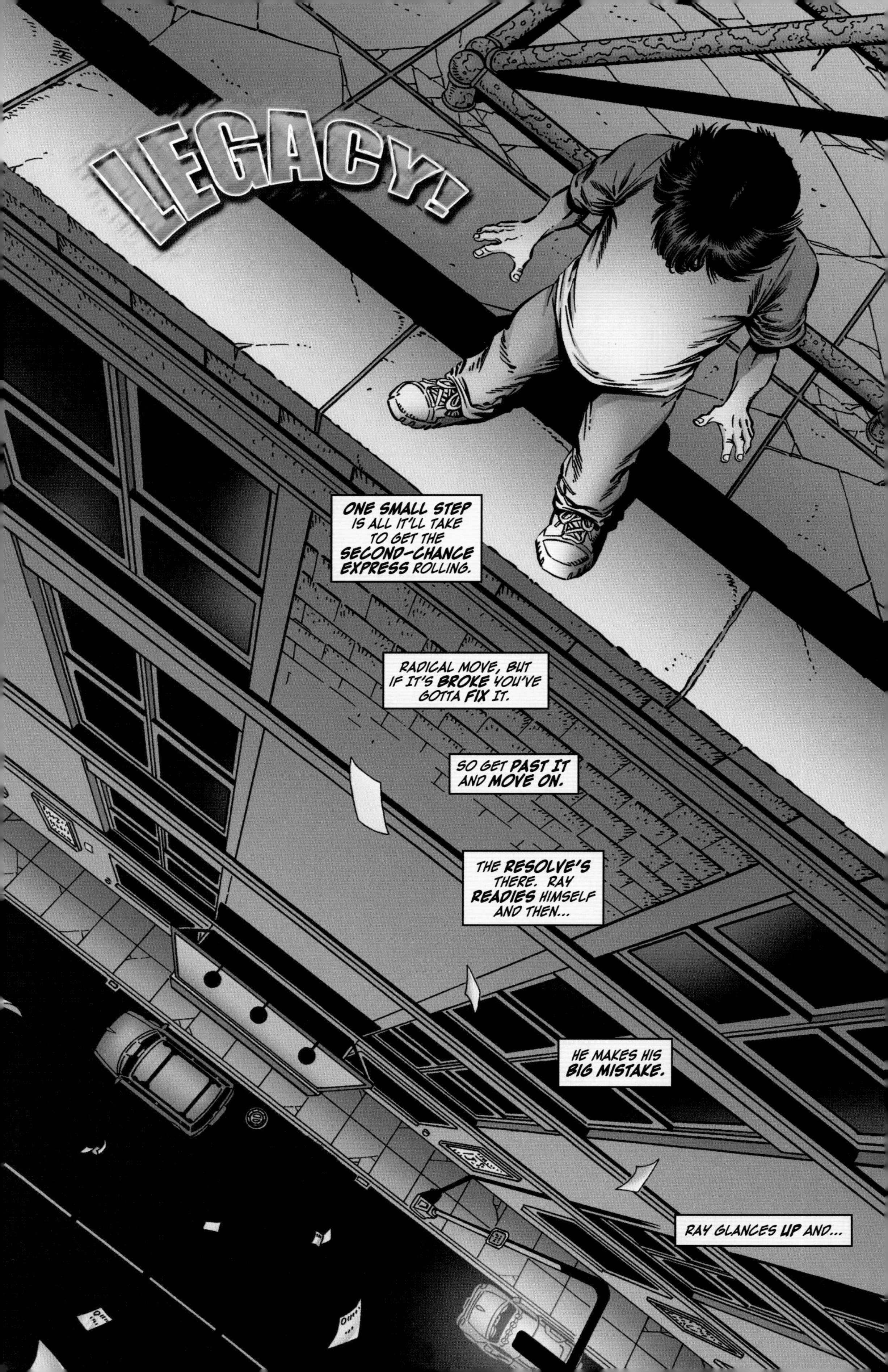
LEGACY!
ONE SMALL STEP IS ALL IT'LL TAKE TO GET THE SECOND-CHANCE EXPRESS ROLLING.
RADICAL MOVE, BUT IF IT'S BROKE YOU'VE GOTTA FIX IT.
SO GET PAST IT AND MOVE ON.
THE RESOLVE'S THERE. RAY READIES HIMSELF AND THEN...
HE MAKES HIS BIG MISTAKE.
RAY GLANCES UP AND...

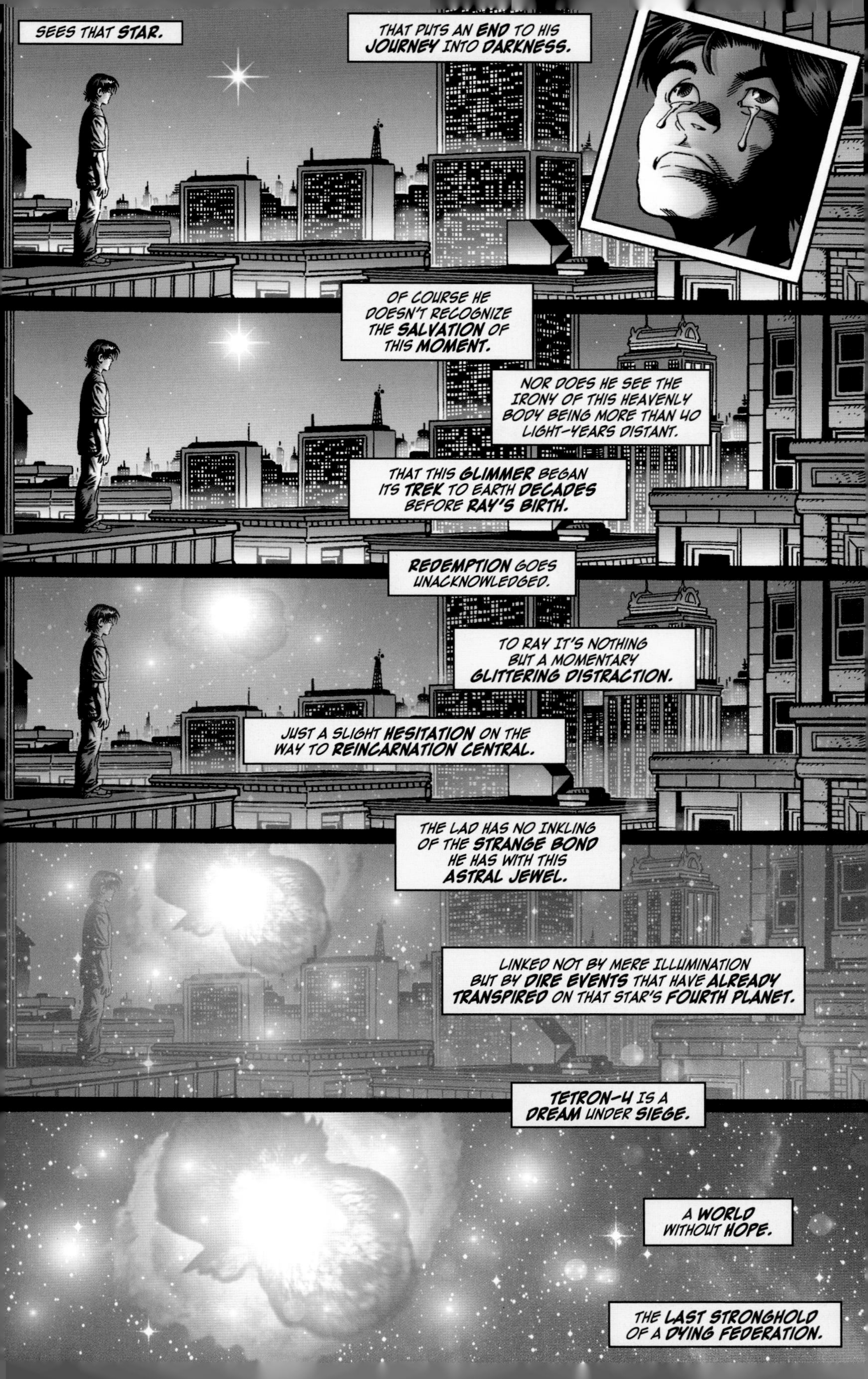
SEES THAT STAR.
THAT PUTS AN END TO HIS JOURNEY INTO DARKNESS.
OF COURSE HE DOESN'T RECOGNIZE THE SALVATION OF THIS MOMENT.
NOR DOES HE SEE THE IRONY OF THIS HEAVENLY BODY BEING MORE THAN 40 LIGHT-YEARS DISTANT.
THAT THIS GLIMMER BEGAN ITS TREK TO EARTH DECADES BEFORE RAY'S BIRTH.
REDEMPTION GOES UNACKNOWLEDGED.
TO RAY IT'S NOTHING BUT A MOMENTARY GLITTERING DISTRACTION.
JUST A SLIGHT HESITATION ON THE WAY TO REINCARNATION CENTRAL.
THE LAD HAS NO INKLING OF THE STRANGE BOND HE HAS WITH THIS ASTRAL JEWEL.
LINKED NOT BY MERE ILLUMINATION BUT BY DIRE EVENTS THAT HAVE ALREADY TRANSPIRED ON THAT STAR'S FOURTH PLANET.
TETRON-4 IS A DREAM UNDER SIEGE.
A WORLD WITHOUT HOPE.
THE LAST STRONGHOLD OF A DYING FEDERATION.

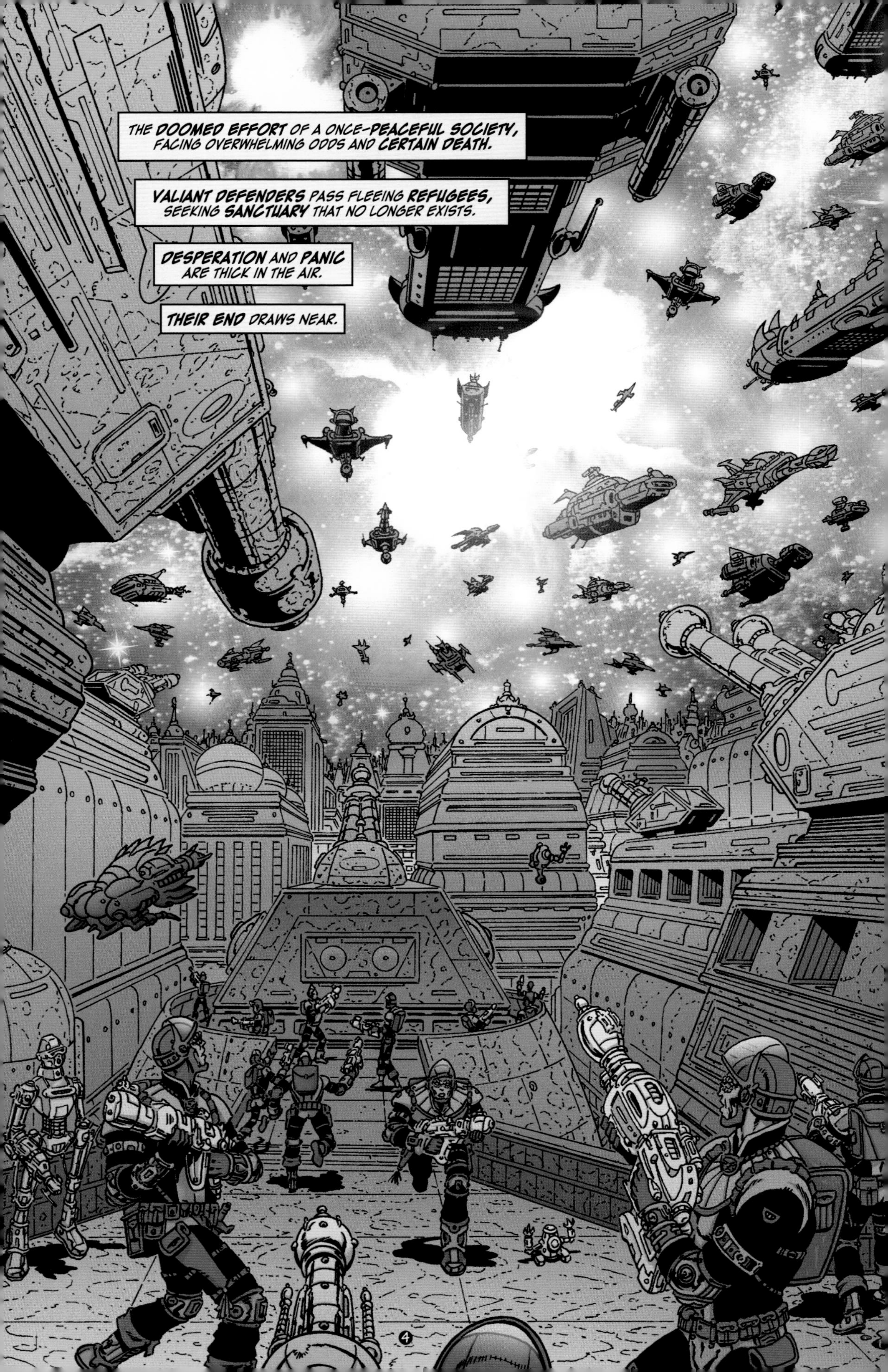
THE DOOMED EFFORT OF A ONCE-PEACEFUL SOCIETY, FACING OVERWHELMING ODDS AND CERTAIN DEATH.
VALIANT DEFENDERS PASS FLEEING REFUGEES, SEEKING SANCTUARY THAT NO LONGER EXISTS.
DESPERATION AND PANIC ARE THICK IN THE AIR.
THEIR END DRAWS NEAR.

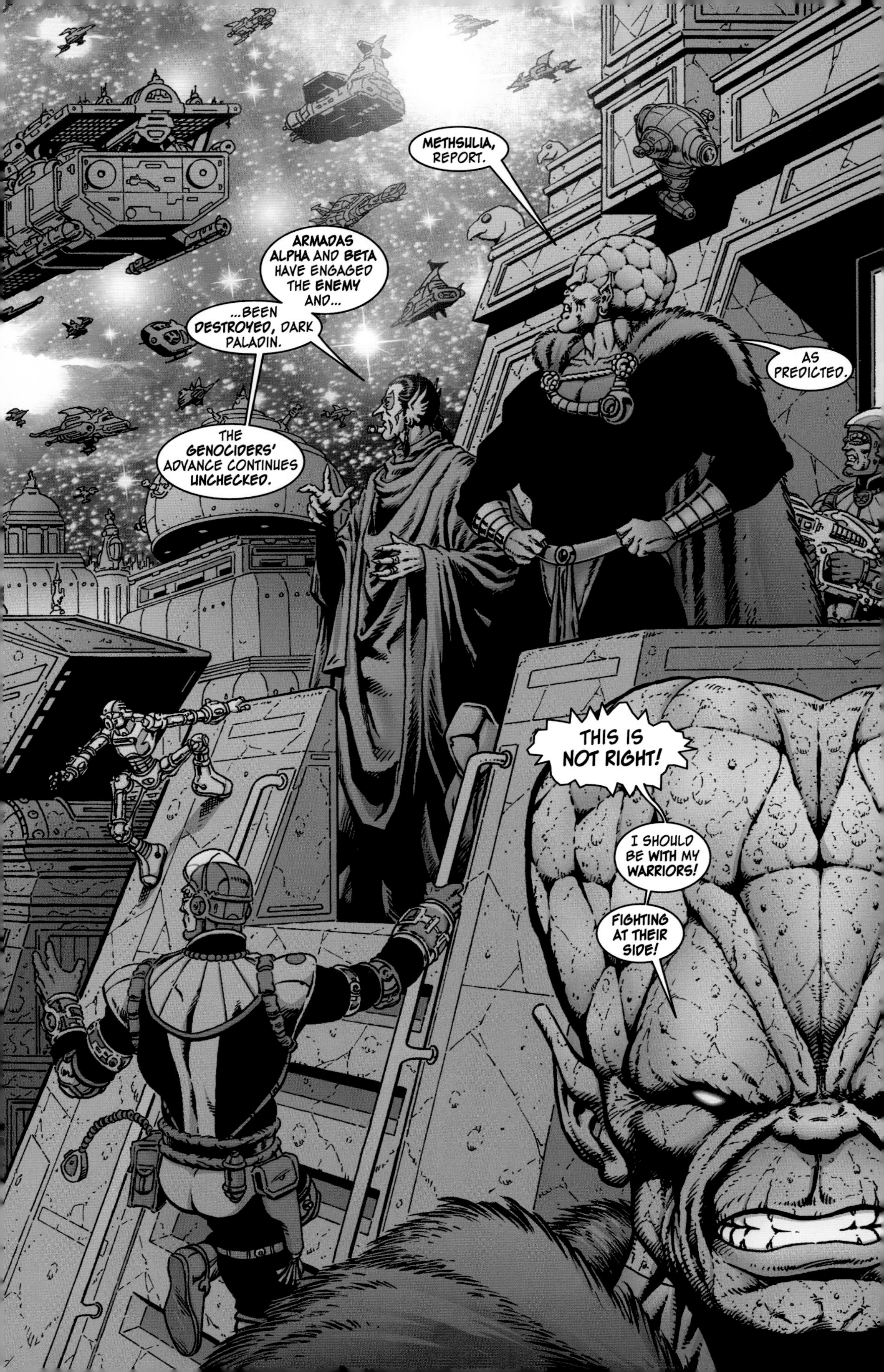
METHSULIA, REPORT.
ARMADAS ALPHA AND BETA HAVE ENGAGED THE ENEMY AND...
...BEEN DESTROYED, DARK PALADIN.
THE GENOCIDERS' ADVANCE CONTINUES UNCHECKED.
AS PREDICTED.
THIS IS NOT RIGHT!
I SHOULD BE WITH MY WARRIORS!
FIGHTING AT THEIR SIDE!

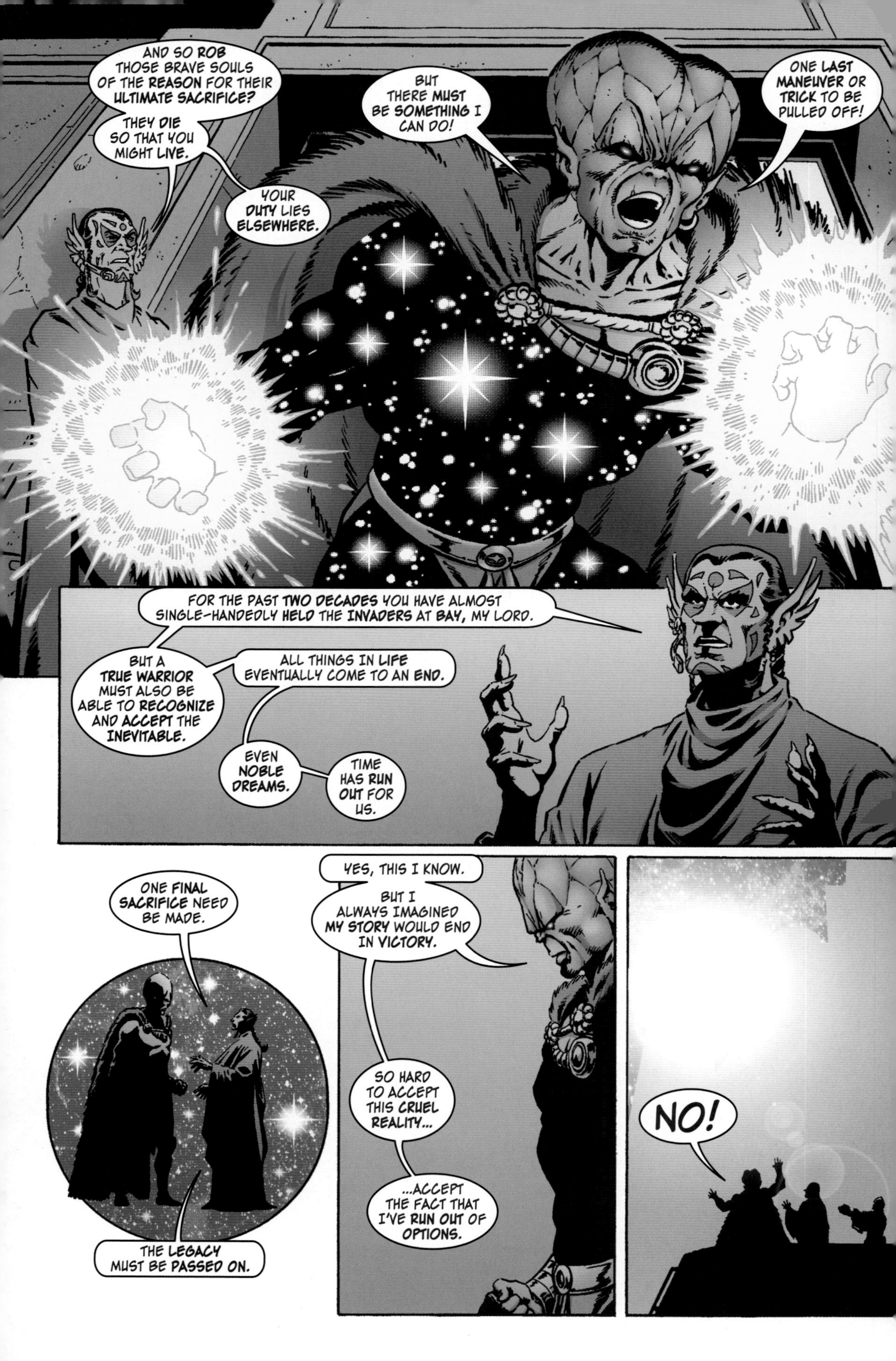
AND SO ROB THOSE BRAVE SOULS OF THE REASON FOR THEIR ULTIMATE SACRIFICE?
THEY DIE SO THAT YOU MIGHT LIVE.
YOUR DUTY LIES ELSEWHERE.
BUT THERE MUST BE SOMETHING I CAN DO!
ONE LAST MANEUVER OR TRICK TO BE PULLED OFF!
FOR THE PAST TWO DECADES YOU HAVE ALMOST SINGLE-HANDEDLY HELD THE INVADERS AT BAY, MY LORD.
BUT A TRUE WARRIOR MUST ALSO BE ABLE TO RECOGNIZE AND ACCEPT THE INEVITABLE.
ALL THINGS IN LIFE EVENTUALLY COME TO AN END.
EVEN NOBLE DREAMS.
TIME HAS RUN OUT FOR US.
ONE FINAL SACRIFICE NEED BE MADE.
THE LEGACY MUST BE PASSED ON.
YES, THIS I KNOW.
BUT I ALWAYS IMAGINED MY STORY WOULD END IN VICTORY.
SO HARD TO ACCEPT THIS CRUEL REALITY...
...ACCEPT THE FACT THAT I'VE RUN OUT OF OPTIONS.
NO!

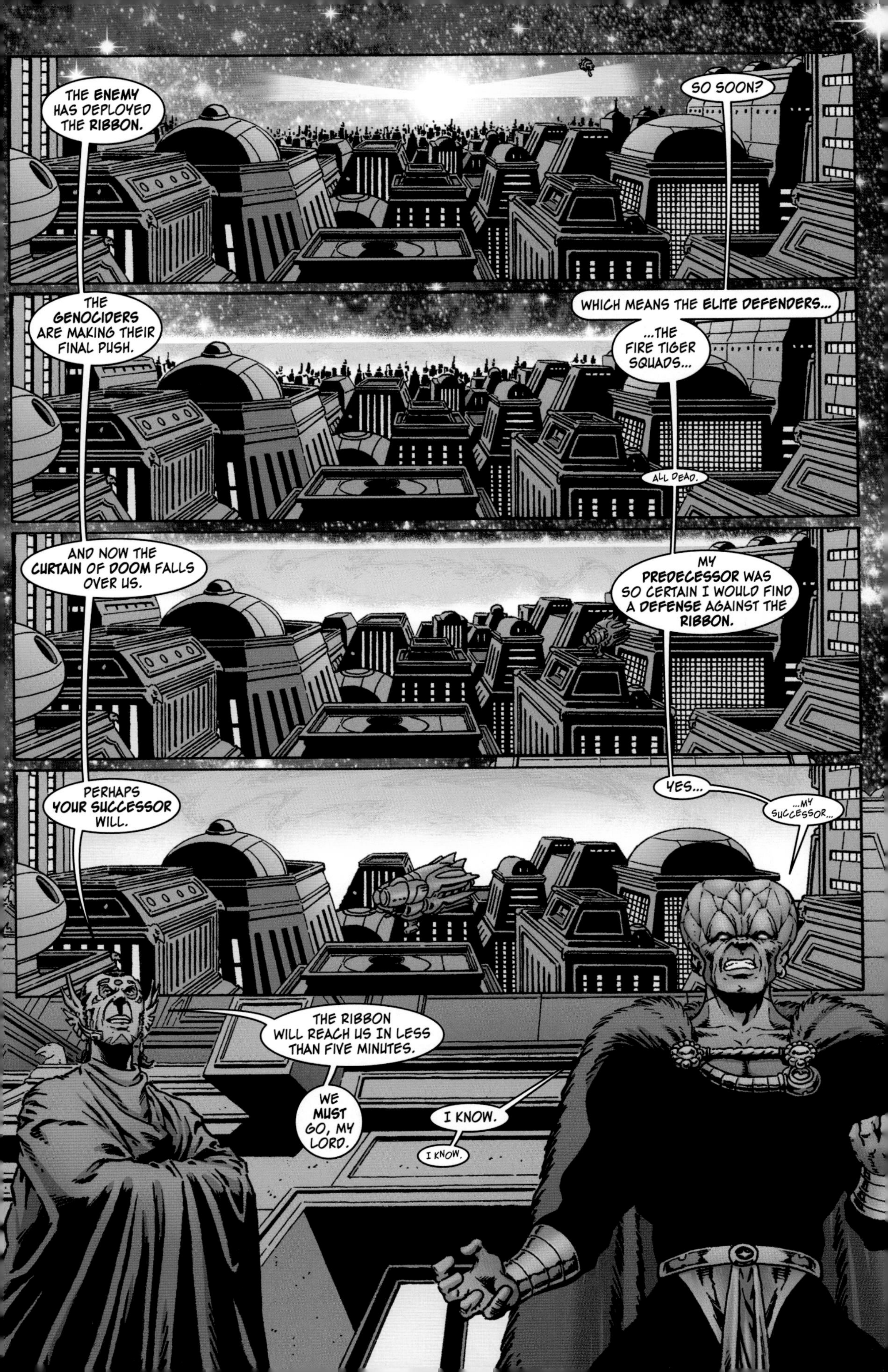

THE ENEMY HAS DEPLOYED THE RIBBON.
SO SOON?
THE GENOCIDERS ARE MAKING THEIR FINAL PUSH.
WHICH MEANS THE ELITE DEFENDERS...
...THE FIRE TIGER SQUADS...
ALL DEAD.
AND NOW THE CURTAIN OF DOOM FALLS OVER US.
MY PREDECESSOR WAS SO CERTAIN I WOULD FIND A DEFENSE AGAINST THE RIBBON.
PERHAPS YOUR SUCCESSOR WILL.
YES...
...MY SUCCESSOR...
THE RIBBON WILL REACH US IN LESS THAN FIVE MINUTES.
WE MUST GO, MY LORD.
I KNOW.
I KNOW.

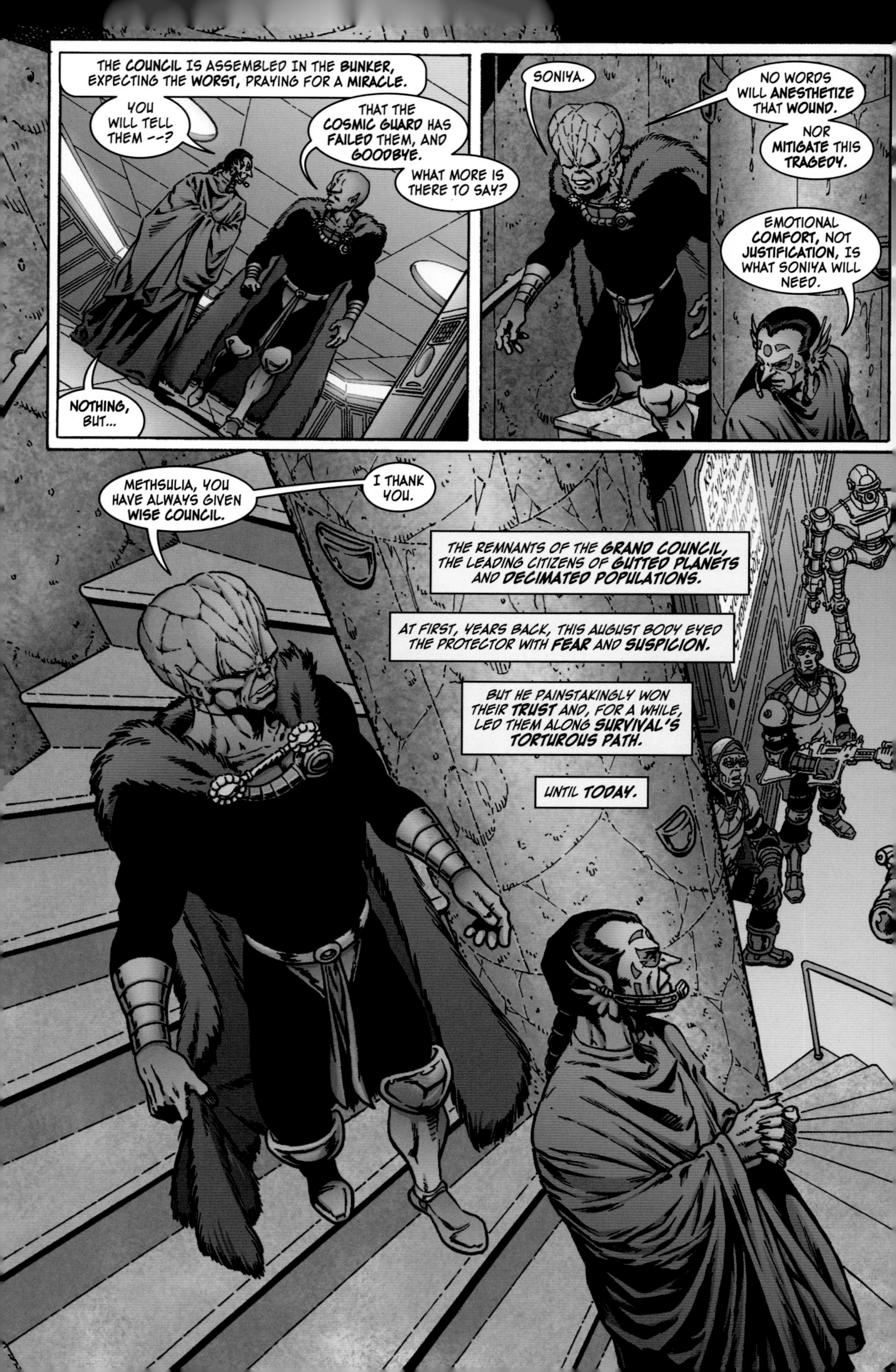
THE COUNCIL IS ASSEMBLED IN THE BUNKER, EXPECTING THE WORST, PRAYING FOR A MIRACLE.
YOU WILL TELL THEM --?
THAT THE COSMIC GUARD HAS FAILED THEM, AND GOODBYE.
WHAT MORE IS THERE TO SAY?
NOTHING, BUT...
SONIYA.
NO WORDS WILL ANESTHETIZE THAT WOUND.
NOR MITIGATE THIS TRAGEDY.
EMOTIONAL COMFORT, NOT JUSTIFICATION, IS WHAT SONIYA WILL NEED.
METHSULIA, YOU HAVE ALWAYS GIVEN WISE COUNCIL.
I THANK YOU.
THE REMNANTS OF THE GRAND COUNCIL, THE LEADING CITIZENS OF GUTTED PLANETS AND DECIMATED POPULATIONS.
AT FIRST, YEARS BACK, THIS AUGUST BODY EYED THE PROTECTOR WITH FEAR AND SUSPICION.
BUT HE PAINSTAKINGLY WON THEIR TRUST AND, FOR A WHILE, LED THEM ALONG SURVIVAL'S TORTUROUS PATH.
UNTIL TODAY.

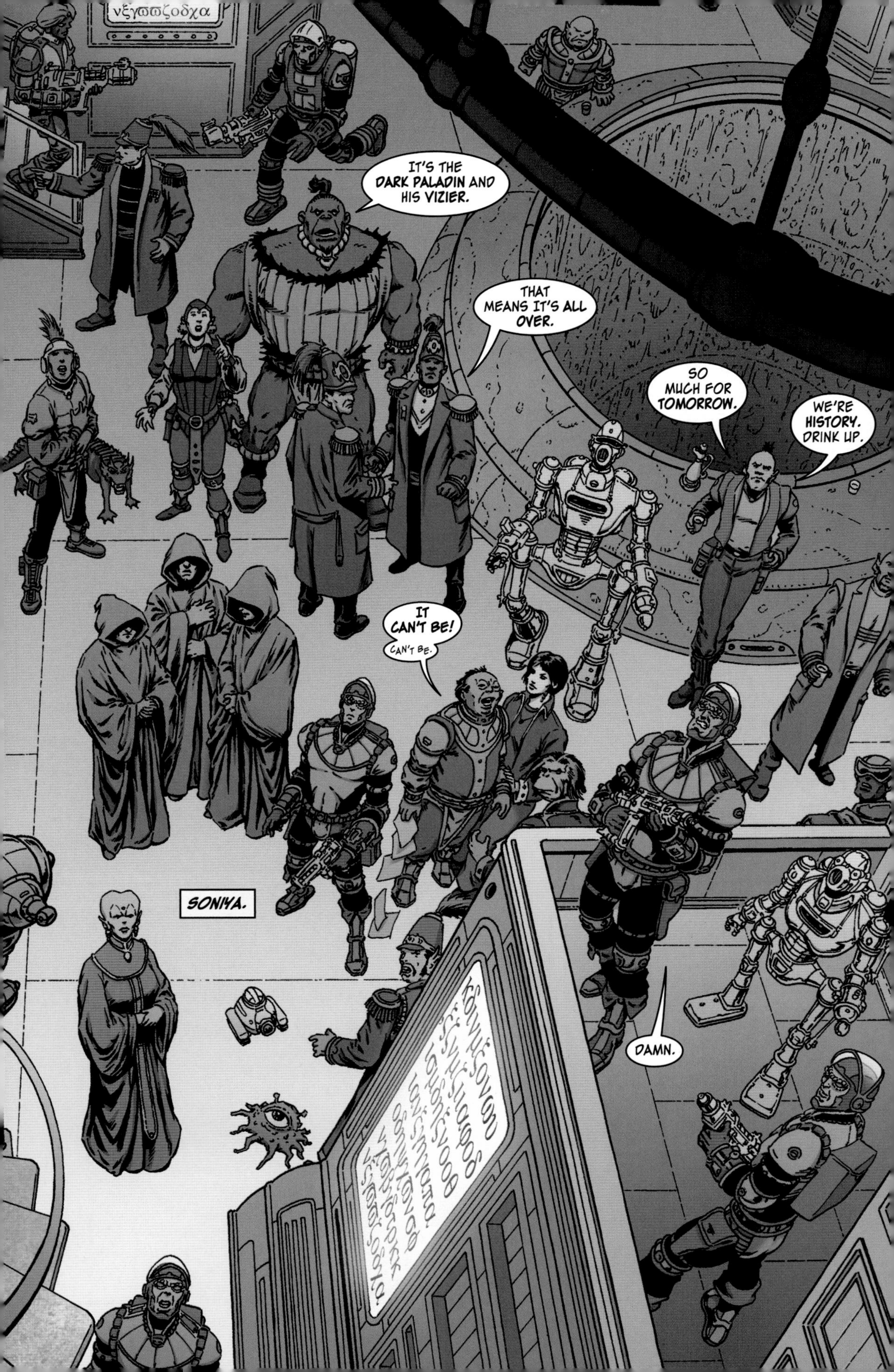

IT'S THE DARK PALADIN AND HIS VIZIER.
THAT MEANS IT'S ALL OVER.
SO MUCH FOR TOMORROW.
WE'RE HISTORY. DRINK UP.
IT CAN'T BE! CAN'T BE.
SONIYA.
DAMN.

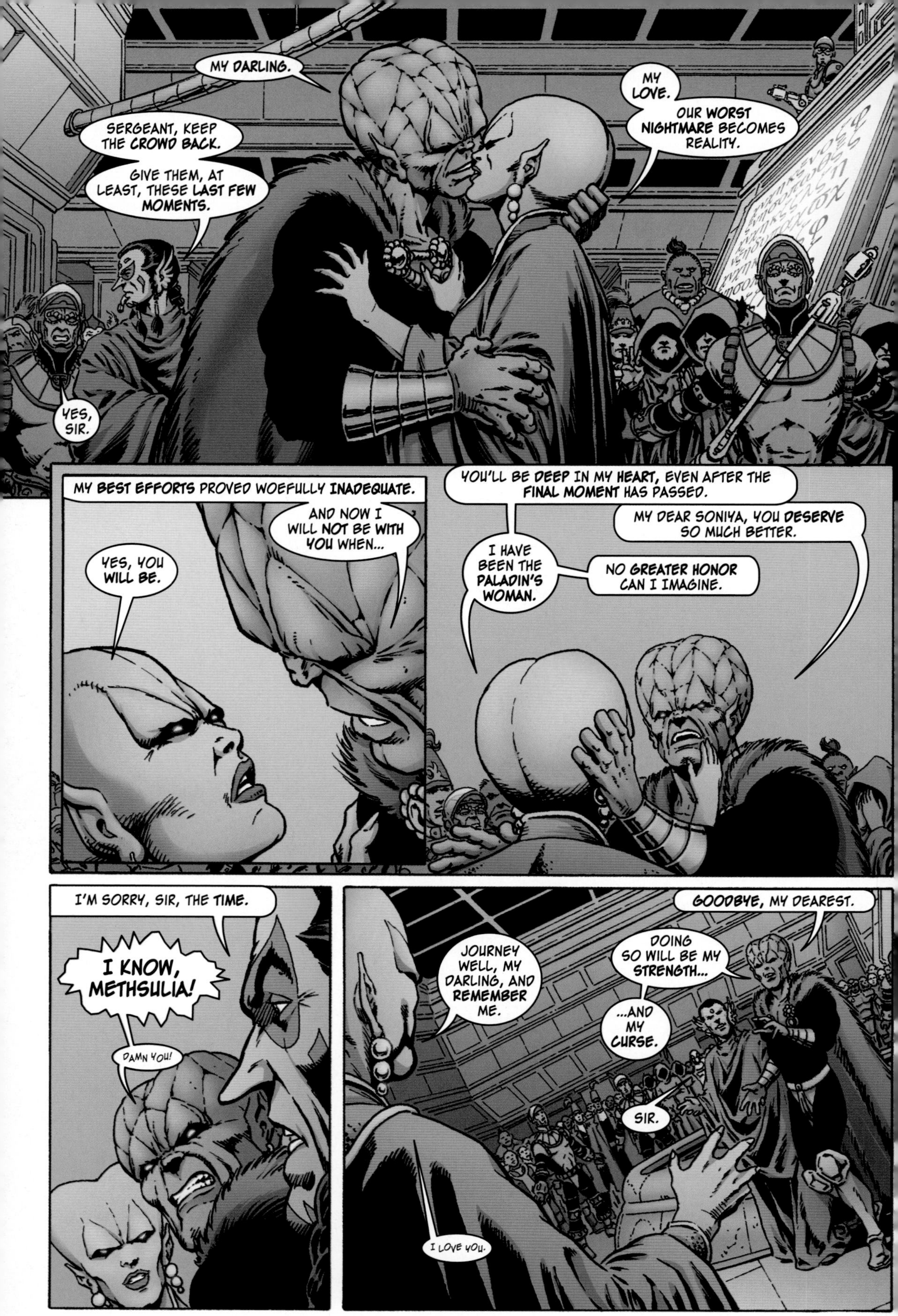
MY DARLING.
SERGEANT, KEEP THE CROWD BACK.
GIVE THEM, AT LEAST, THESE LAST FEW MOMENTS.
MY LOVE.
OUR WORST NIGHTMARE BECOMES REALITY.
YES, SIR.
MY BEST EFFORTS PROVED WOEFULLY INADEQUATE.
AND NOW I WILL NOT BE WITH YOU WHEN...
YES, YOU WILL BE.
YOU'LL BE DEEP IN MY HEART, EVEN AFTER THE FINAL MOMENT HAS PASSED.
MY DEAR SONIYA, YOU DESERVE SO MUCH BETTER.
I HAVE BEEN THE PALADIN'S WOMAN.
NO GREATER HONOR CAN I IMAGINE.
I'M SORRY, SIR, THE TIME.
I KNOW, METHSULIA!
DAMN YOU!
GOODBYE, MY DEAREST.
JOURNEY WELL, MY DARLING, AND REMEMBER ME.
DOING SO WILL BE MY STRENGTH...
...AND MY CURSE.
SIR.
I LOVE YOU.

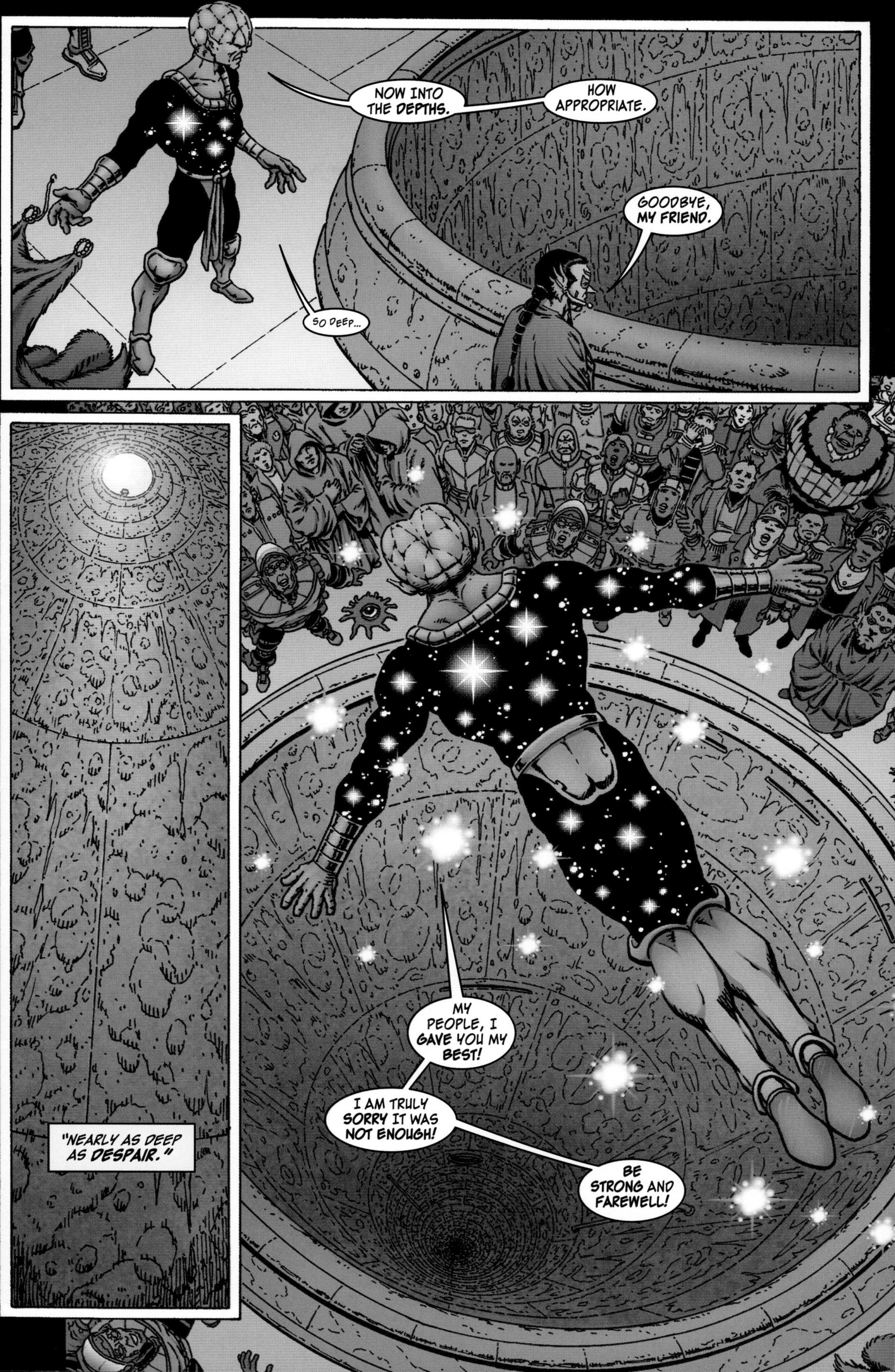
NOW INTO THE DEPTHS.
HOW APPROPRIATE.
GOODBYE, MY FRIEND.
SO DEEP...
"NEARLY AS DEEP AS DESPAIR."
MY PEOPLE, I GAVE YOU MY BEST!
I AM TRULY SORRY IT WAS NOT ENOUGH!
BE STRONG AND FAREWELL!

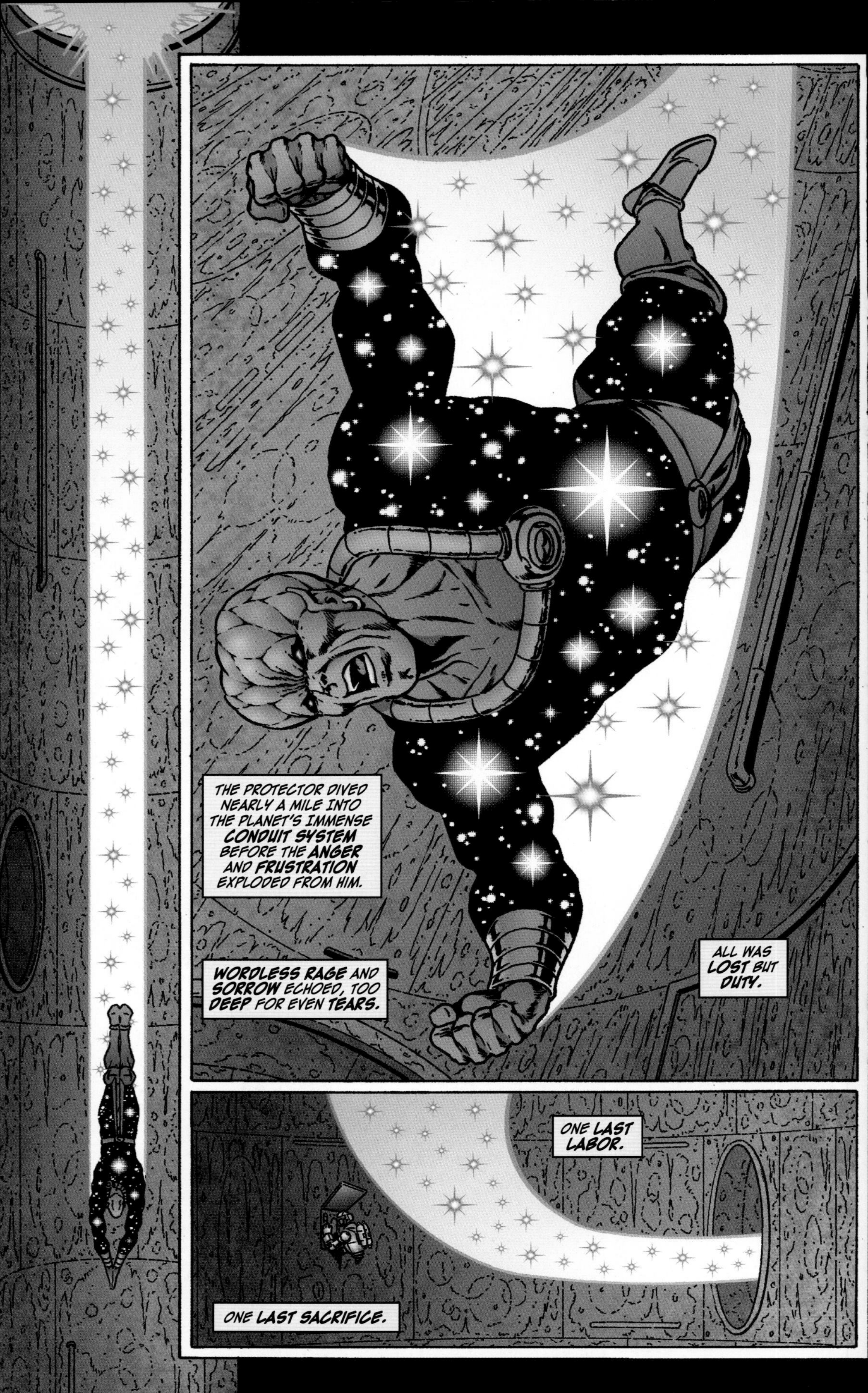

THE PROTECTOR DIVED NEARLY A MILE INTO THE PLANET'S IMMENSE CONDUIT SYSTEM BEFORE THE ANGER AND FRUSTRATION EXPLODED FROM HIM.
WORDLESS RAGE AND SORROW ECHOED, TOO DEEP FOR EVEN TEARS.
ALL WAS LOST BUT DUTY.
ONE LAST LABOR.
ONE LAST SACRIFICE.

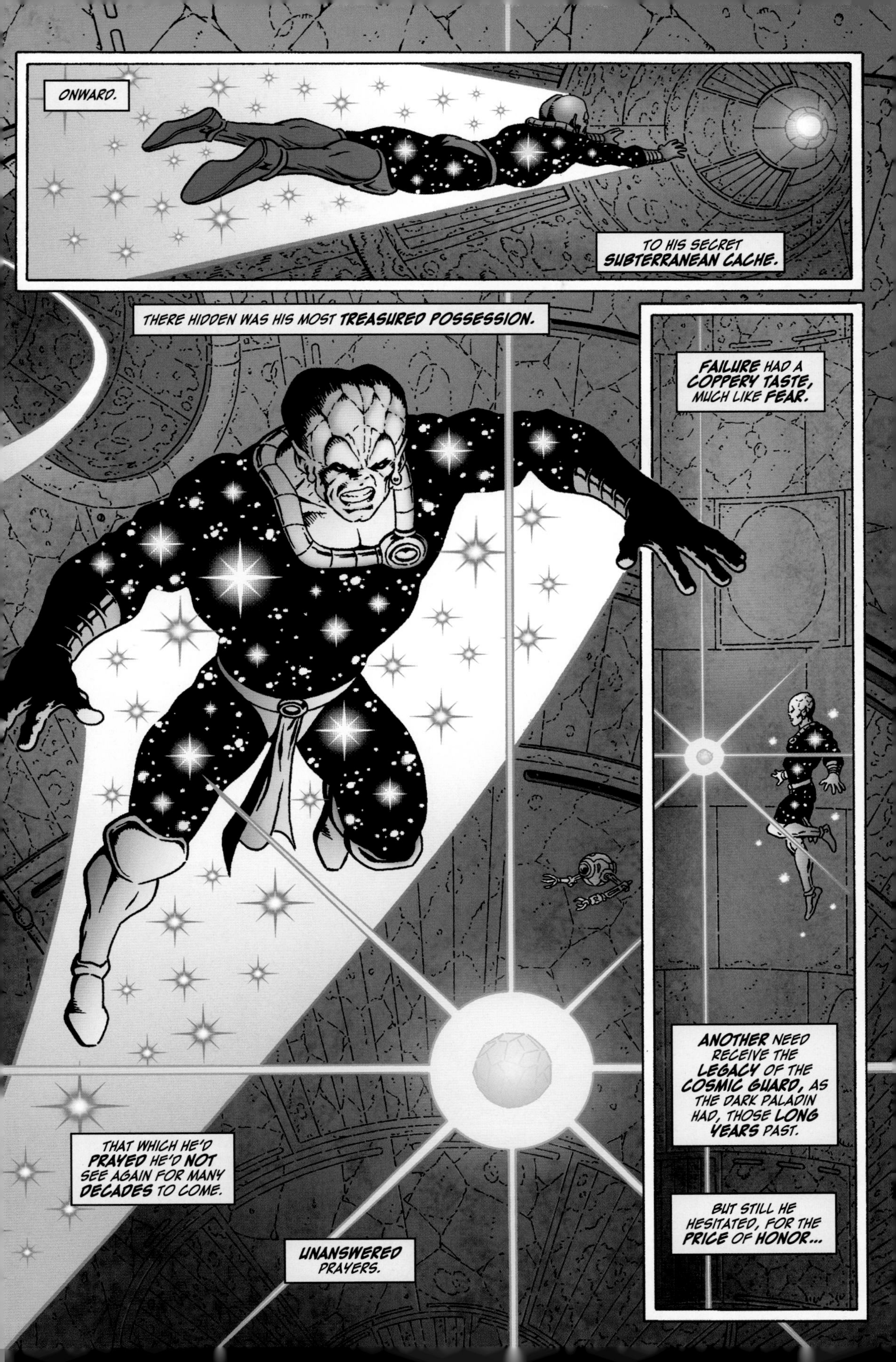
ONWARD.
TO HIS SECRET SUBTERRANEAN CACHE.
THERE HIDDEN WAS HIS MOST TREASURED POSSESSION.
THAT WHICH HE'D PRAYED HE'D NOT SEE AGAIN FOR MANY DECADES TO COME.
UNANSWERED PRAYERS.
FAILURE HAD A COPPERY TASTE, MUCH LIKE FEAR.
ANOTHER NEED RECEIVE THE LEGACY OF THE COSMIC GUARD, AS THE DARK PALADIN HAD, THOSE LONG YEARS PAST.
BUT STILL HE HESITATED, FOR THE PRICE OF HONOR...

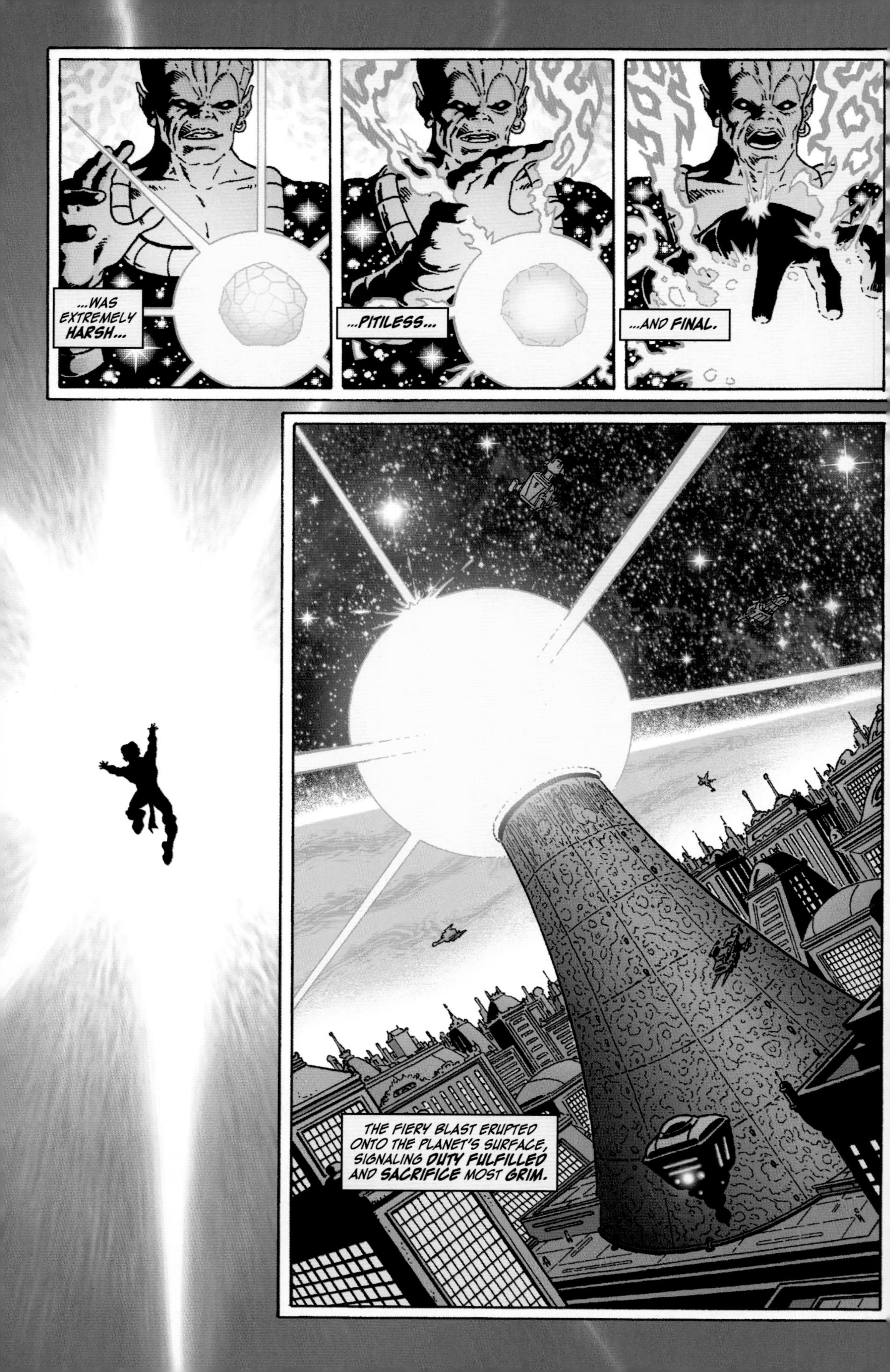
...WAS EXTREMELY HARSH...
...PITILESS...
...AND FINAL.
THE FIERY BLAST ERUPTED ONTO THE PLANET'S SURFACE, SIGNALING DUTY FULFILLED AND SACRIFICE MOST GRIM.

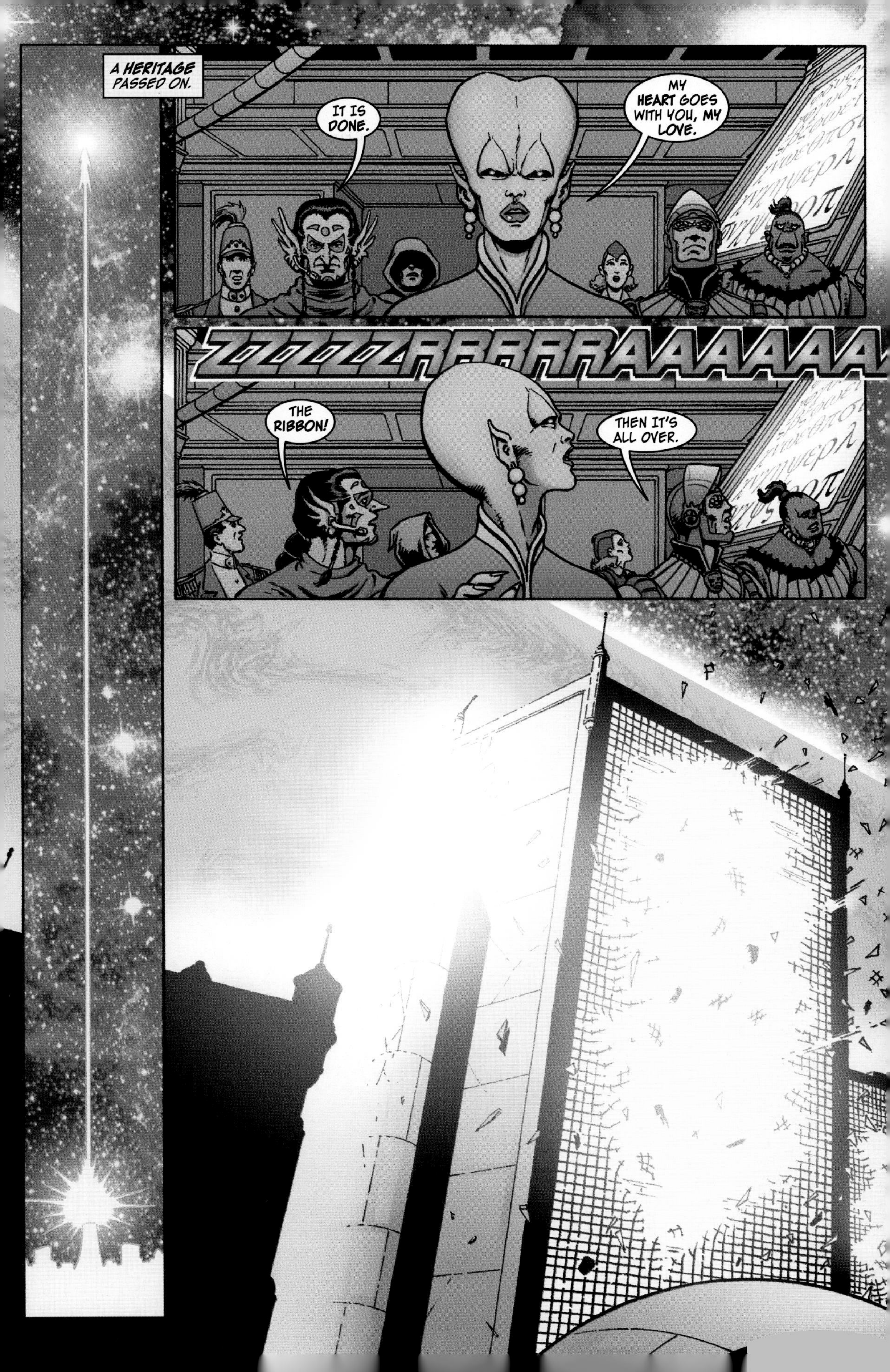

A HERITAGE PASSED ON.
IT IS DONE.
MY HEART GOES WITH YOU, MY LOVE.
ZZZZZZRRRRRRAAAAAAA
THE RIBBON!
THEN IT'S ALL OVER.

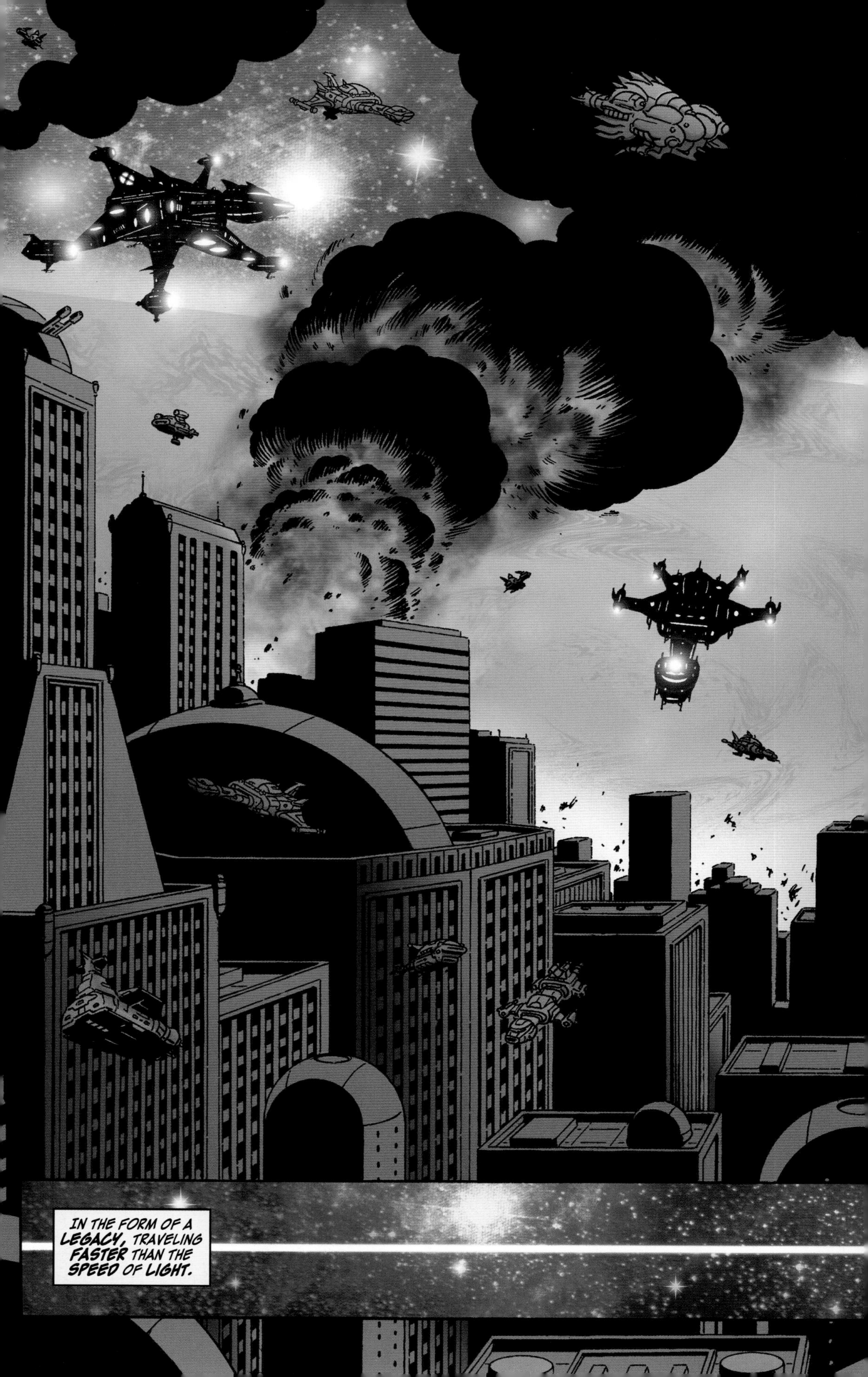
IN THE FORM OF A LEGACY, TRAVELING FASTER THAN THE SPEED OF LIGHT.

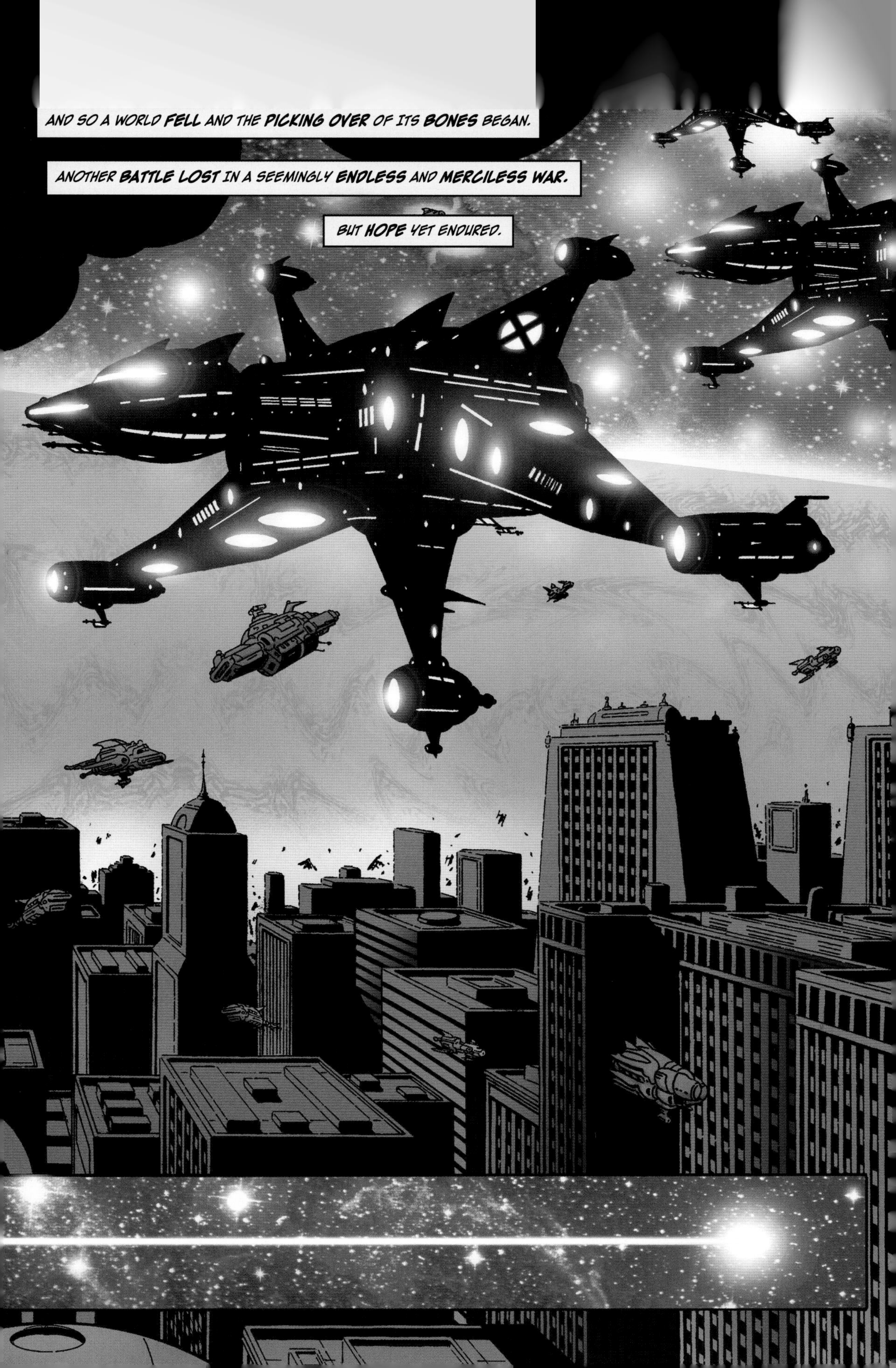
AND SO A WORLD FELL AND THE PICKING OVER OF ITS BONES BEGAN.
ANOTHER BATTLE LOST IN A SEEMINGLY ENDLESS AND MERCILESS WAR.
BUT HOPE YET ENDURED.

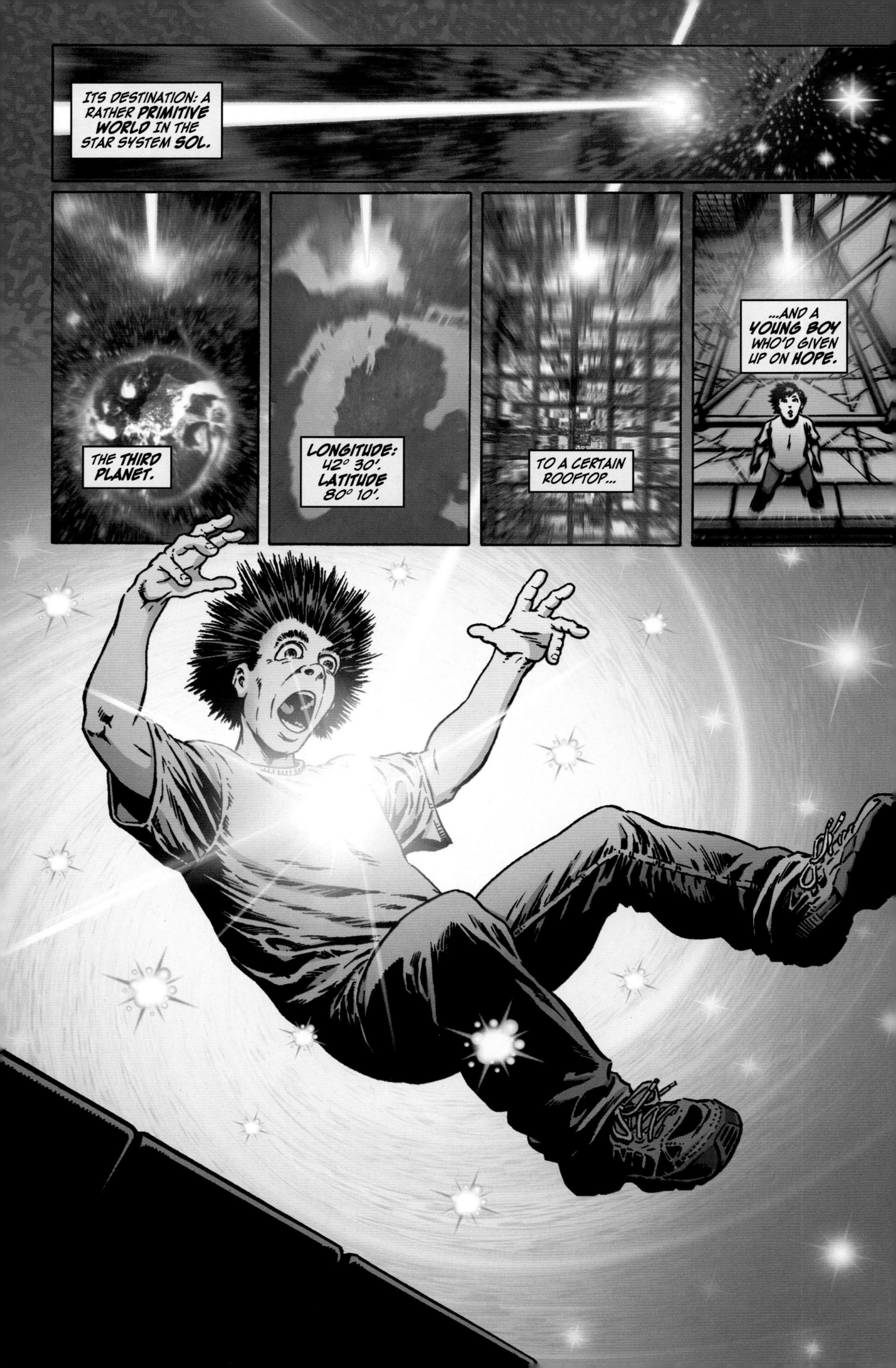
ITS DESTINATION: A RATHER PRIMITIVE WORLD IN THE STAR SYSTEM SOL.
THE THIRD PLANET.
LONGITUDE: 42° 30'. LATITUDE 80° 10'.
TO A CERTAIN ROOFTOP...
...AND A YOUNG BOY WHO'D GIVEN UP ON HOPE.

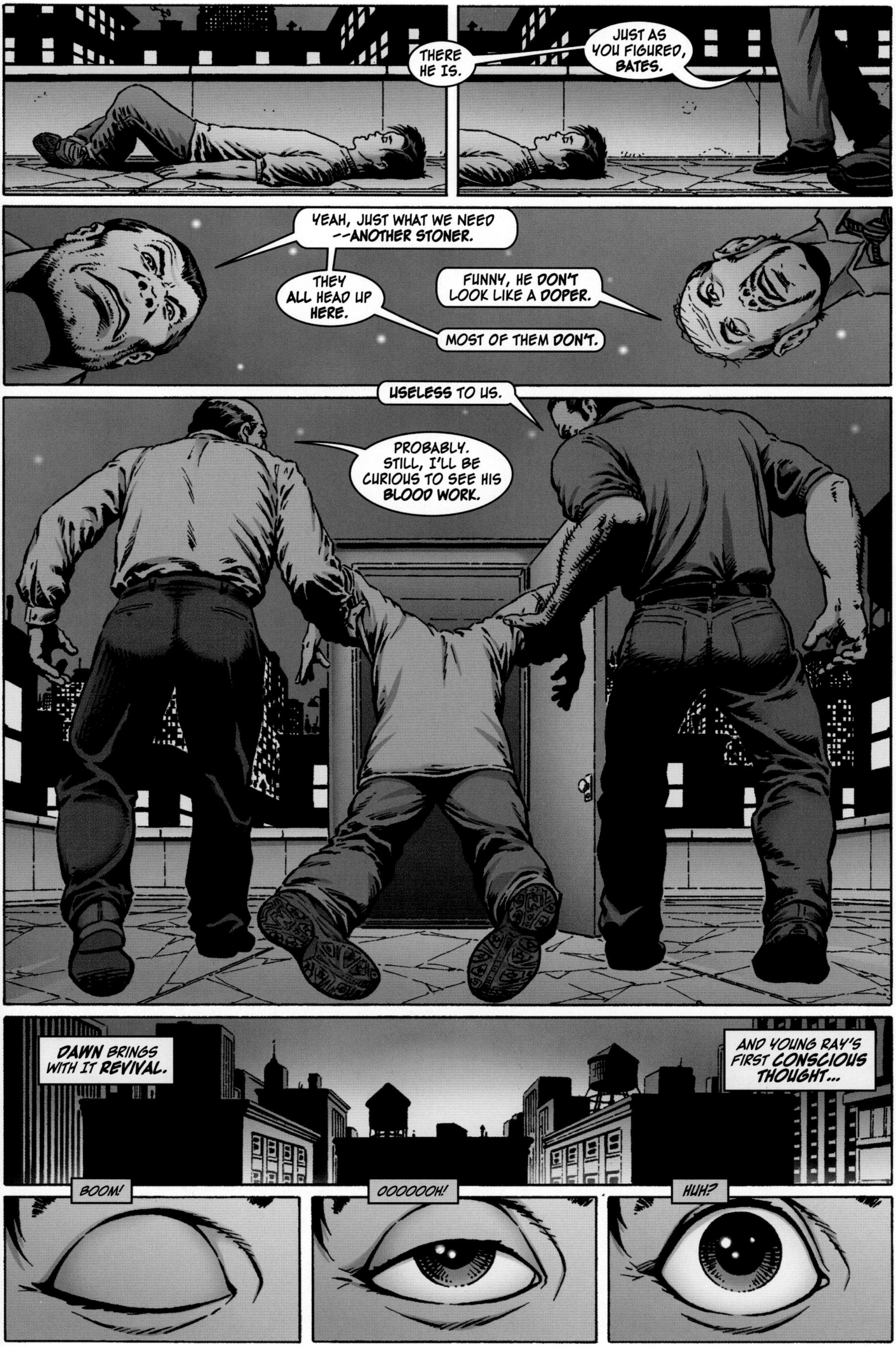
THERE HE IS.
JUST AS YOU FIGURED, BATES.
YEAH, JUST WHAT WE NEED --ANOTHER STONER.
THEY ALL HEAD UP HERE.
FUNNY, HE DON'T LOOK LIKE A DOPER.
MOST OF THEM DON'T.
USELESS TO US.
PROBABLY. STILL, I'LL BE CURIOUS TO SEE HIS BLOOD WORK.
DAWN BRINGS WITH IT REVIVAL.
AND YOUNG RAY'S FIRST CONSCIOUS THOUGHT...
BOOM!
OOOOOOH!
HUH?

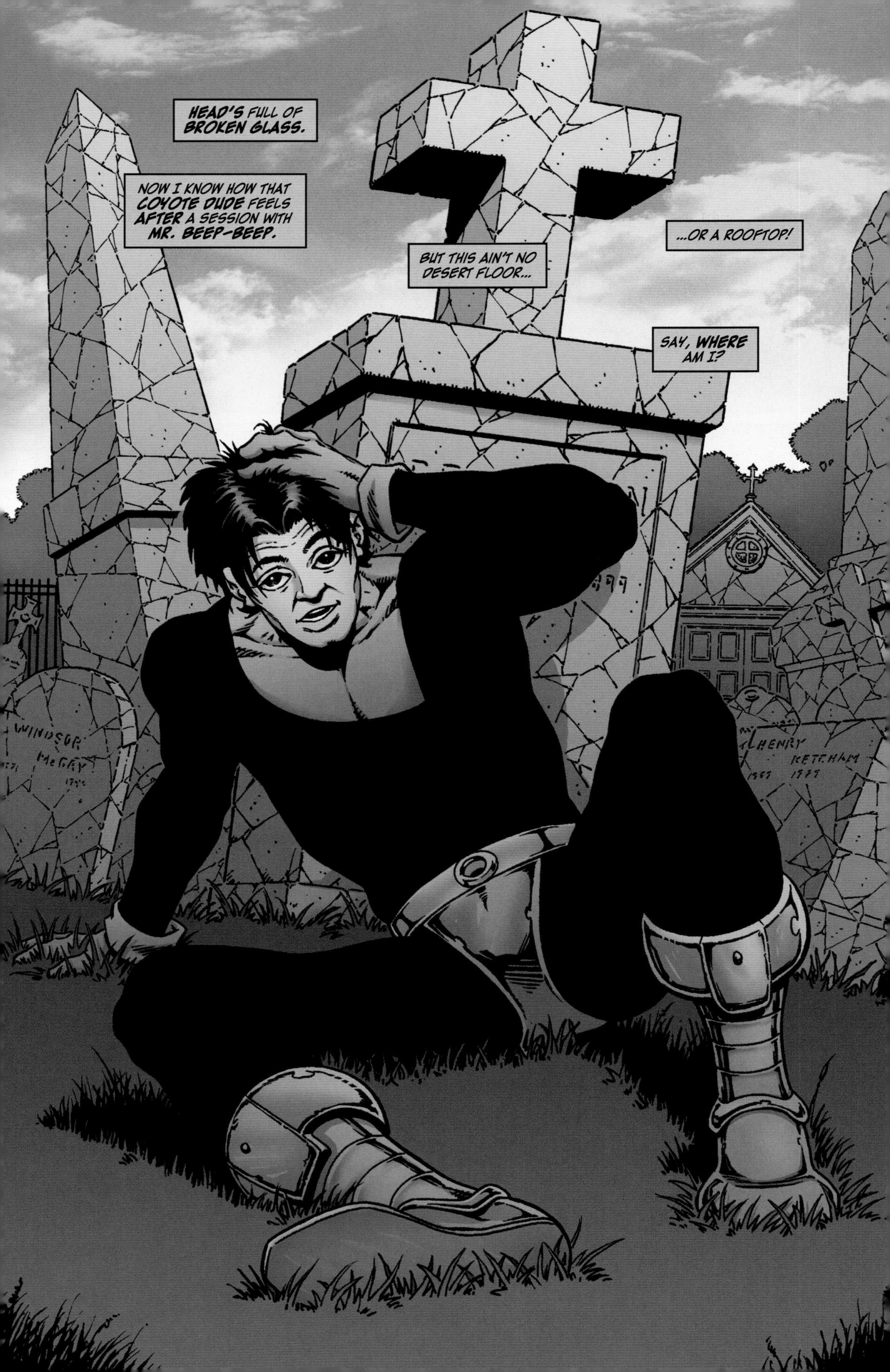
HEAD'S FULL OF BROKEN GLASS.
NOW I KNOW HOW THAT COYOTE DUDE FEELS AFTER A SESSION WITH MR. BEEP-BEEP.
BUT THIS AIN'T NO DESERT FLOOR...
...OR A ROOFTOP!
SAY, WHERE AM I?

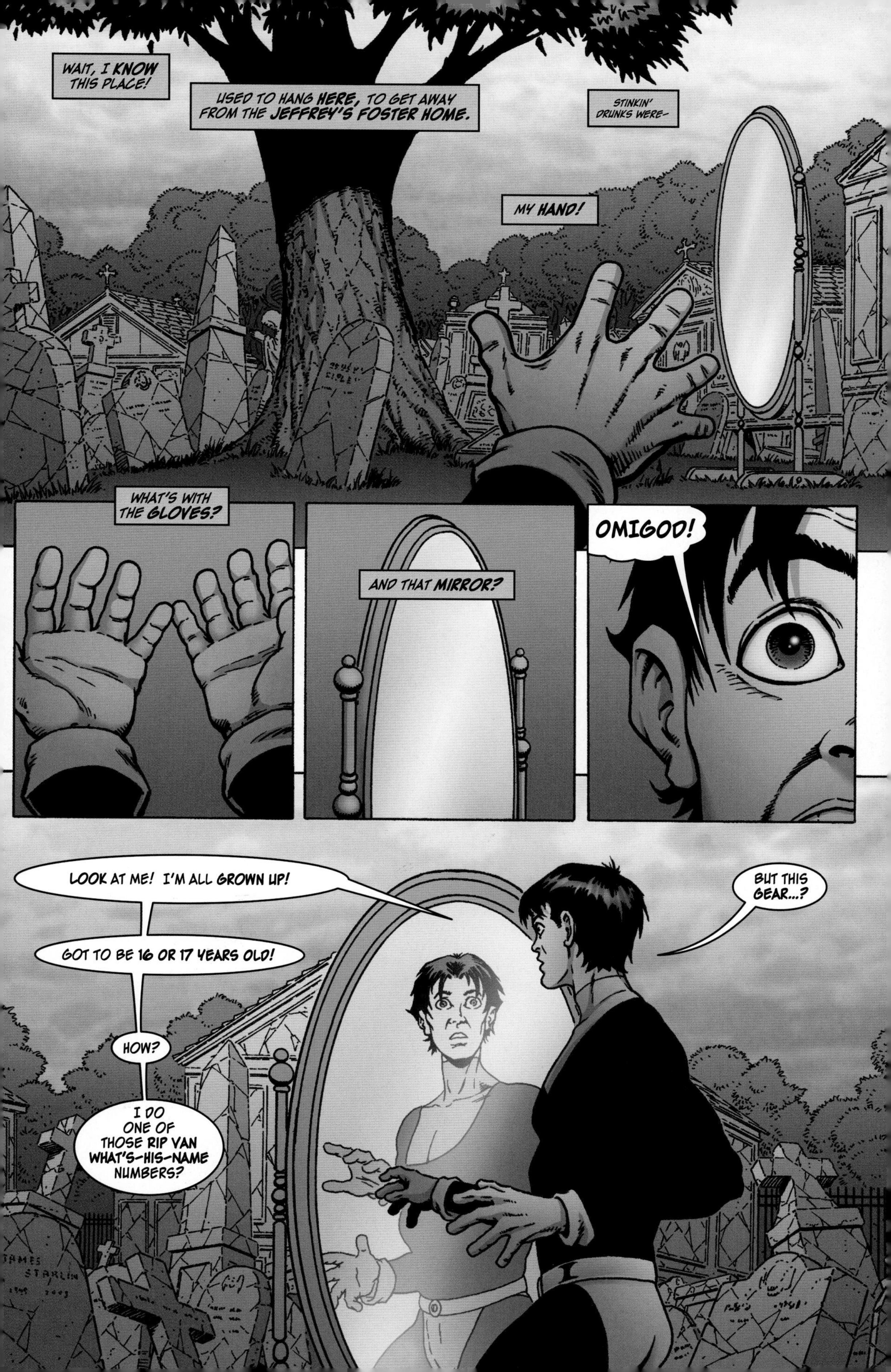

WAIT, I KNOW THIS PLACE!
USED TO HANG HERE, TO GET AWAY FROM THE JEFFREY'S FOSTER HOME.
STINKIN' DRUNKS WERE-
MY HAND!
WHAT'S WITH THE GLOVES?
AND THAT MIRROR?
OMIGOD!
LOOK AT ME! I'M ALL GROWN UP!
GOT TO BE 16 OR 17 YEARS OLD!
HOW?
I DO ONE OF THOSE RIP VAN WHAT'S-HIS-NAME NUMBERS?
BUT THIS GEAR...?

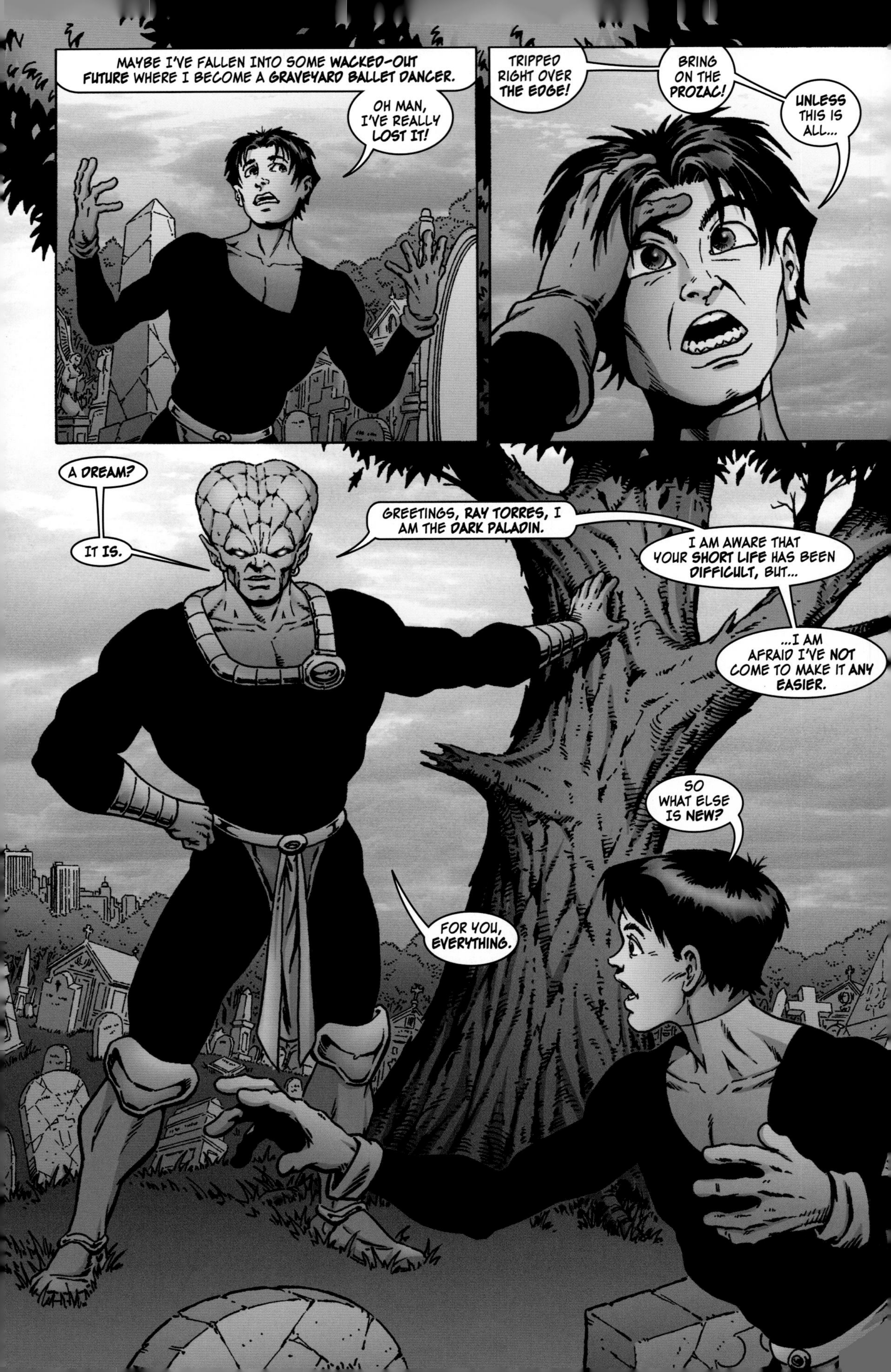
MAYBE I'VE FALLEN INTO SOME WACKED-OUT FUTURE WHERE I BECOME A GRAVEYARD BALLET DANCER.
OH MAN, I'VE REALLY LOST IT!
TRIPPED RIGHT OVER THE EDGE!
BRING ON THE PROZAC!
UNLESS THIS IS ALL...
A DREAM?
IT IS.
GREETINGS, RAY TORRES, I AM THE DARK PALADIN.
I AM AWARE THAT YOUR SHORT LIFE HAS BEEN DIFFICULT, BUT...
...I AM AFRAID I'VE NOT COME TO MAKE IT ANY EASIER.
SO WHAT ELSE IS NEW?
FOR YOU, EVERYTHING.

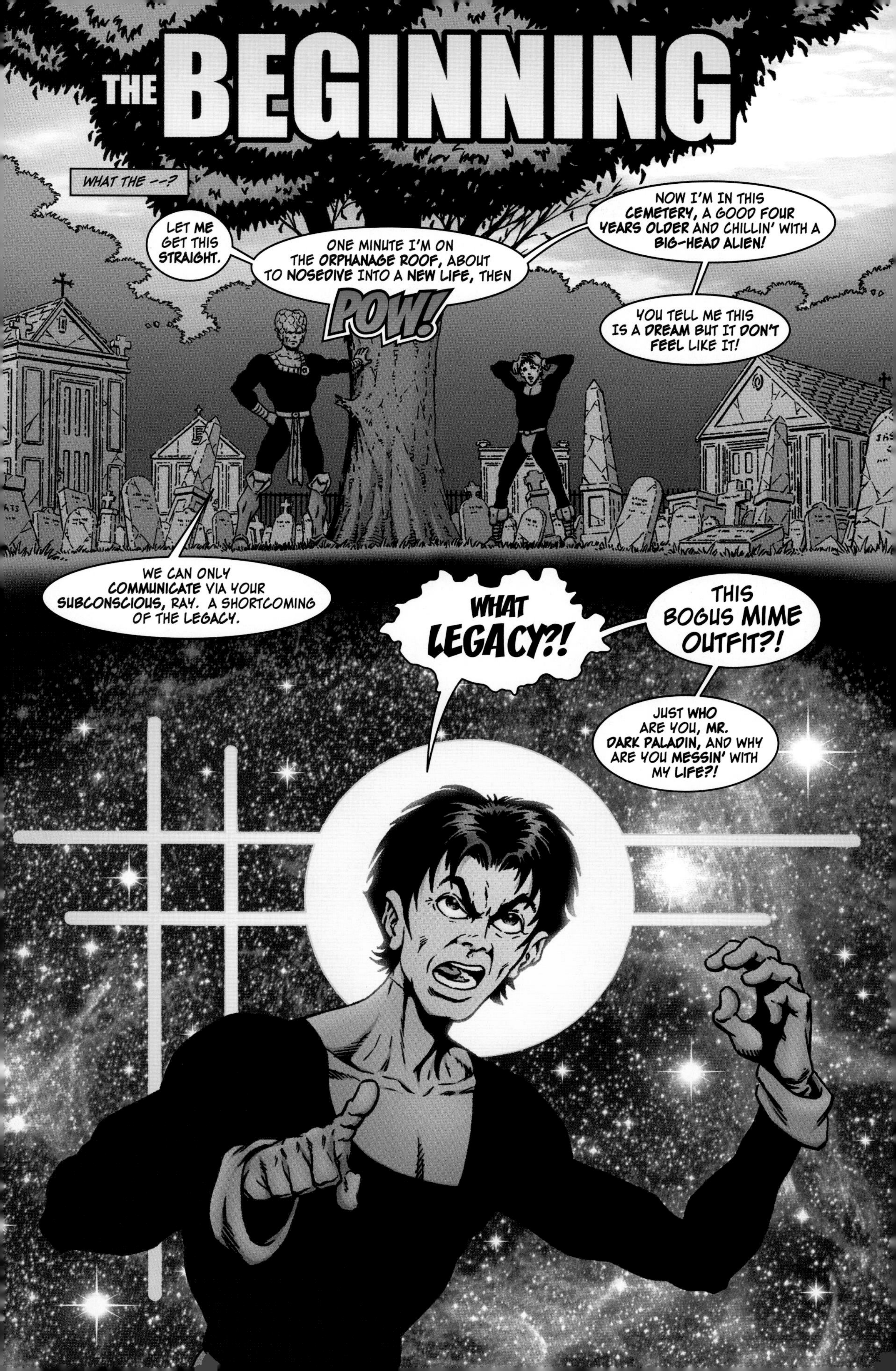
THE BEGINNING
WHAT THE --?
LET ME GET THIS STRAIGHT.
ONE MINUTE I'M ON THE ORPHANAGE ROOF, ABOUT TO NOSEDIVE INTO A NEW LIFE, THEN
POW!
NOW I'M IN THIS CEMETERY, A GOOD FOUR YEARS OLDER AND CHILLIN' WITH A BIG-HEAD ALIEN!
YOU TELL ME THIS IS A DREAM BUT IT DON'T FEEL LIKE IT!
WE CAN ONLY COMMUNICATE VIA YOUR SUBCONSCIOUS, RAY. A SHORTCOMING OF THE LEGACY.
WHAT LEGACY?!
THIS BOGUS MIME OUTFIT?!
JUST WHO ARE YOU, MR. DARK PALADIN, AND WHY ARE YOU MESSIN' WITH MY LIFE?!

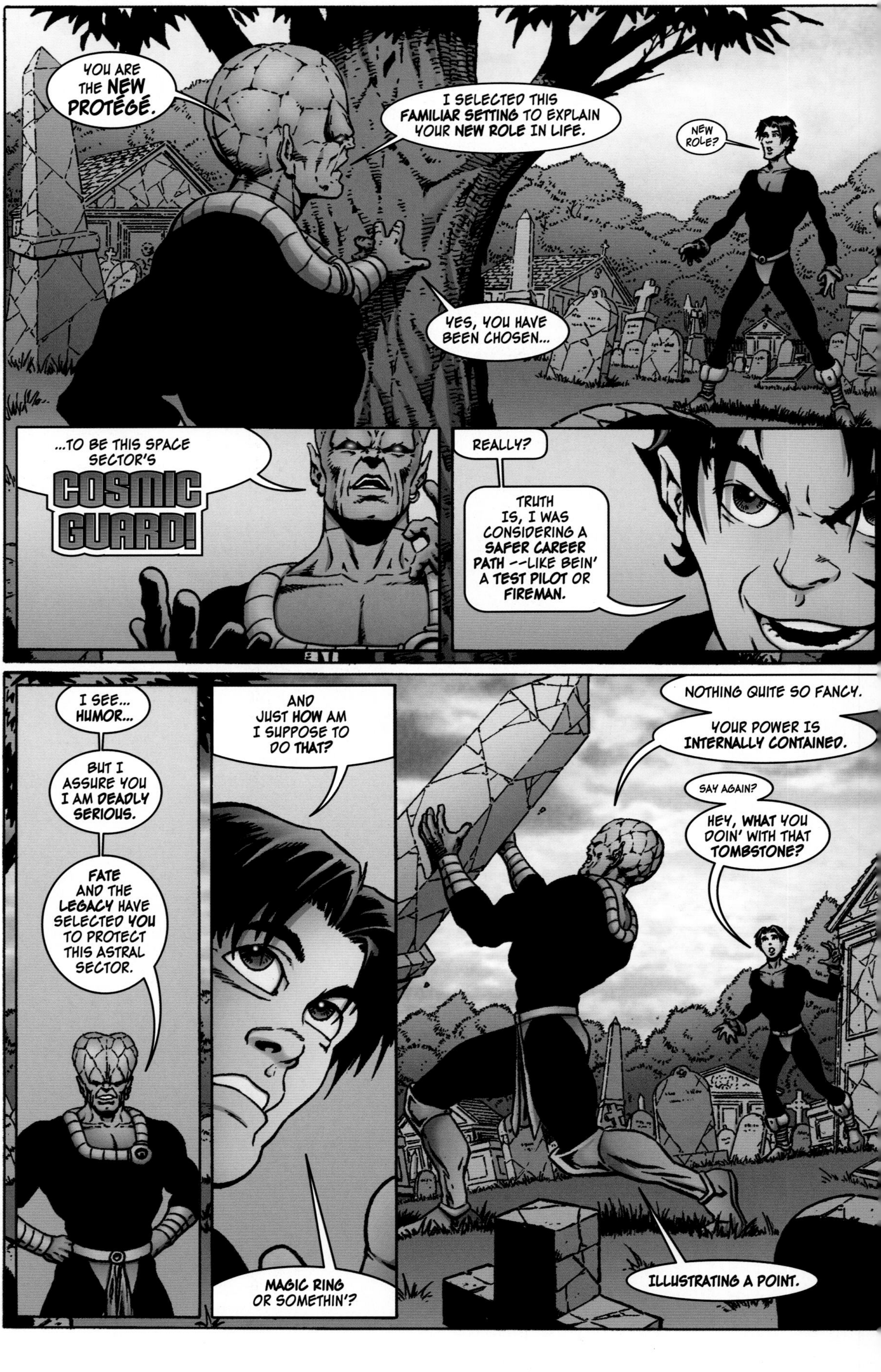

YOU ARE THE NEW PROTÉGÉ.
I SELECTED THIS FAMILIAR SETTING TO EXPLAIN YOUR NEW ROLE IN LIFE.
NEW ROLE?
YES, YOU HAVE BEEN CHOSEN...
...TO BE THIS SPACE SECTOR'S
COSMIC GUARD!
REALLY?
TRUTH IS, I WAS CONSIDERING A SAFER CAREER PATH --LIKE BEIN' A TEST PILOT OR FIREMAN.
I SEE... HUMOR...
BUT I ASSURE YOU I AM DEADLY SERIOUS.
FATE AND THE LEGACY HAVE SELECTED YOU TO PROTECT THIS ASTRAL SECTOR.
AND JUST HOW AM I SUPPOSE TO DO THAT?
MAGIC RING OR SOMETHIN'?
NOTHING QUITE SO FANCY.
YOUR POWER IS INTERNALLY CONTAINED.
SAY AGAIN?
HEY, WHAT YOU DOIN' WITH THAT TOMBSTONE?
ILLUSTRATING A POINT.

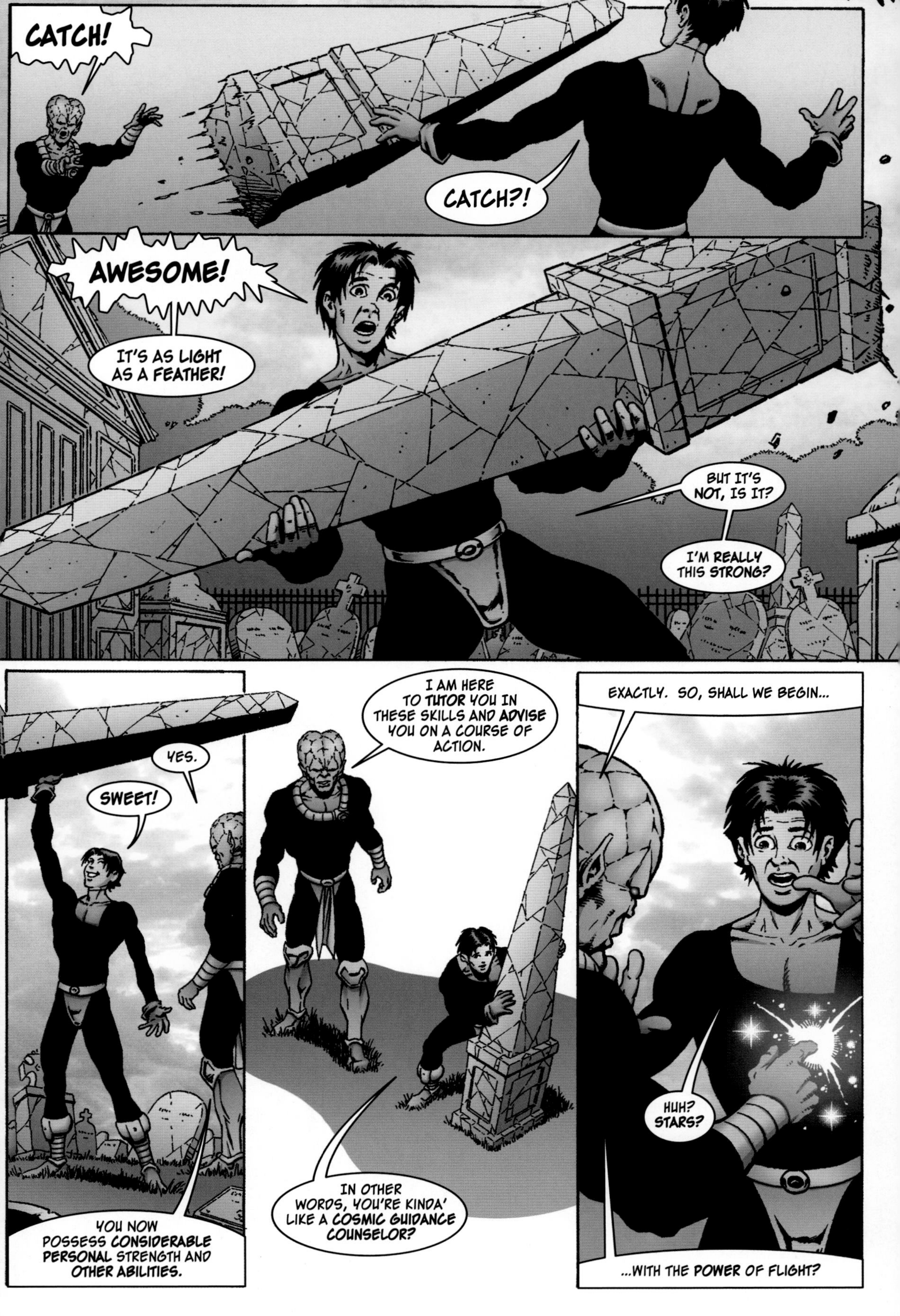
CATCH!
CATCH?!
AWESOME!
IT'S AS LIGHT AS A FEATHER!
BUT IT'S NOT, IS IT?
I'M REALLY THIS STRONG?
YES.
SWEET!
YOU NOW POSSESS CONSIDERABLE PERSONAL STRENGTH AND OTHER ABILITIES.
I AM HERE TO TUTOR YOU IN THESE SKILLS AND ADVISE YOU ON A COURSE OF ACTION.
IN OTHER WORDS, YOU'RE KINDA' LIKE A COSMIC GUIDANCE COUNSELOR?
EXACTLY. SO, SHALL WE BEGIN...
HUH? STARS?
...WITH THE POWER OF FLIGHT?

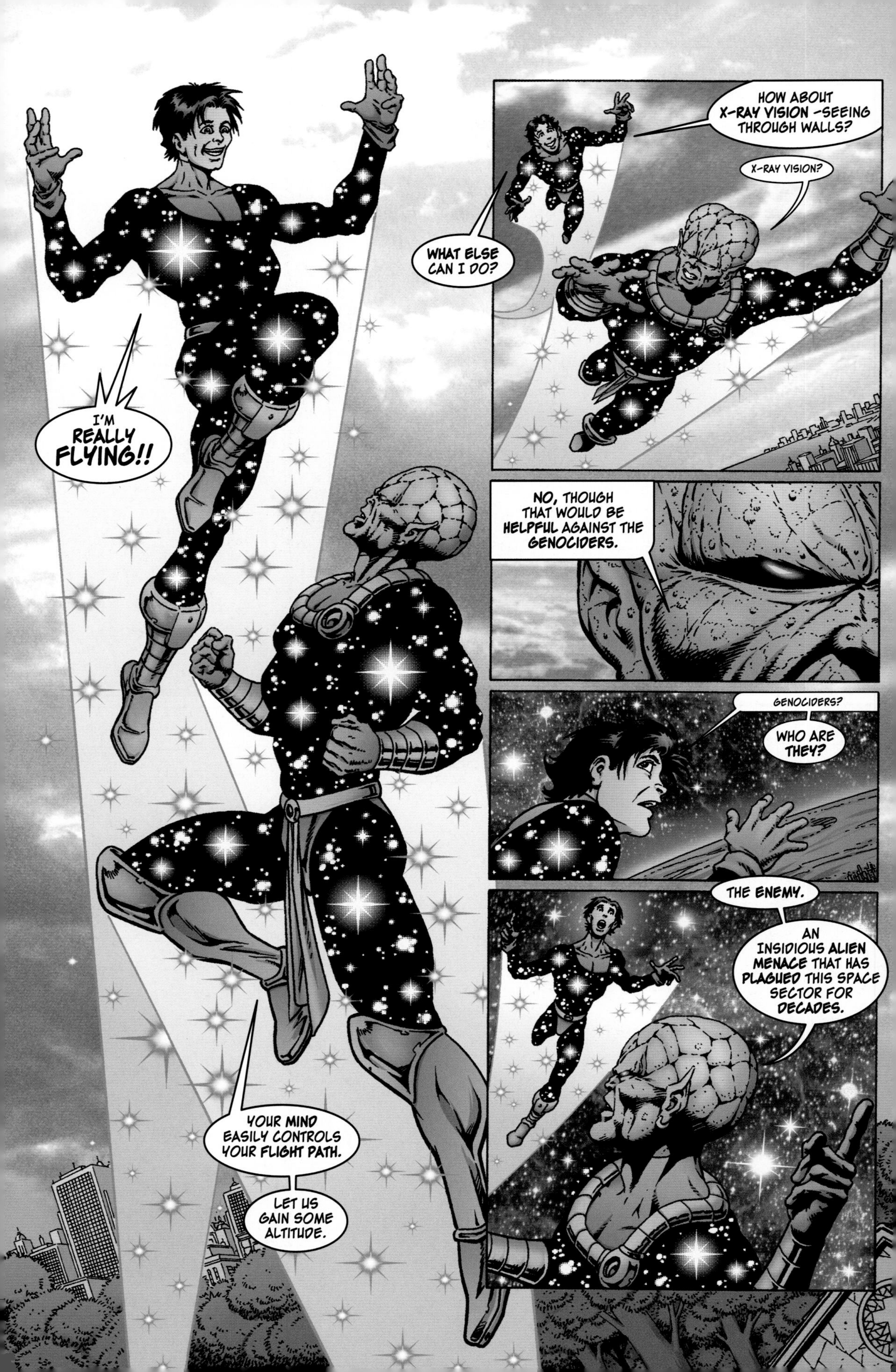
I'M REALLY FLYING!!
YOUR MIND EASILY CONTROLS YOUR FLIGHT PATH.
LET US GAIN SOME ALTITUDE.
WHAT ELSE CAN I DO?
HOW ABOUT X-RAY VISION -SEEING THROUGH WALLS?
X-RAY VISION?
NO, THOUGH THAT WOULD BE HELPFUL AGAINST THE GENOCIDERS.
GENOCIDERS?
WHO ARE THEY?
THE ENEMY.
AN INSIDIOUS ALIEN MENACE THAT HAS PLAGUED THIS SPACE SECTOR FOR DECADES.

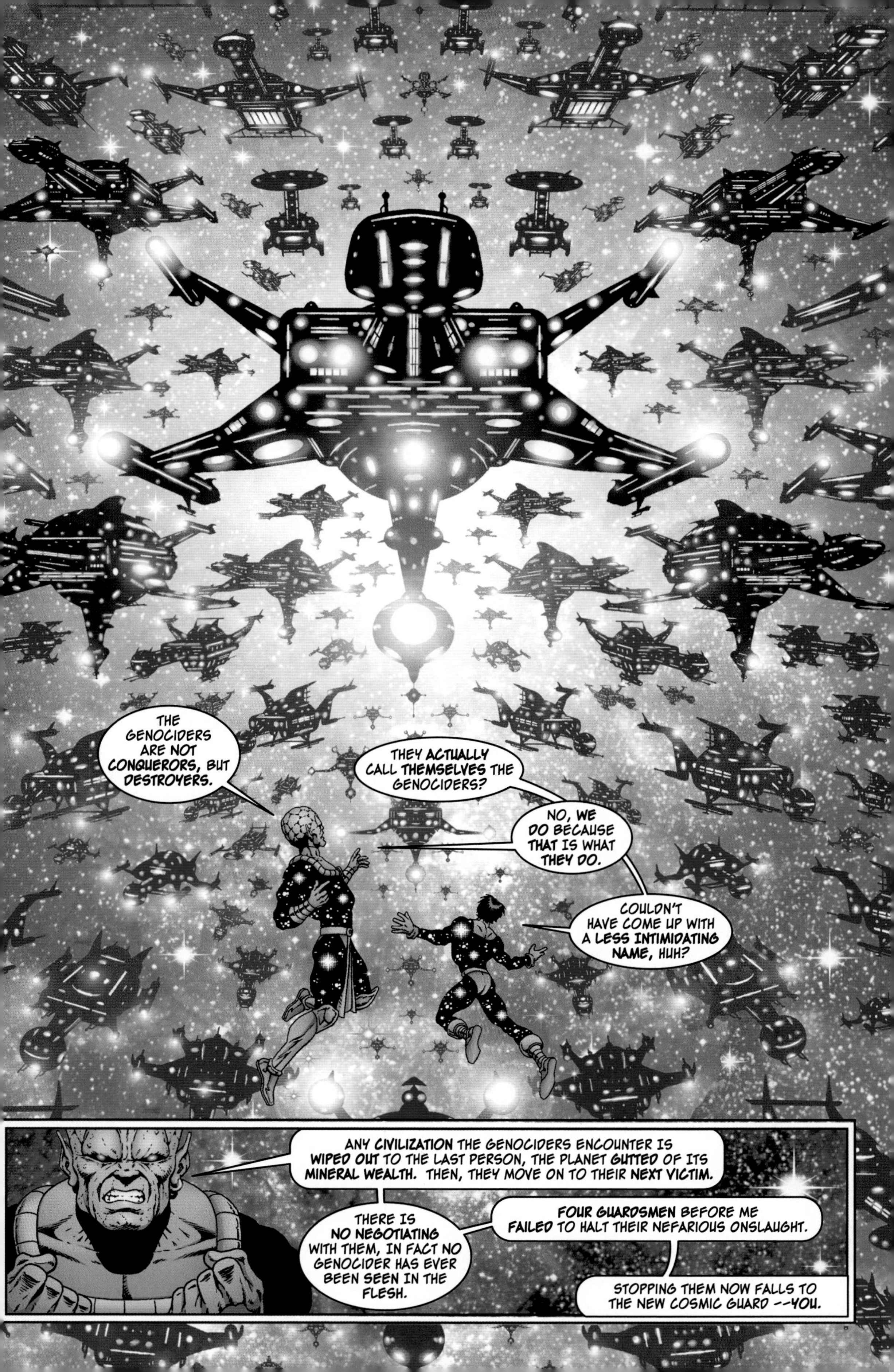

THE GENOCIDERS ARE NOT CONQUERORS, BUT DESTROYERS.
THEY ACTUALLY CALL THEMSELVES THE GENOCIDERS?
NO, WE DO BECAUSE THAT IS WHAT THEY DO.
COULDN'T HAVE COME UP WITH A LESS INTIMIDATING NAME, HUH?
ANY CIVILIZATION THE GENOCIDERS ENCOUNTER IS WIPED OUT TO THE LAST PERSON, THE PLANET GUTTED OF ITS MINERAL WEALTH. THEN, THEY MOVE ON TO THEIR NEXT VICTIM.
THERE IS NO NEGOTIATING WITH THEM, IN FACT NO GENOCIDER HAS EVER BEEN SEEN IN THE FLESH.
FOUR GUARDSMEN BEFORE ME FAILED TO HALT THEIR NEFARIOUS ONSLAUGHT.
STOPPING THEM NOW FALLS TO THE NEW COSMIC GUARD --YOU.

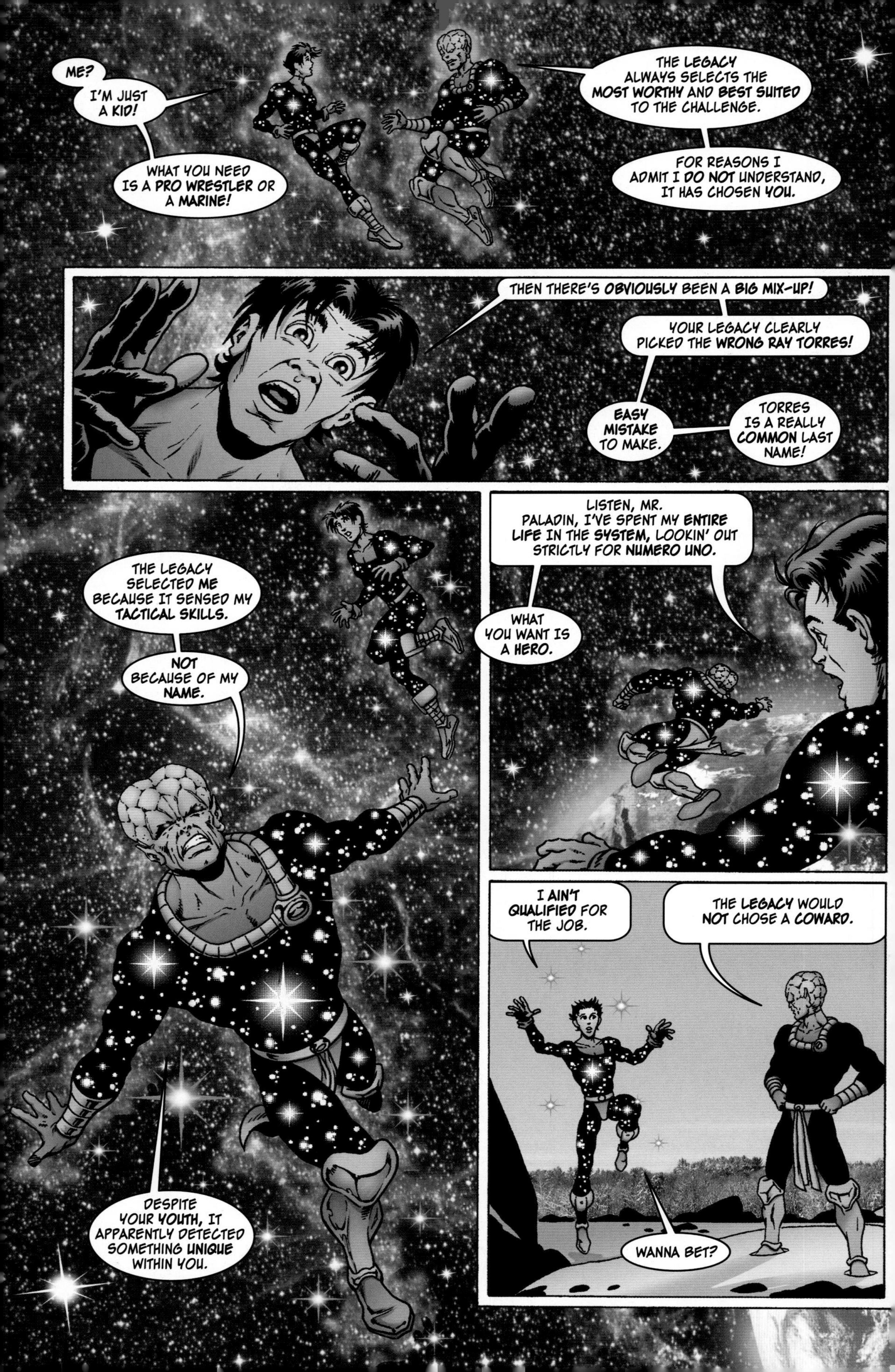

ME?
I'M JUST A KID!
WHAT YOU NEED IS A PRO WRESTLER OR A MARINE!
THE LEGACY ALWAYS SELECTS THE MOST WORTHY AND BEST SUITED TO THE CHALLENGE.
FOR REASONS I ADMIT I DO NOT UNDERSTAND, IT HAS CHOSEN YOU.
THEN THERE'S OBVIOUSLY BEEN A BIG MIX-UP!
YOUR LEGACY CLEARLY PICKED THE WRONG RAY TORRES!
TORRES IS A REALLY COMMON LAST NAME!
EASY MISTAKE TO MAKE.
THE LEGACY SELECTED ME BECAUSE IT SENSED MY TACTICAL SKILLS.
NOT BECAUSE OF MY NAME.
DESPITE YOUR YOUTH, IT APPARENTLY DETECTED SOMETHING UNIQUE WITHIN YOU.
LISTEN, MR. PALADIN, I'VE SPENT MY ENTIRE LIFE IN THE SYSTEM, LOOKIN' OUT STRICTLY FOR NUMERO UNO.
WHAT YOU WANT IS A HERO.
I AIN'T QUALIFIED FOR THE JOB.
THE LEGACY WOULD NOT CHOSE A COWARD.
WANNA BET?

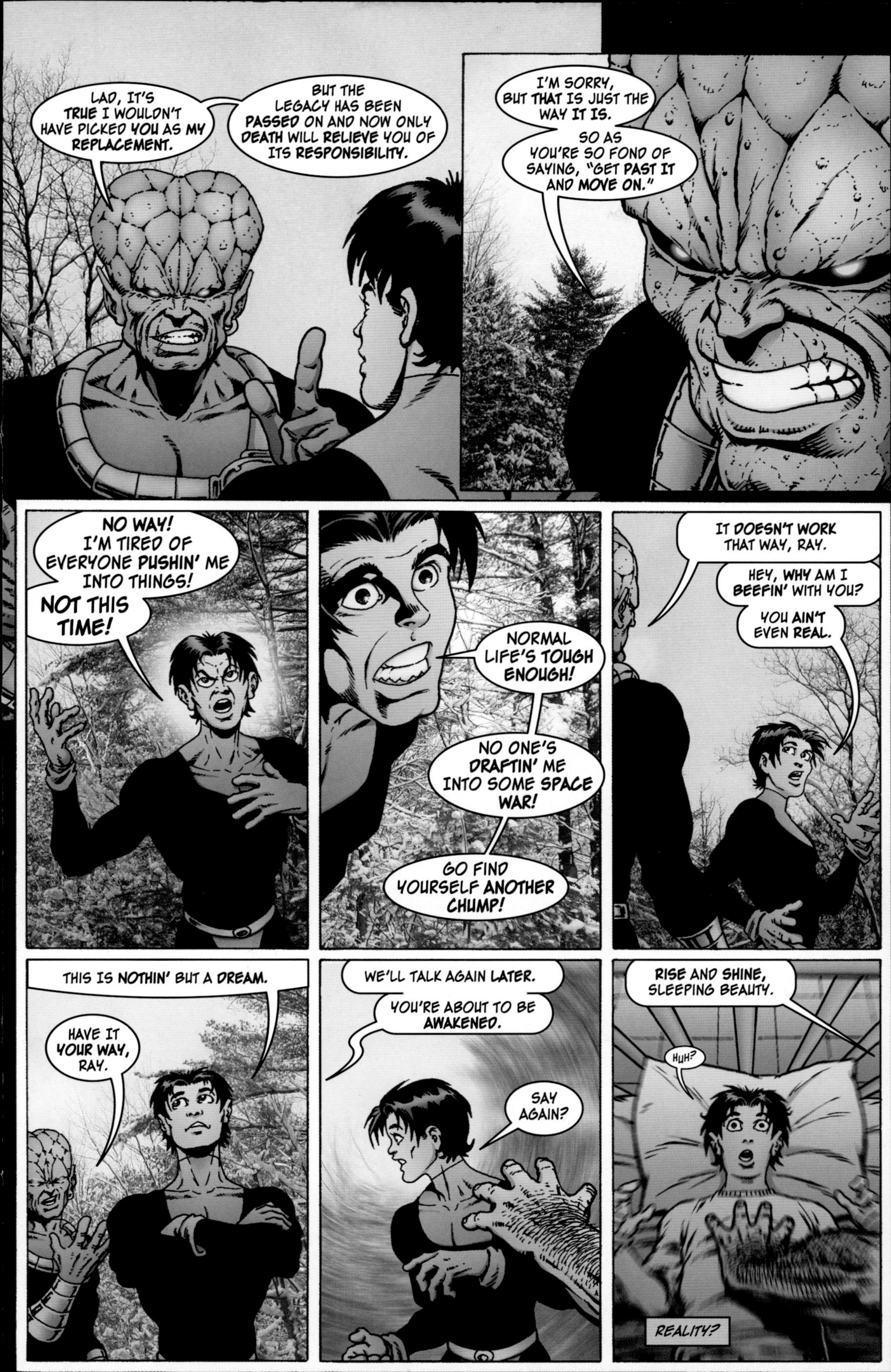
LAD, IT'S TRUE I WOULDN'T HAVE PICKED YOU AS MY REPLACEMENT.
BUT THE LEGACY HAS BEEN PASSED ON AND NOW ONLY DEATH WILL RELIEVE YOU OF ITS RESPONSIBILITY.
I'M SORRY, BUT THAT IS JUST THE WAY IT IS.
SO AS YOU'RE SO FOND OF SAYING, "GET PAST IT AND MOVE ON."
NO WAY! I'M TIRED OF EVERYONE PUSHIN' ME INTO THINGS!
NOT THIS TIME!
NORMAL LIFE'S TOUGH ENOUGH!
NO ONE'S DRAFTIN' ME INTO SOME SPACE WAR!
GO FIND YOURSELF ANOTHER CHUMP!
IT DOESN'T WORK THAT WAY, RAY.
HEY, WHY AM I BEEFIN' WITH YOU?
YOU AIN'T EVEN REAL.
THIS IS NOTHIN' BUT A DREAM.
HAVE IT YOUR WAY, RAY.
WE'LL TALK AGAIN LATER.
YOU'RE ABOUT TO BE AWAKENED.
SAY AGAIN?
RISE AND SHINE, SLEEPING BEAUTY.
HUH?
REALITY?

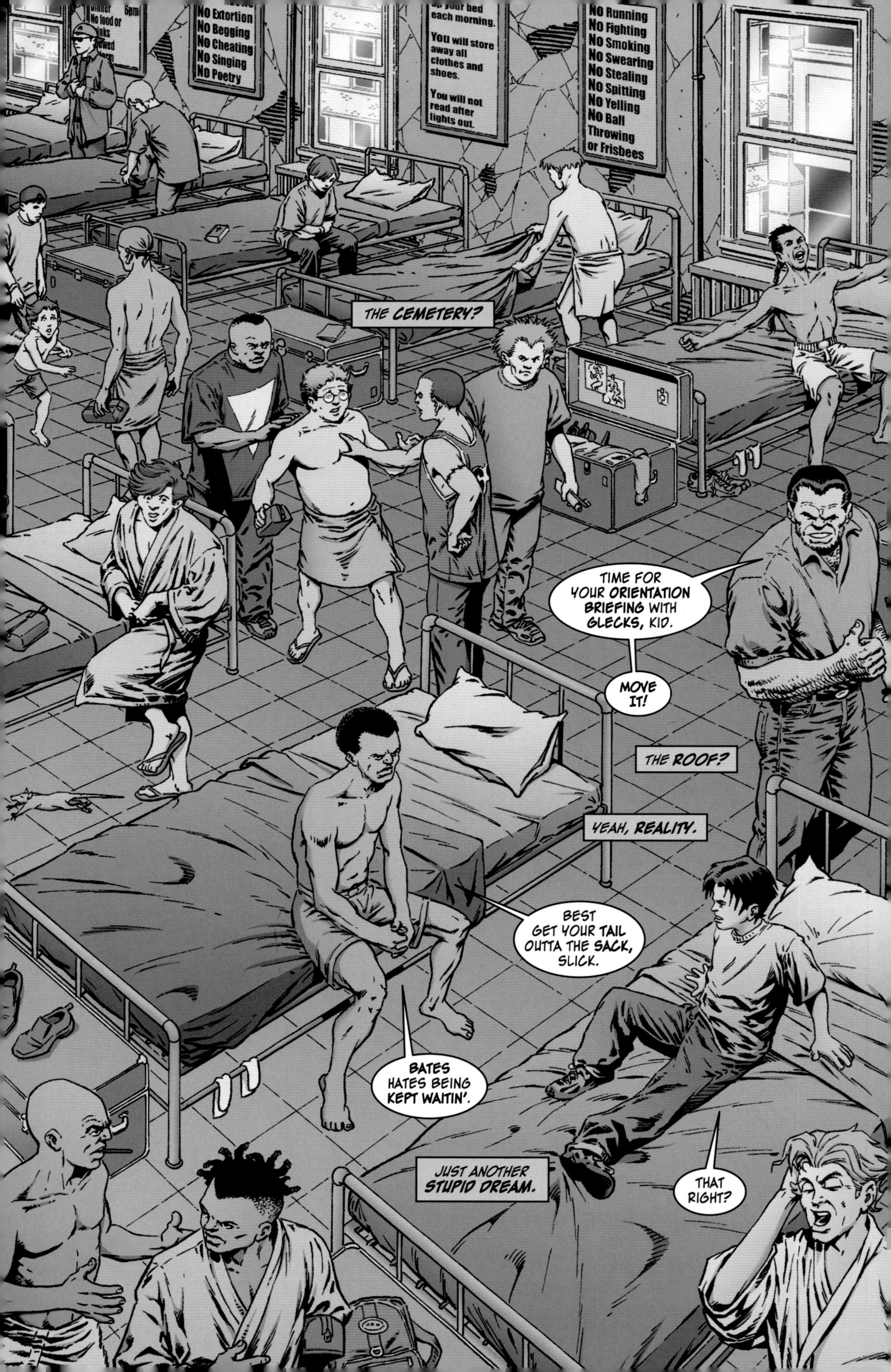
NO Extortion
NO Begging
NO Cheating
NO Singing
NO Poetry
each morning.
You will store away all clothes and shoes.
You will not read after lights out.
NO Running
NO Fighting
NO Smoking
NO Swearing
NO Stealing
NO Spitting
NO Yelling
NO Ball Throwing or Frisbees
THE CEMETERY?
TIME FOR YOUR ORIENTATION BRIEFING WITH GLECKS, KID.
MOVE IT!
THE ROOF?
YEAH, REALITY.
BEST GET YOUR TAIL OUTTA THE SACK, SLICK.
BATES HATES BEING KEPT WAITIN'.
JUST ANOTHER STUPID DREAM.
THAT RIGHT?

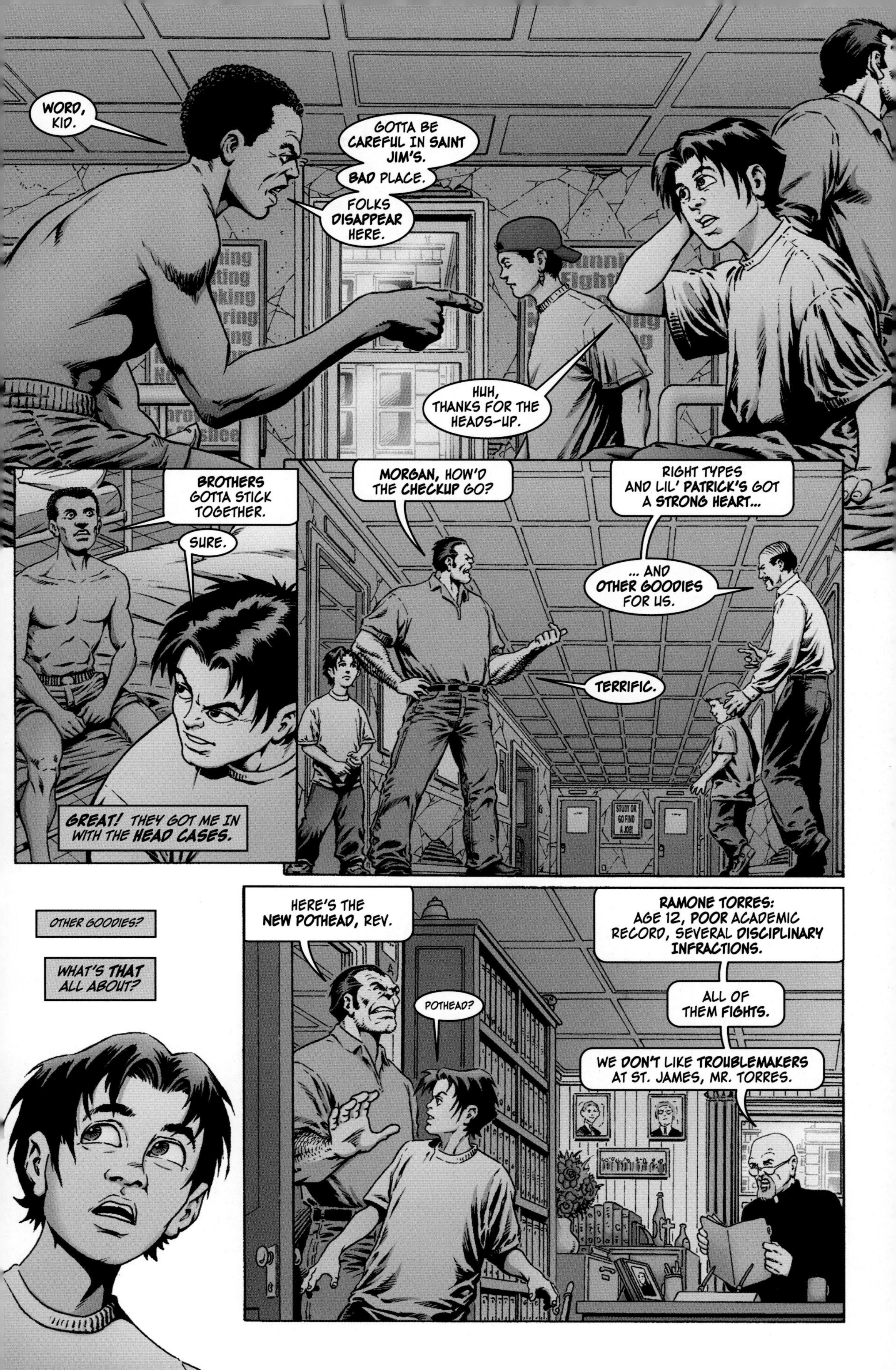
WORD, KID.
GOTTA BE CAREFUL IN SAINT JIM'S.
BAD PLACE.
FOLKS DISAPPEAR HERE.
HUH, THANKS FOR THE HEADS-UP.
BROTHERS GOTTA STICK TOGETHER.
SURE.
GREAT! THEY GOT ME IN WITH THE HEAD CASES.
MORGAN, HOW'D THE CHECKUP GO?
RIGHT TYPES AND LIL' PATRICK'S GOT A STRONG HEART...
... AND OTHER GOODIES FOR US.
TERRIFIC.
STUDY OR GO FIND A JOB!
OTHER GOODIES?
WHAT'S THAT ALL ABOUT?
HERE'S THE NEW POTHEAD, REV.
POTHEAD?
RAMONE TORRES: AGE 12, POOR ACADEMIC RECORD, SEVERAL DISCIPLINARY INFRACTIONS.
ALL OF THEM FIGHTS.
WE DON'T LIKE TROUBLEMAKERS AT ST. JAMES, MR. TORRES.

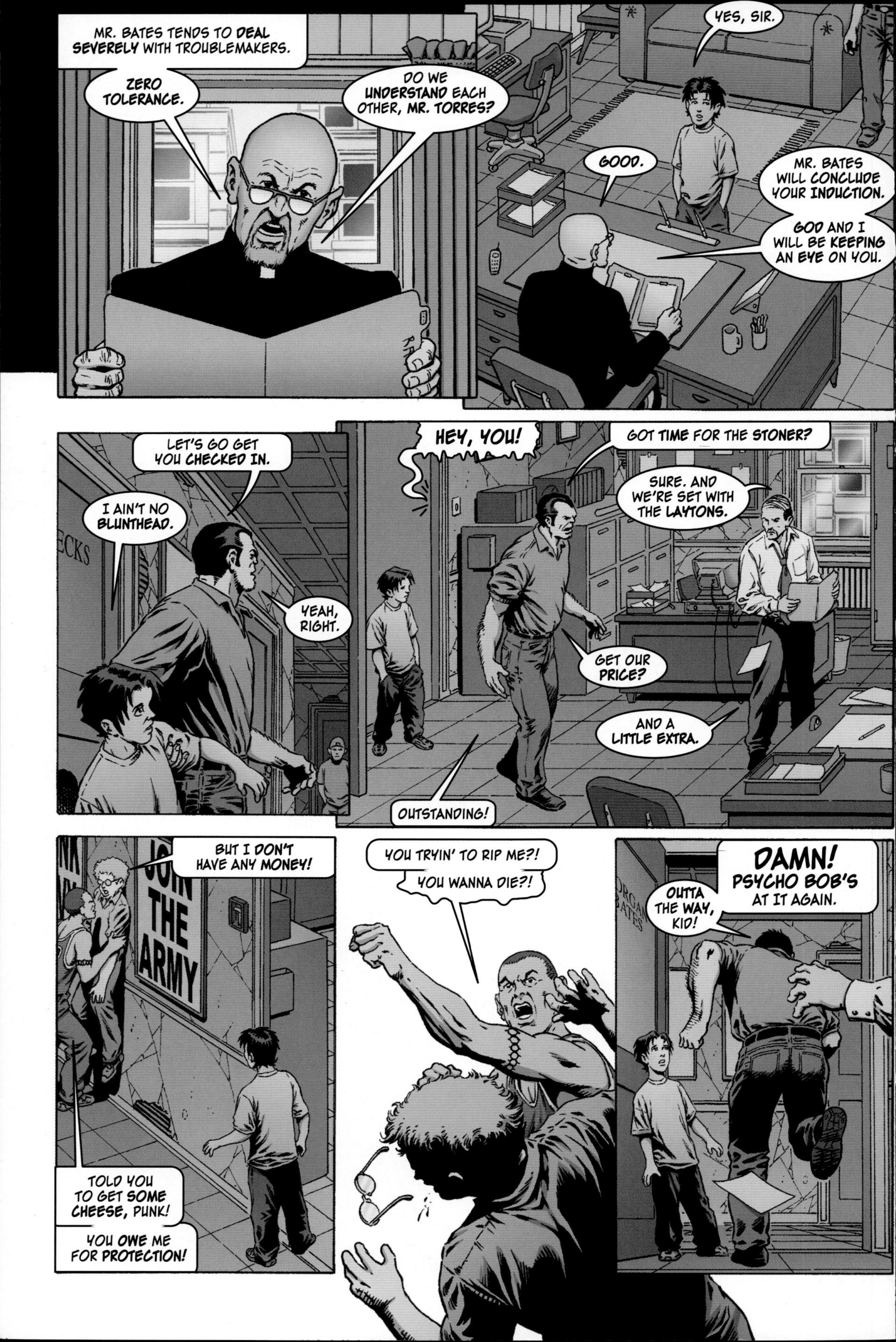
MR. BATES TENDS TO DEAL SEVERELY WITH TROUBLEMAKERS.
ZERO TOLERANCE.
DO WE UNDERSTAND EACH OTHER, MR. TORRES?
YES, SIR.
GOOD.
MR. BATES WILL CONCLUDE YOUR INDUCTION.
GOD AND I WILL BE KEEPING AN EYE ON YOU.
LET'S GO GET YOU CHECKED IN.
I AIN'T NO BLUNTHEAD.
YEAH, RIGHT.
HEY, YOU!
GOT TIME FOR THE STONER?
SURE. AND WE'RE SET WITH THE LAYTONS.
GET OUR PRICE?
AND A LITTLE EXTRA.
OUTSTANDING!
JOIN THE ARMY
BUT I DON'T HAVE ANY MONEY!
TOLD YOU TO GET SOME CHEESE, PUNK!
YOU OWE ME FOR PROTECTION!
YOU TRYIN' TO RIP ME?!
YOU WANNA DIE?!
DAMN! PSYCHO BOB'S AT IT AGAIN.
OUTTA THE WAY, KID!

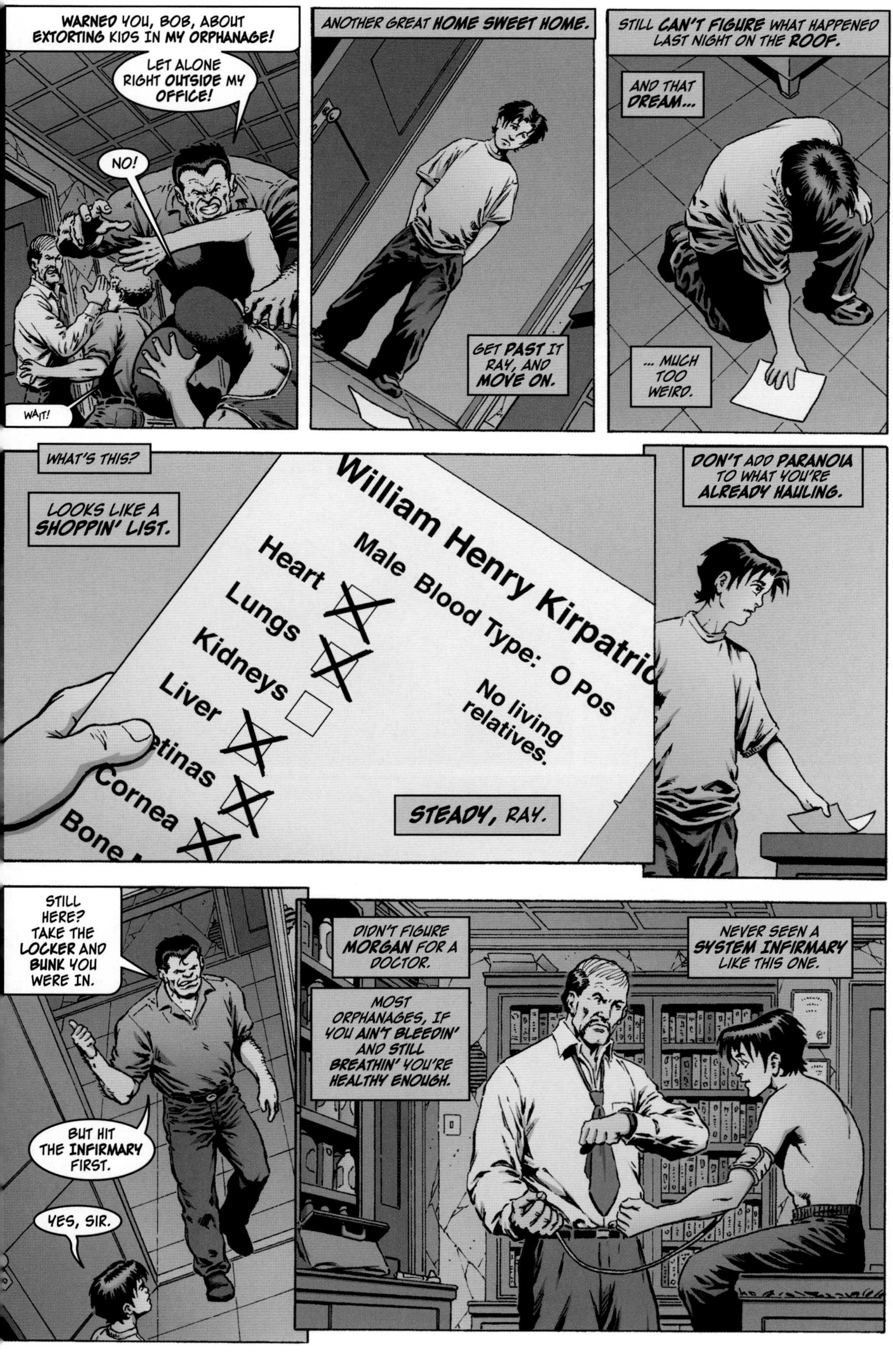
WARNED YOU, BOB, ABOUT EXTORTING KIDS IN MY ORPHANAGE!
LET ALONE RIGHT OUTSIDE MY OFFICE!
NO!
WAIT!
ANOTHER GREAT HOME SWEET HOME.
GET PAST IT RAY, AND MOVE ON.
STILL CAN'T FIGURE WHAT HAPPENED LAST NIGHT ON THE ROOF.
AND THAT DREAM...
... MUCH TOO WEIRD.
WHAT'S THIS?
LOOKS LIKE A SHOPPIN' LIST.
William Henry Kirpatric
Male Blood Type: O Pos
Heart
Lungs
Kidneys
Liver
etinas
Cornea
Bone
No living relatives.
STEADY, RAY.
DON'T ADD PARANOIA TO WHAT YOU'RE ALREADY HAULING.
STILL HERE? TAKE THE LOCKER AND BUNK YOU WERE IN.
BUT HIT THE INFIRMARY FIRST.
YES, SIR.
DIDN'T FIGURE MORGAN FOR A DOCTOR.
MOST ORPHANAGES, IF YOU AIN'T BLEEDIN' AND STILL BREATHIN' YOU'RE HEALTHY ENOUGH.
NEVER SEEN A SYSTEM INFIRMARY LIKE THIS ONE.

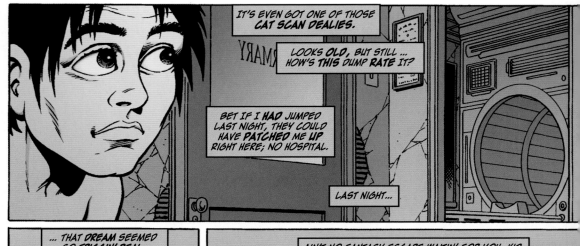

IT'S EVEN GOT ONE OF THOSE *CAT SCAN DEALIES.*

LOOKS *OLD,* BUT STILL ... HOW'S *THIS DUMP* RATE IT?

BET IF I *HAD* JUMPED LAST NIGHT, THEY COULD HAVE *PATCHED* ME *UP* RIGHT HERE; NO HOSPITAL.

LAST NIGHT...

... THAT DREAM SEEMED SO *FRIGGIN'* REAL.

FELT THAT *GRAVESTONE* IN MY HANDS.

YOU'RE TRIPPIN', RAY.

AIN'T NO FANTASY ESCAPE WAITIN' FOR YOU, KID.

BETTER *SETTLE* IN AND *LEARN* HOW *THINGS WORK* AROUND HERE.

JUST REMEMBER: KEEP YOUR LIP *SHUT,* HEAD *DOWN* AND STAY *OUTTA--*

OH, *BOY!*

THIS IS SO *NOT RIGHT.*

TEACH YOU TO HOLD OUT ON ME!

AIN'T YOUR PROBLEM, RAY.

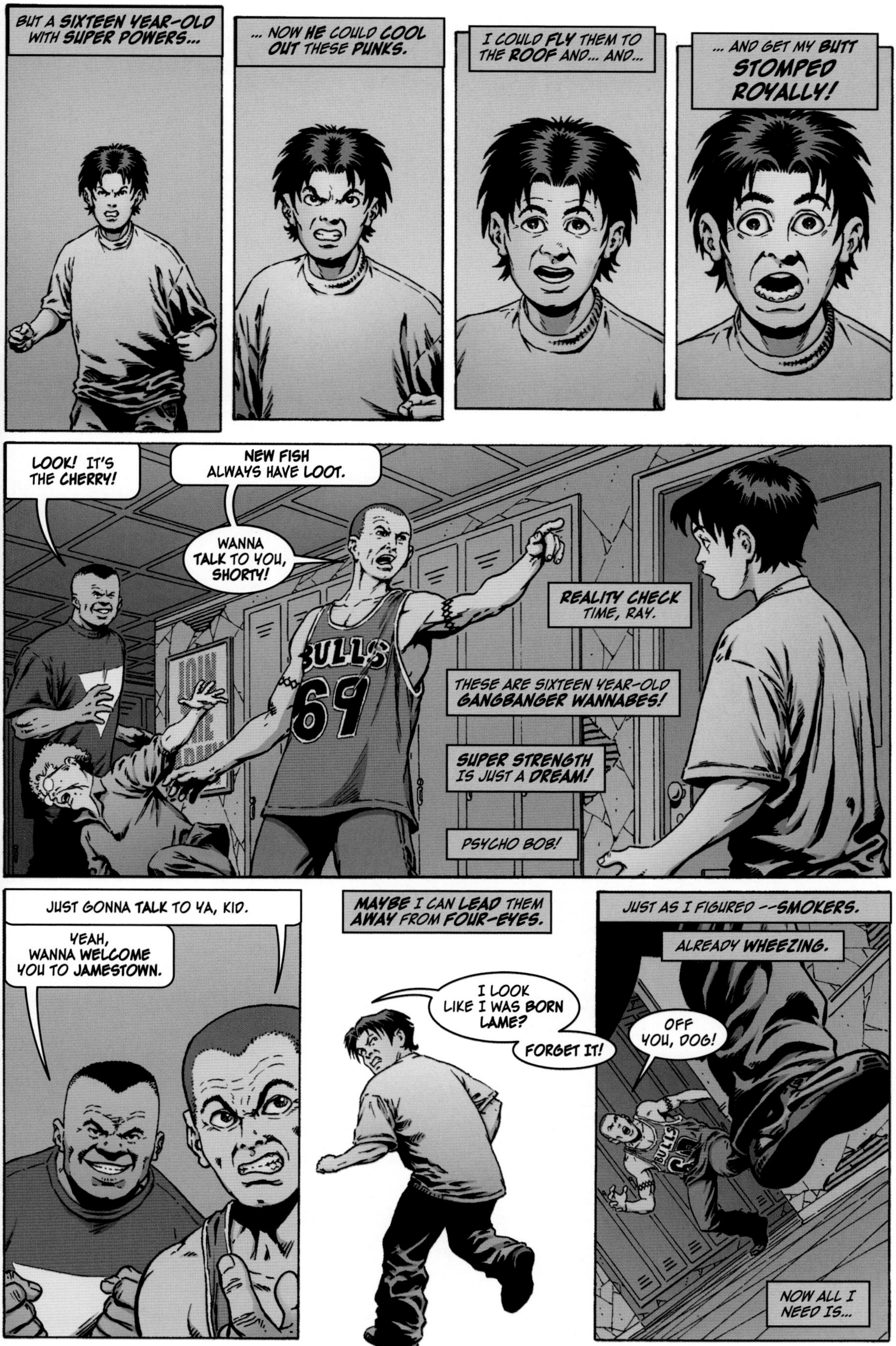
BUT A SIXTEEN YEAR-OLD WITH SUPER POWERS...
... NOW HE COULD COOL OUT THESE PUNKS.
I COULD FLY THEM TO THE ROOF AND... AND...
... AND GET MY BUTT STOMPED ROYALLY!
LOOK! IT'S THE CHERRY!
NEW FISH ALWAYS HAVE LOOT.
WANNA TALK TO YOU, SHORTY!
REALITY CHECK TIME, RAY.
THESE ARE SIXTEEN YEAR-OLD GANGBANGER WANNABES!
SUPER STRENGTH IS JUST A DREAM!
PSYCHO BOB!
BULLS 69
JUST GONNA TALK TO YA, KID.
YEAH, WANNA WELCOME YOU TO JAMESTOWN.
MAYBE I CAN LEAD THEM AWAY FROM FOUR-EYES.
I LOOK LIKE I WAS BORN LAME?
FORGET IT!
JUST AS I FIGURED --SMOKERS.
ALREADY WHEEZING.
OFF YOU, DOG!
NOW ALL I NEED IS...

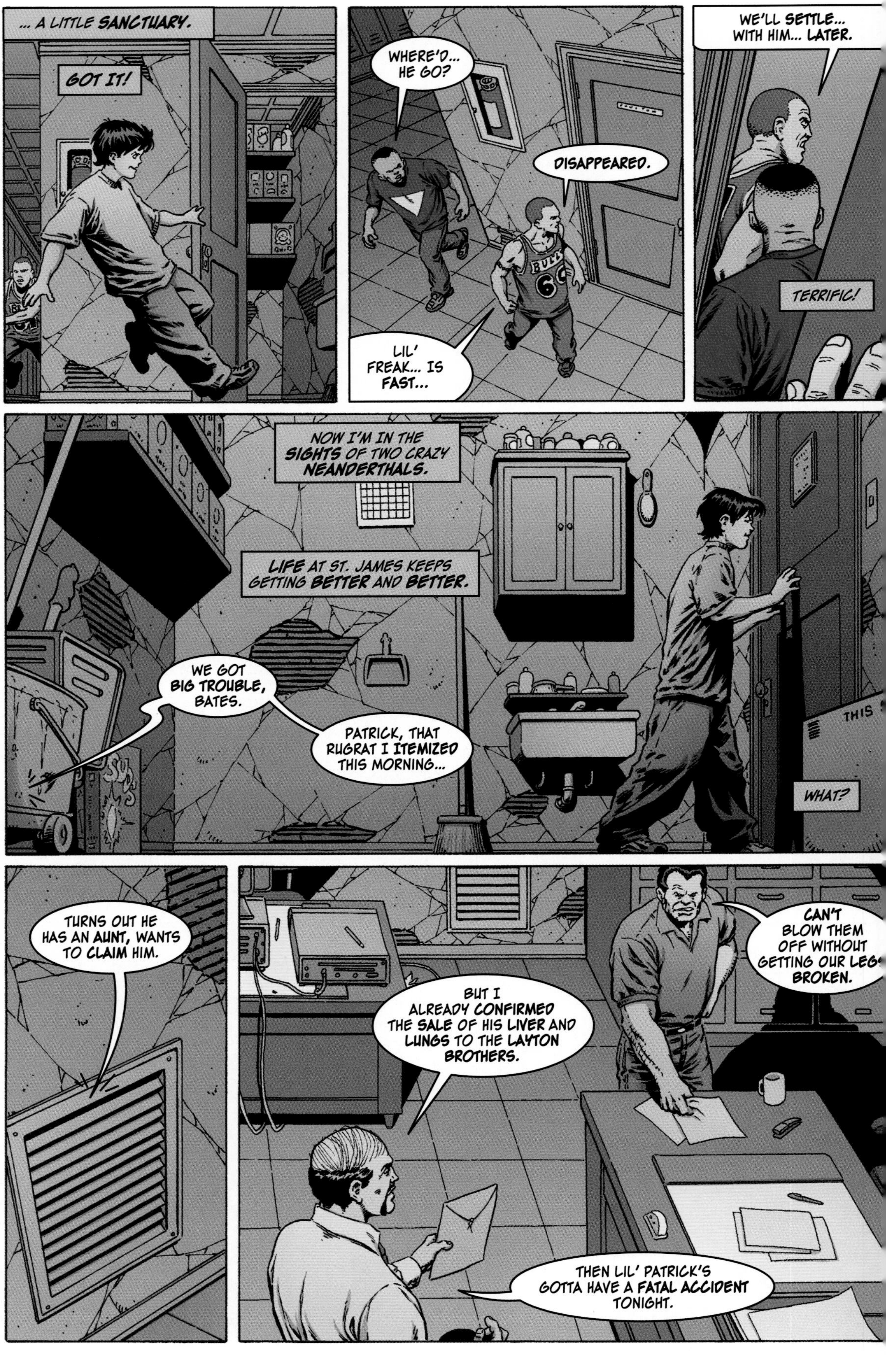

... A LITTLE SANCTUARY.
GOT IT!
WHERE'D... HE GO?
DISAPPEARED.
LIL' FREAK... IS FAST...
WE'LL SETTLE... WITH HIM... LATER.
TERRIFIC!
NOW I'M IN THE SIGHTS OF TWO CRAZY NEANDERTHALS.
LIFE AT ST. JAMES KEEPS GETTING BETTER AND BETTER.
WE GOT BIG TROUBLE, BATES.
PATRICK, THAT RUGRAT I ITEMIZED THIS MORNING...
WHAT?
TURNS OUT HE HAS AN AUNT, WANTS TO CLAIM HIM.
BUT I ALREADY CONFIRMED THE SALE OF HIS LIVER AND LUNGS TO THE LAYTON BROTHERS.
CAN'T BLOW THEM OFF WITHOUT GETTING OUR LEGS BROKEN.
THEN LIL' PATRICK'S GOTTA HAVE A FATAL ACCIDENT TONIGHT.

YEAH, ANOTHER TRAGIC BRAIN INJURY.
THEY'RE ACTUALLY GONNA TAKE OUT THAT KID...
... AND SELL HIS ORGANS!
FRIGGIN' GHOULS!
AND THERE AIN'T A THING I CAN DO TO SAVE HIM.
HANDS DOWN, THIS IS DEFINITELY THE WORST ORPHANAGE YET!
PRETTY SWEET, HUH, MOM AND DAD?
IN THIS PHOTO I SWIPED FROM MY FILE...
... YOU BOTH LOOK LIKE ALL-RIGHT, CARING PEOPLE.
JACK'S
CHEQUES
GIROS
MONEY
ORDERS
CHECKS
CASH
SO WHAT HAPPENED TO YOU?
WHERE'D YOU GO?
INCOME TAXES REPARED
WHY'D YOU DESERT ME?
CAN'T IMAGINE THIS IS THE LIFE YOU WANTED FOR ME.
BUT IT'S WHAT I'M STUCK WITH.
NOW ALL I GOT TO DO IS SURVIVE IT.
SUDS

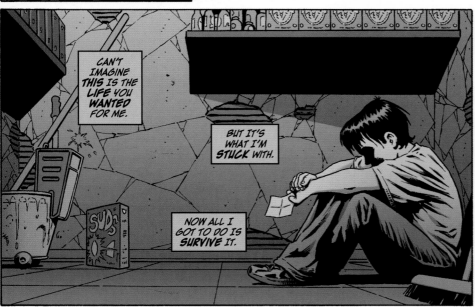

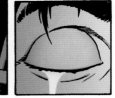

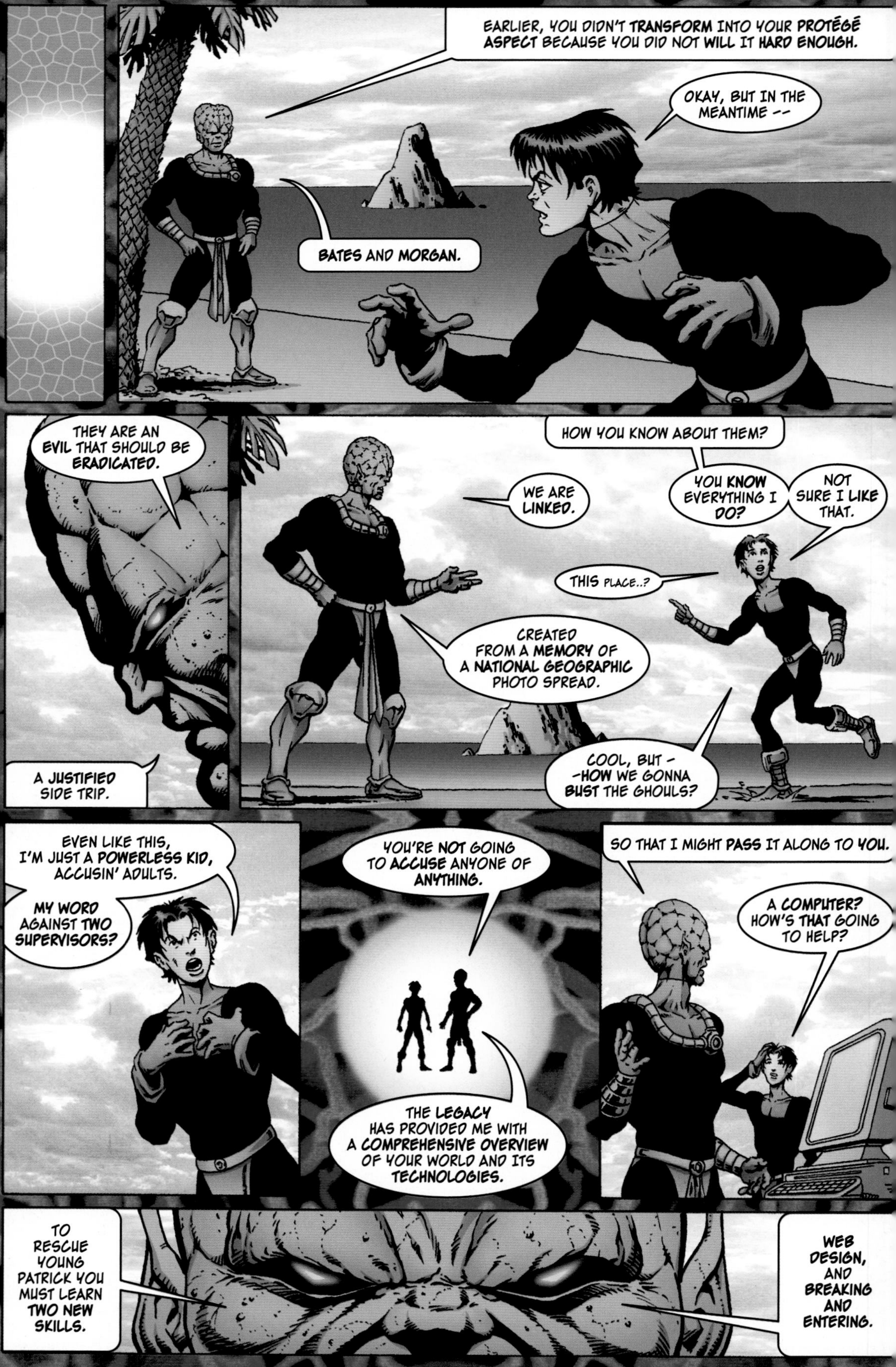
EARLIER, YOU DIDN'T TRANSFORM INTO YOUR PROTÉGÉ ASPECT BECAUSE YOU DID NOT WILL IT HARD ENOUGH.
OKAY, BUT IN THE MEANTIME --
BATES AND MORGAN.
THEY ARE AN EVIL THAT SHOULD BE ERADICATED.
A JUSTIFIED SIDE TRIP.
HOW YOU KNOW ABOUT THEM?
WE ARE LINKED.
YOU KNOW EVERYTHING I DO?
NOT SURE I LIKE THAT.
THIS PLACE..?
CREATED FROM A MEMORY OF A NATIONAL GEOGRAPHIC PHOTO SPREAD.
COOL, BUT -
-HOW WE GONNA BUST THE GHOULS?
EVEN LIKE THIS, I'M JUST A POWERLESS KID, ACCUSIN' ADULTS.
MY WORD AGAINST TWO SUPERVISORS?
YOU'RE NOT GOING TO ACCUSE ANYONE OF ANYTHING.
THE LEGACY HAS PROVIDED ME WITH A COMPREHENSIVE OVERVIEW OF YOUR WORLD AND ITS TECHNOLOGIES.
SO THAT I MIGHT PASS IT ALONG TO YOU.
A COMPUTER? HOW'S THAT GOING TO HELP?
TO RESCUE YOUNG PATRICK YOU MUST LEARN TWO NEW SKILLS.
WEB DESIGN, AND BREAKING AND ENTERING.

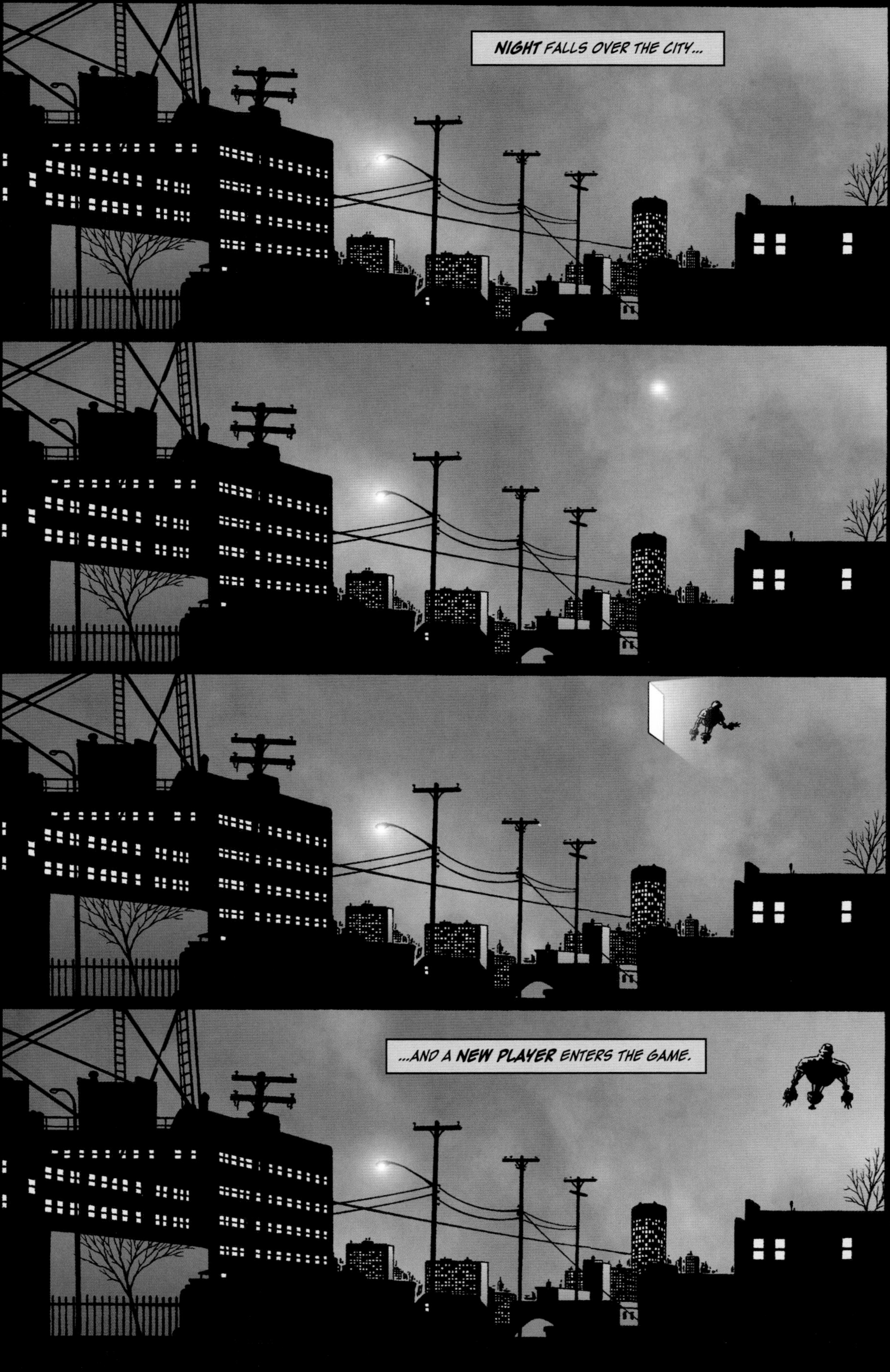
NIGHT FALLS OVER THE CITY...
...AND A NEW PLAYER ENTERS THE GAME.

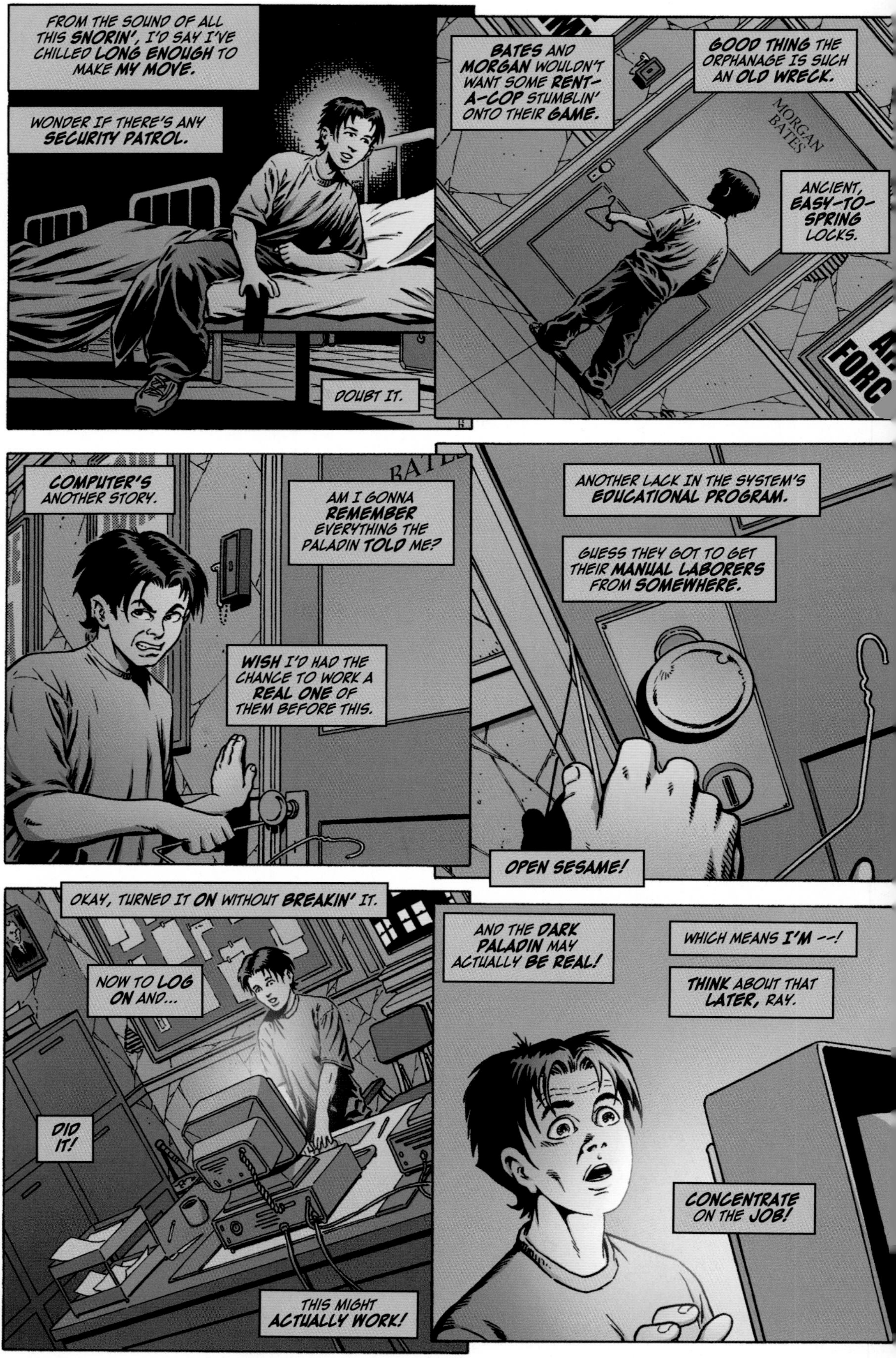
FROM THE SOUND OF ALL THIS SNORIN', I'D SAY I'VE CHILLED LONG ENOUGH TO MAKE MY MOVE.
WONDER IF THERE'S ANY SECURITY PATROL.
DOUBT IT.
BATES AND MORGAN WOULDN'T WANT SOME RENT-A-COP STUMBLIN' ONTO THEIR GAME.
GOOD THING THE ORPHANAGE IS SUCH AN OLD WRECK.
MORGAN
BATES
ANCIENT, EASY-TO-SPRING LOCKS.
COMPUTER'S ANOTHER STORY.
AM I GONNA REMEMBER EVERYTHING THE PALADIN TOLD ME?
WISH I'D HAD THE CHANCE TO WORK A REAL ONE OF THEM BEFORE THIS.
ANOTHER LACK IN THE SYSTEM'S EDUCATIONAL PROGRAM.
GUESS THEY GOT TO GET THEIR MANUAL LABORERS FROM SOMEWHERE.
OPEN SESAME!
OKAY, TURNED IT ON WITHOUT BREAKIN' IT.
NOW TO LOG ON AND...
DID IT!
THIS MIGHT ACTUALLY WORK!
AND THE DARK PALADIN MAY ACTUALLY BE REAL!
WHICH MEANS I'M --!
THINK ABOUT THAT LATER, RAY.
CONCENTRATE ON THE JOB!

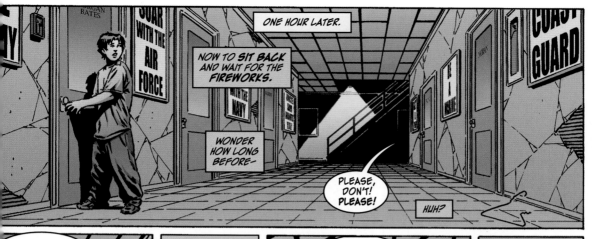

ONE HOUR LATER.

NOW TO SIT BACK AND WAIT FOR THE FIREWORKS.

WONDER HOW LONG BEFORE—

PLEASE, DON'T! PLEASE!

HUH?

DON'T MAKE ME DISAPPEAR!

I'LL BE GOOD!

I PROMISE!

BATES AND MORGAN WITH THAT KID...

PATRICK!

WE'RE JUST GOING TO THE ROOF FOR SOME AIR, KID.

SETTLE DOWN.

PLEASE!

"ANOTHER TRAGIC BRAIN INJURY."

THEY'RE GONNA —–!

QUIT YOUR WHINING, KID.

YOU'RE GONNA WAKE EVERYBODY UP.

I JUST CAN'T LET THIS GO DOWN!

CAN'T!

WON'T!

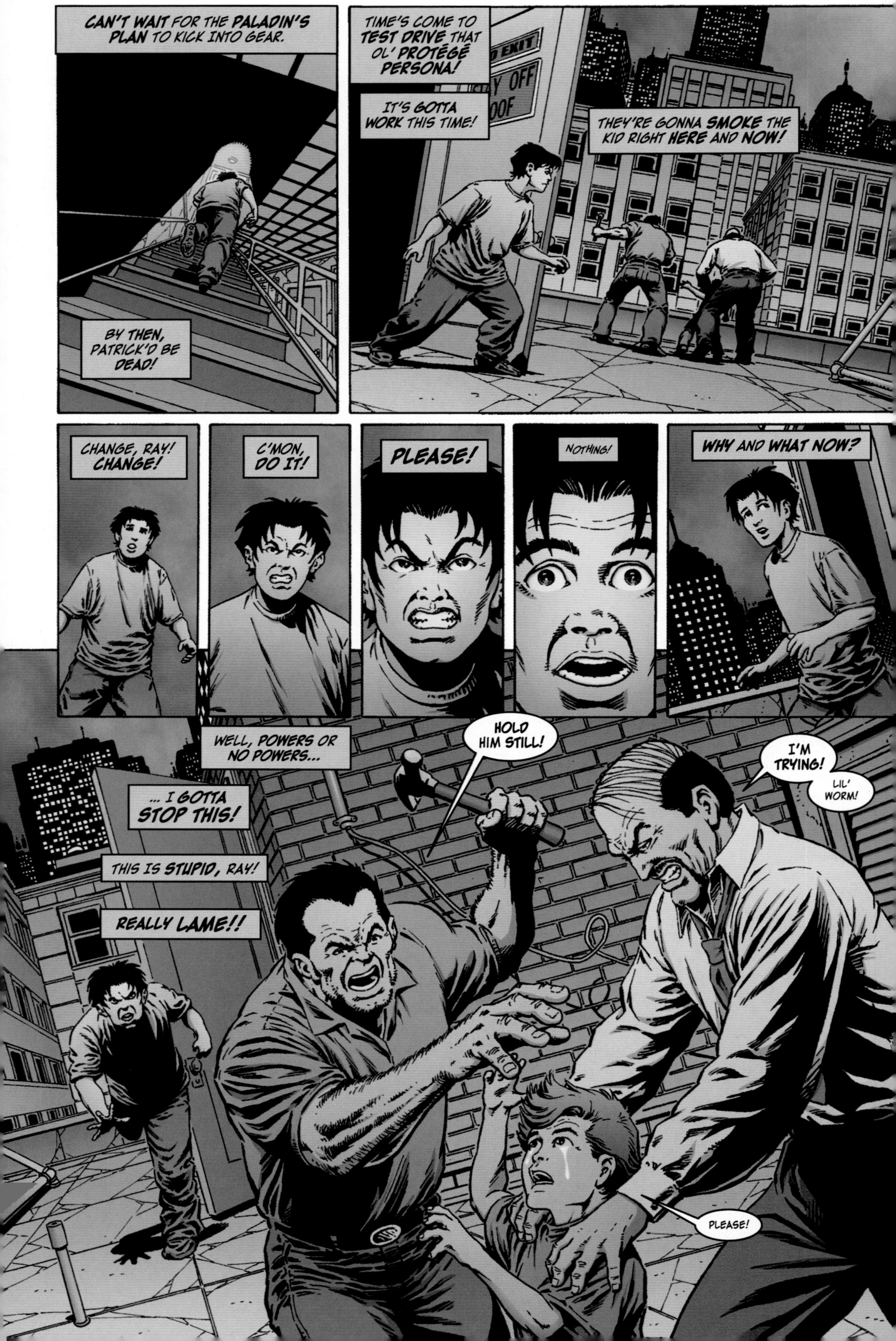
CAN'T WAIT FOR THE PALADIN'S PLAN TO KICK INTO GEAR.
BY THEN, PATRICK'D BE DEAD!
TIME'S COME TO TEST DRIVE THAT OL' PROTÉGÉ PERSONA!
IT'S GOTTA WORK THIS TIME!
THEY'RE GONNA SMOKE THE KID RIGHT HERE AND NOW!
CHANGE, RAY! CHANGE!
C'MON, DO IT!
PLEASE!
NOTHING!
WHY AND WHAT NOW?
WELL, POWERS OR NO POWERS...
... I GOTTA STOP THIS!
THIS IS STUPID, RAY!
REALLY LAME!!
HOLD HIM STILL!
I'M TRYING!
LIL' WORM!
PLEASE!

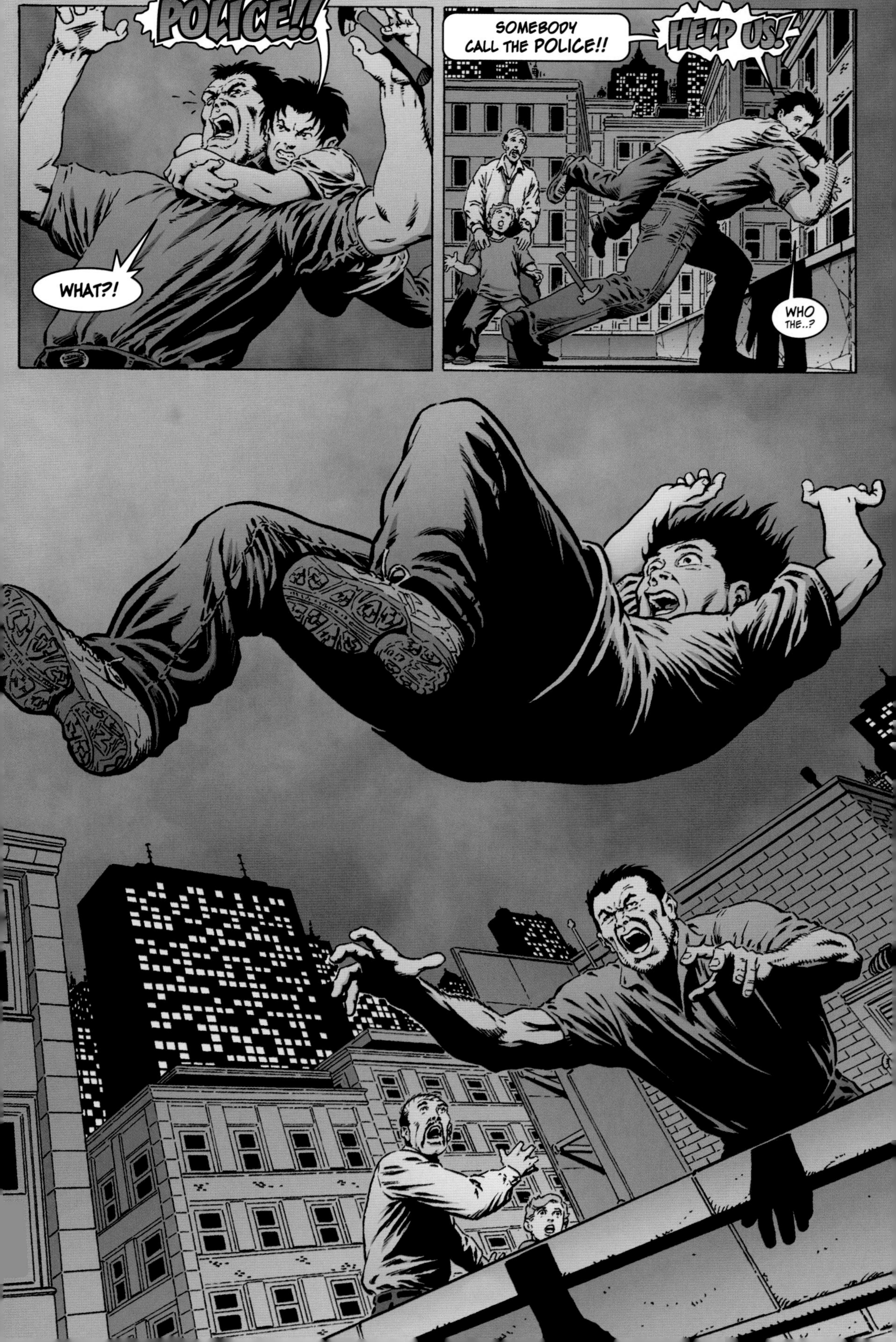
POLICE!!
WHAT?!
SOMEBODY CALL THE POLICE!!
HELP US!
WHO THE..?

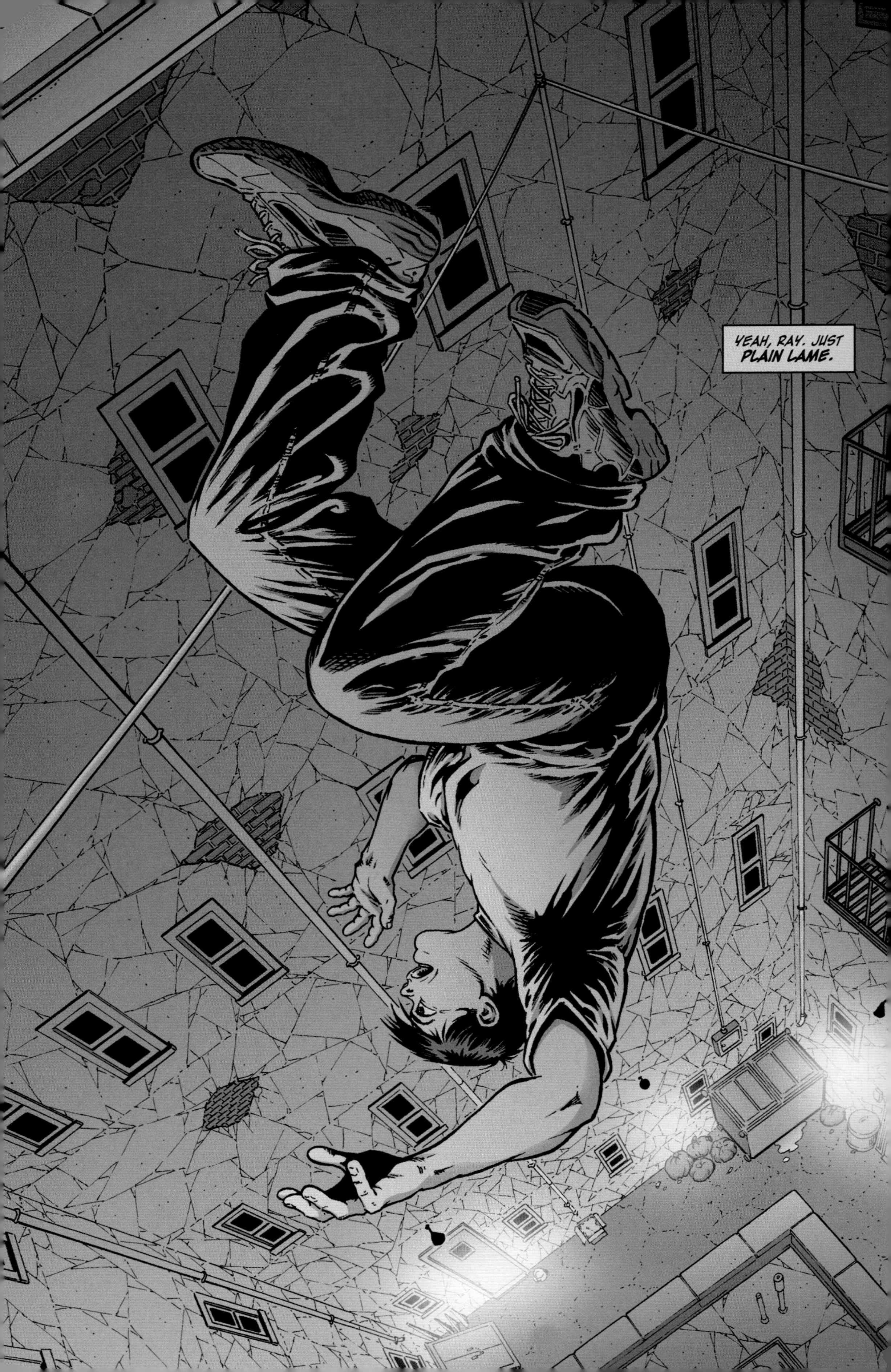
YEAH, RAY. JUST PLAIN LAME.

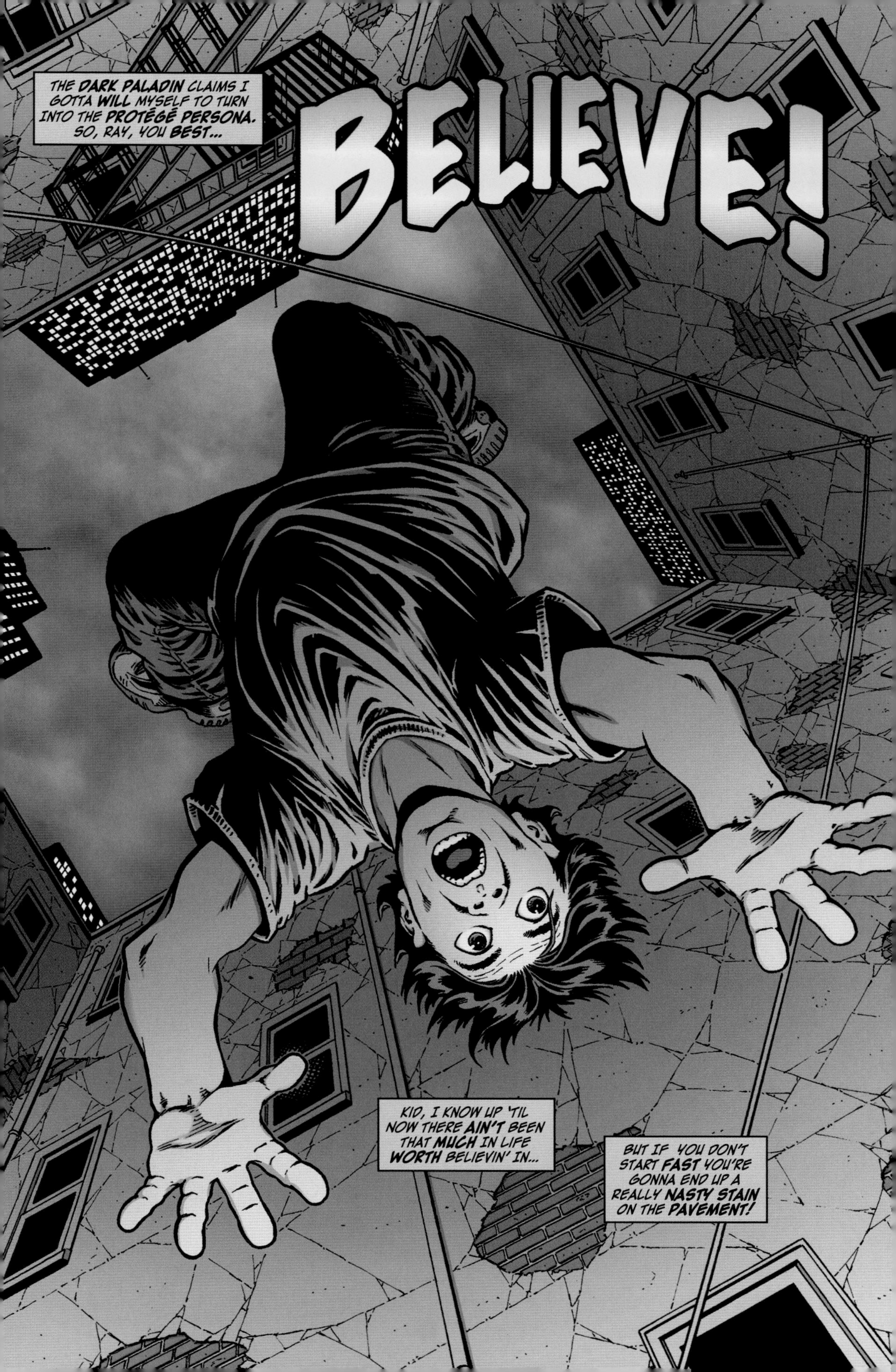
THE DARK PALADIN CLAIMS I GOTTA WILL MYSELF TO TURN INTO THE PROTÉGÉ PERSONA. SO, RAY, YOU BEST...
BELIEVE!
KID, I KNOW UP 'TIL NOW THERE AIN'T BEEN THAT MUCH IN LIFE WORTH BELIEVIN' IN...
BUT IF YOU DON'T START FAST YOU'RE GONNA END UP A REALLY NASTY STAIN ON THE PAVEMENT!

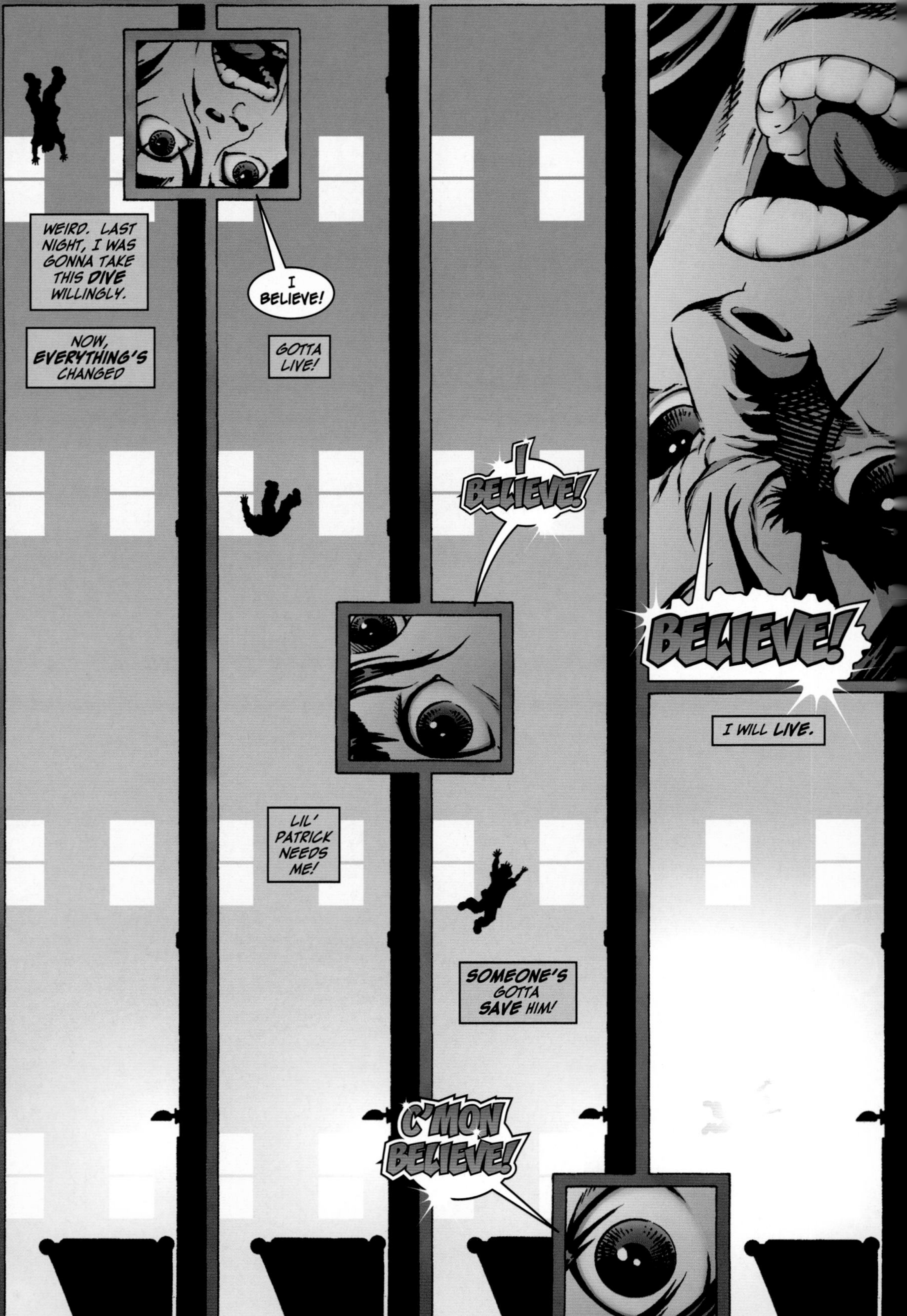

WEIRD. LAST NIGHT, I WAS GONNA TAKE THIS DIVE WILLINGLY.
NOW, EVERYTHING'S CHANGED
I BELIEVE!
GOTTA LIVE!
LIL' PATRICK NEEDS ME!
I BELIEVE!
SOMEONE'S GOTTA SAVE HIM!
C'MON BELIEVE!
BELIEVE!
I WILL LIVE.

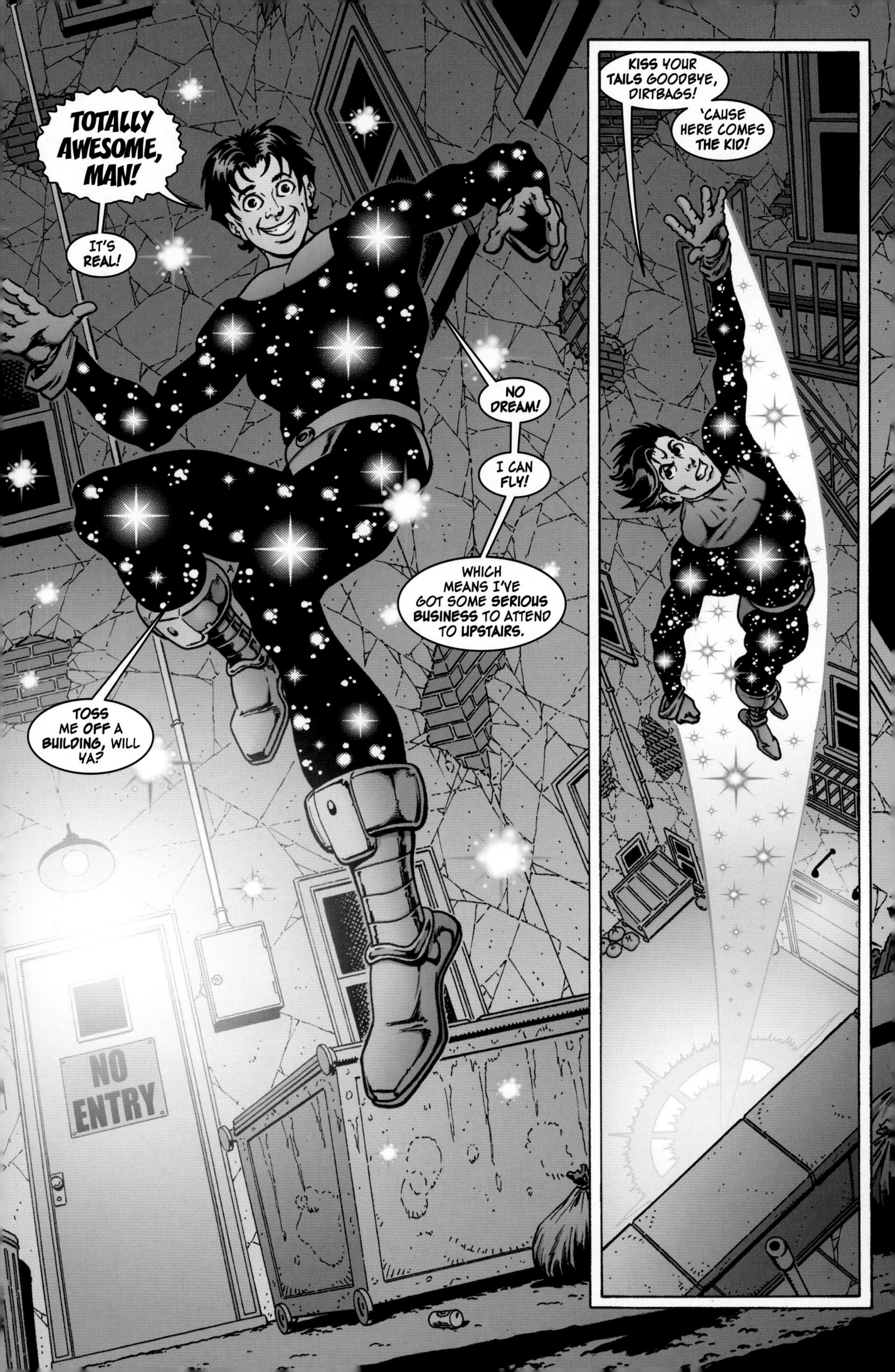
TOTALLY AWESOME, MAN!
IT'S REAL!
NO DREAM!
I CAN FLY!
WHICH MEANS I'VE GOT SOME SERIOUS BUSINESS TO ATTEND TO UPSTAIRS.
TOSS ME OFF A BUILDING, WILL YA?
NO ENTRY
KISS YOUR TAILS GOODBYE, DIRTBAGS!
'CAUSE HERE COMES THE KID!

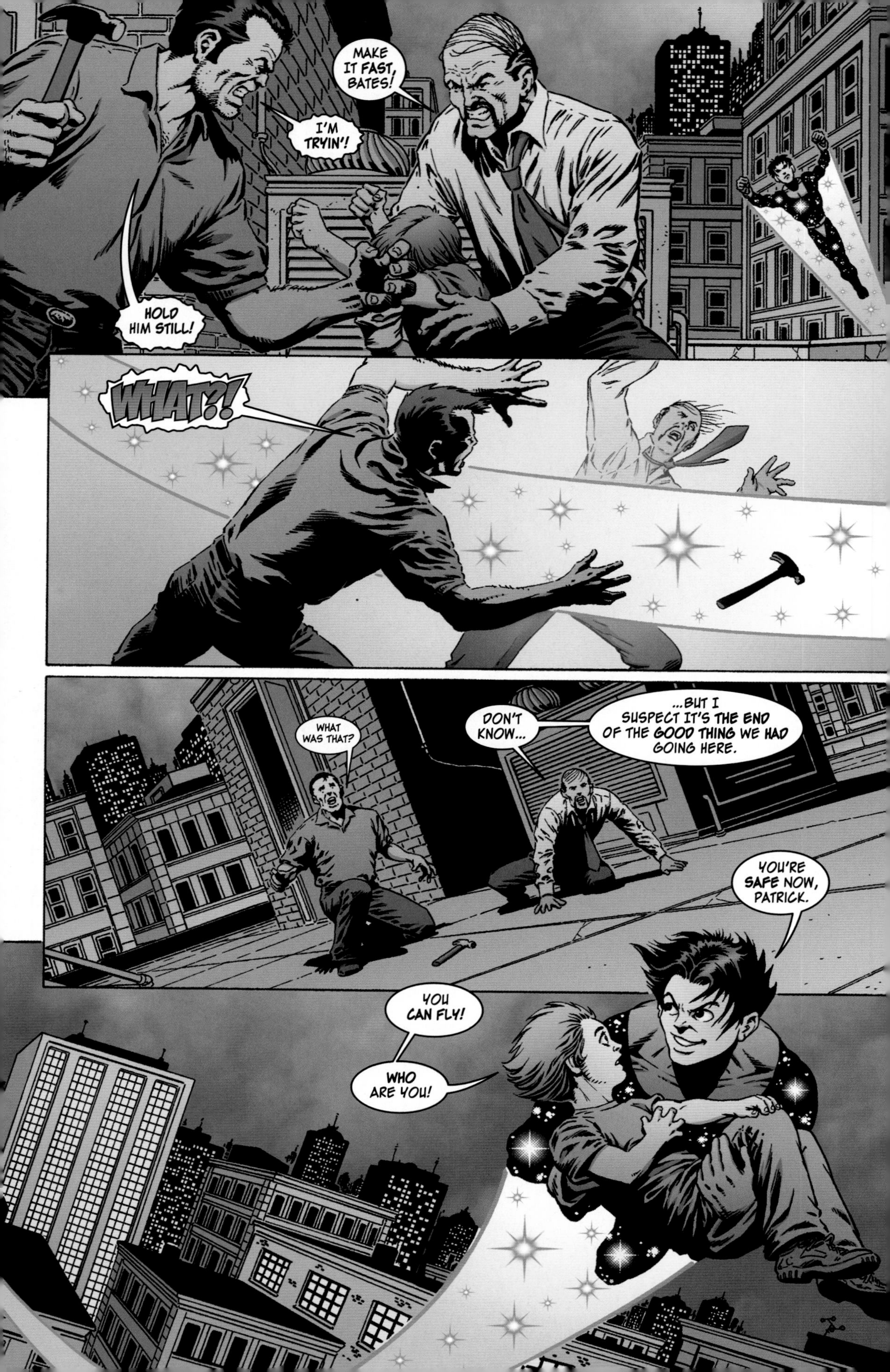
MAKE IT FAST, BATES!
I'M TRYIN'!
HOLD HIM STILL!
WHAT?!
WHAT WAS THAT?
DON'T KNOW...
...BUT I SUSPECT IT'S THE END OF THE GOOD THING WE HAD GOING HERE.
YOU'RE SAFE NOW, PATRICK.
YOU CAN FLY!
WHO ARE YOU!

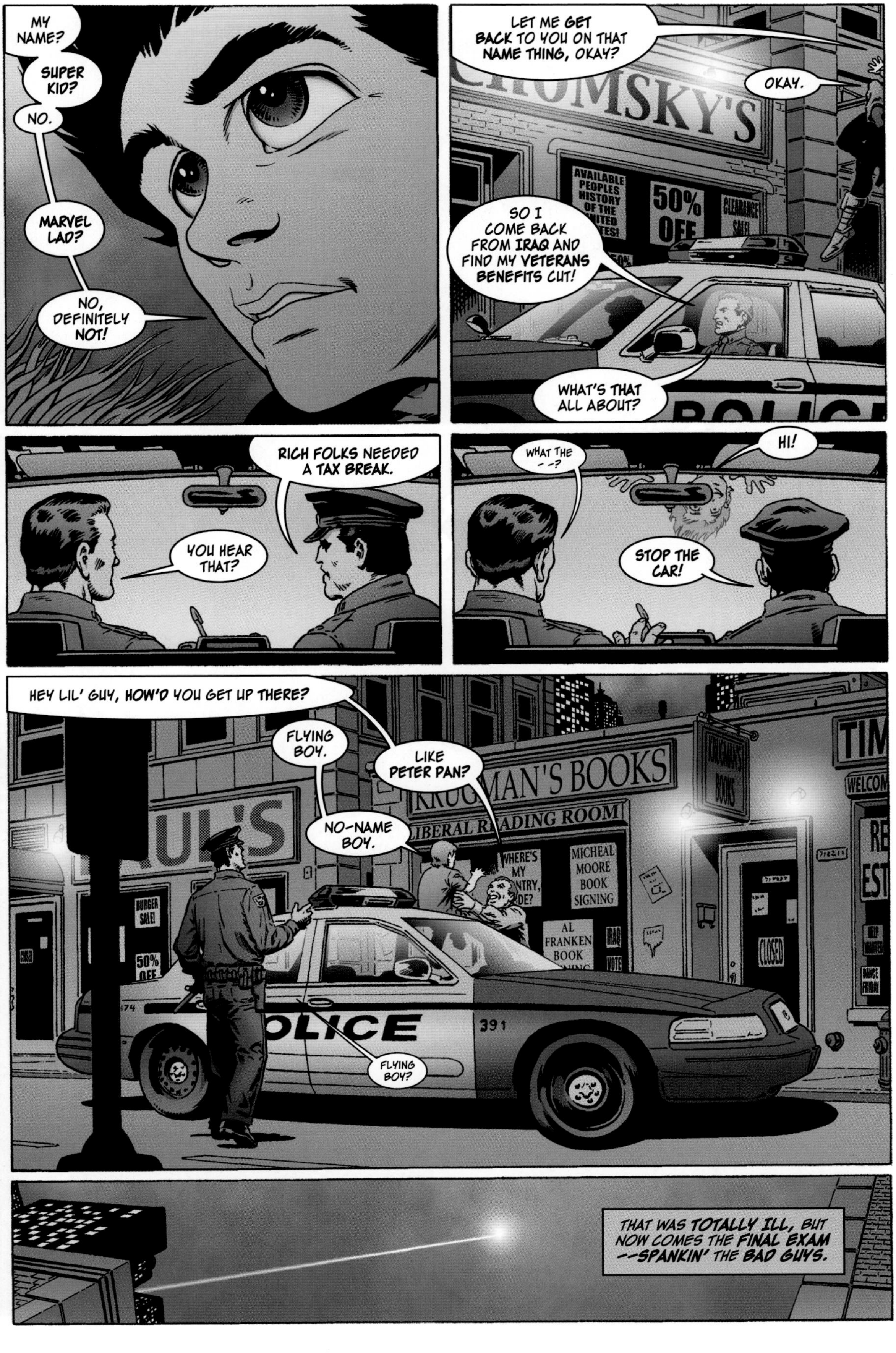
MY NAME?
SUPER KID?
NO.
MARVEL LAD?
NO, DEFINITELY NOT!
LET ME GET BACK TO YOU ON THAT NAME THING, OKAY?
OKAY.
CHOMSKY'S
AVAILABLE PEOPLES HISTORY OF THE UNITED STATES!
50% OFF
CLEARANCE SALE!
SO I COME BACK FROM IRAQ AND FIND MY VETERANS BENEFITS CUT!
WHAT'S THAT ALL ABOUT?
RICH FOLKS NEEDED A TAX BREAK.
YOU HEAR THAT?
WHAT THE --?
HI!
STOP THE CAR!
HEY LIL' GUY, HOW'D YOU GET UP THERE?
FLYING BOY.
LIKE PETER PAN?
NO-NAME BOY.
KRUGMAN'S BOOKS
LIBERAL READING ROOM
MICHEAL MOORE BOOK SIGNING
AL FRANKEN BOOK
BURGER SALE!
CLOSED
POLICE
391
FLYING BOY?
THAT WAS TOTALLY ILL, BUT NOW COMES THE FINAL EXAM --SPANKIN' THE BAD GUYS.

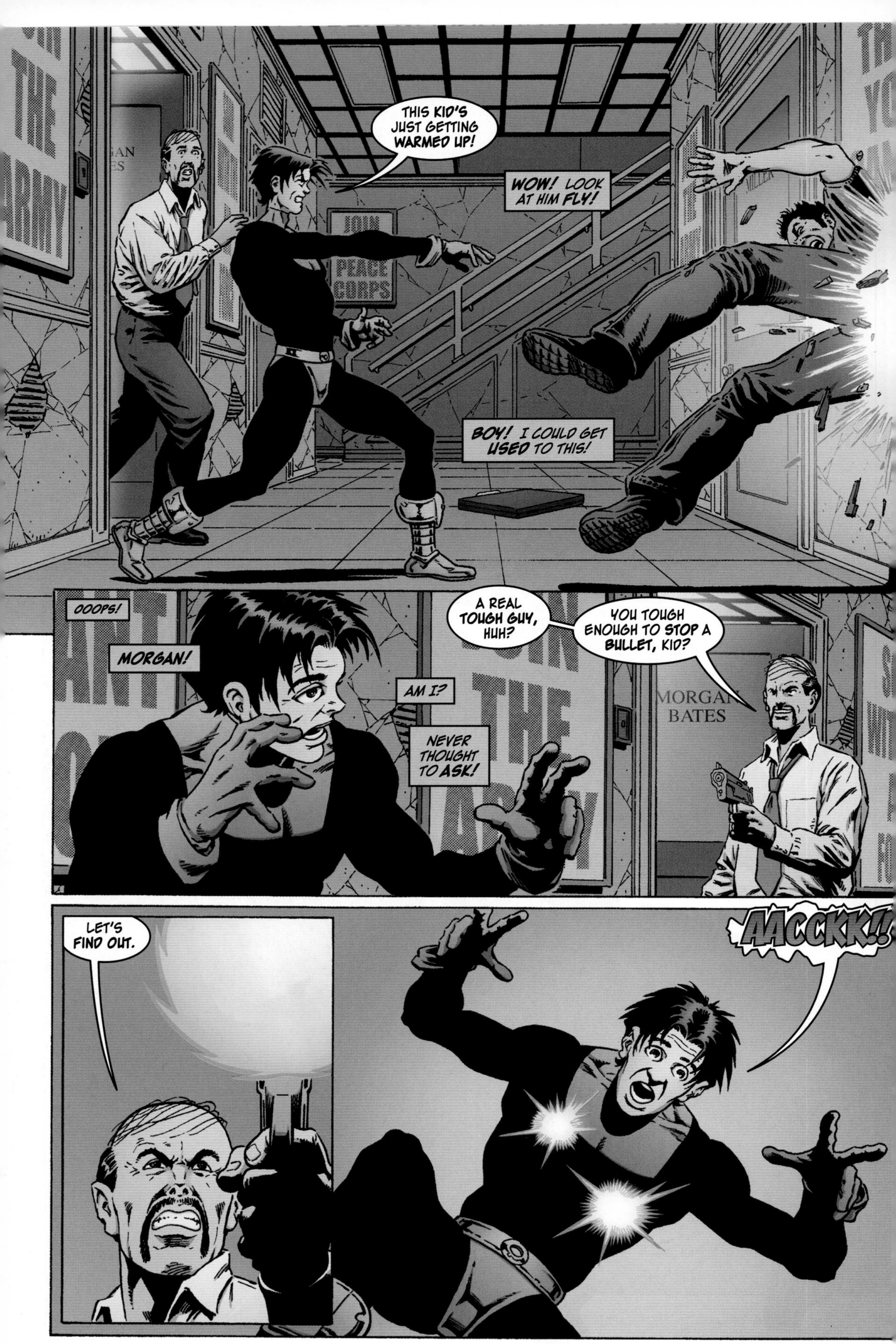
THIS KID'S JUST GETTING WARMED UP!
WOW! LOOK AT HIM FLY!
BOY! I COULD GET USED TO THIS!
JOIN PEACE CORPS
OOOPS!
MORGAN!
AM I?
NEVER THOUGHT TO ASK!
A REAL TOUGH GUY, HUH?
YOU TOUGH ENOUGH TO STOP A BULLET, KID?
MORGAN BATES
LET'S FIND OUT.
AACCKK!!

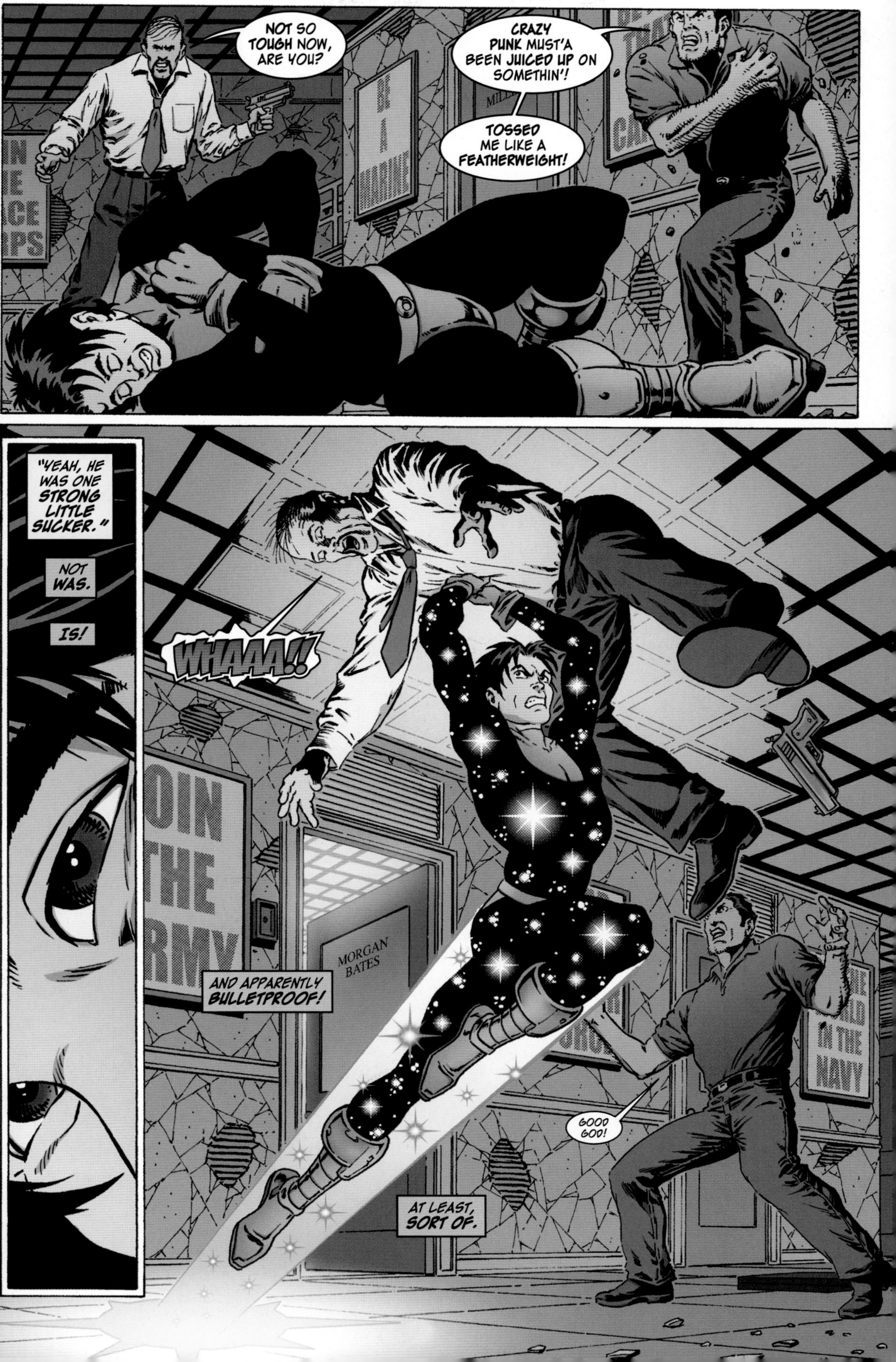
NOT SO TOUGH NOW, ARE YOU?
CRAZY PUNK MUST'A BEEN JUICED UP ON SOMETHIN'!
TOSSED ME LIKE A FEATHERWEIGHT!
BE A MARINE
"YEAH, HE WAS ONE STRONG LITTLE SUCKER."
NOT WAS.
IS!
WHAAA!!
MORGAN BATES
AND APPARENTLY BULLETPROOF!
IN THE NAVY
GOOD GOD!
AT LEAST, SORT OF.

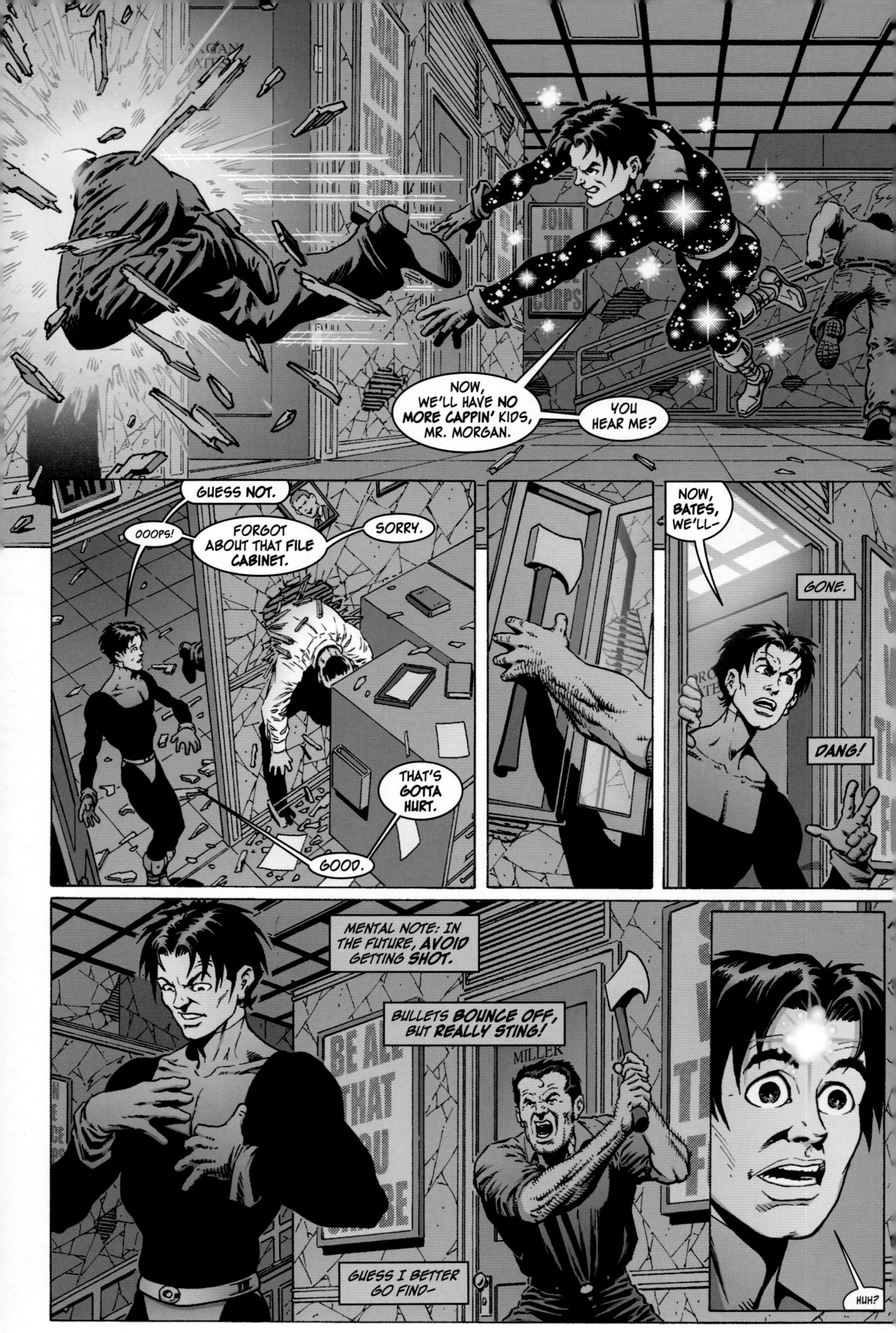
NOW, WE'LL HAVE NO MORE CAPPIN' KIDS, MR. MORGAN.
YOU HEAR ME?
GUESS NOT.
OOOPS!
FORGOT ABOUT THAT FILE CABINET.
SORRY.
THAT'S GOTTA HURT.
GOOD.
NOW, BATES, WE'LL-
GONE.
DANG!
MENTAL NOTE: IN THE FUTURE, AVOID GETTING SHOT.
BULLETS BOUNCE OFF, BUT REALLY STING!
GUESS I BETTER GO FIND-
HUH?

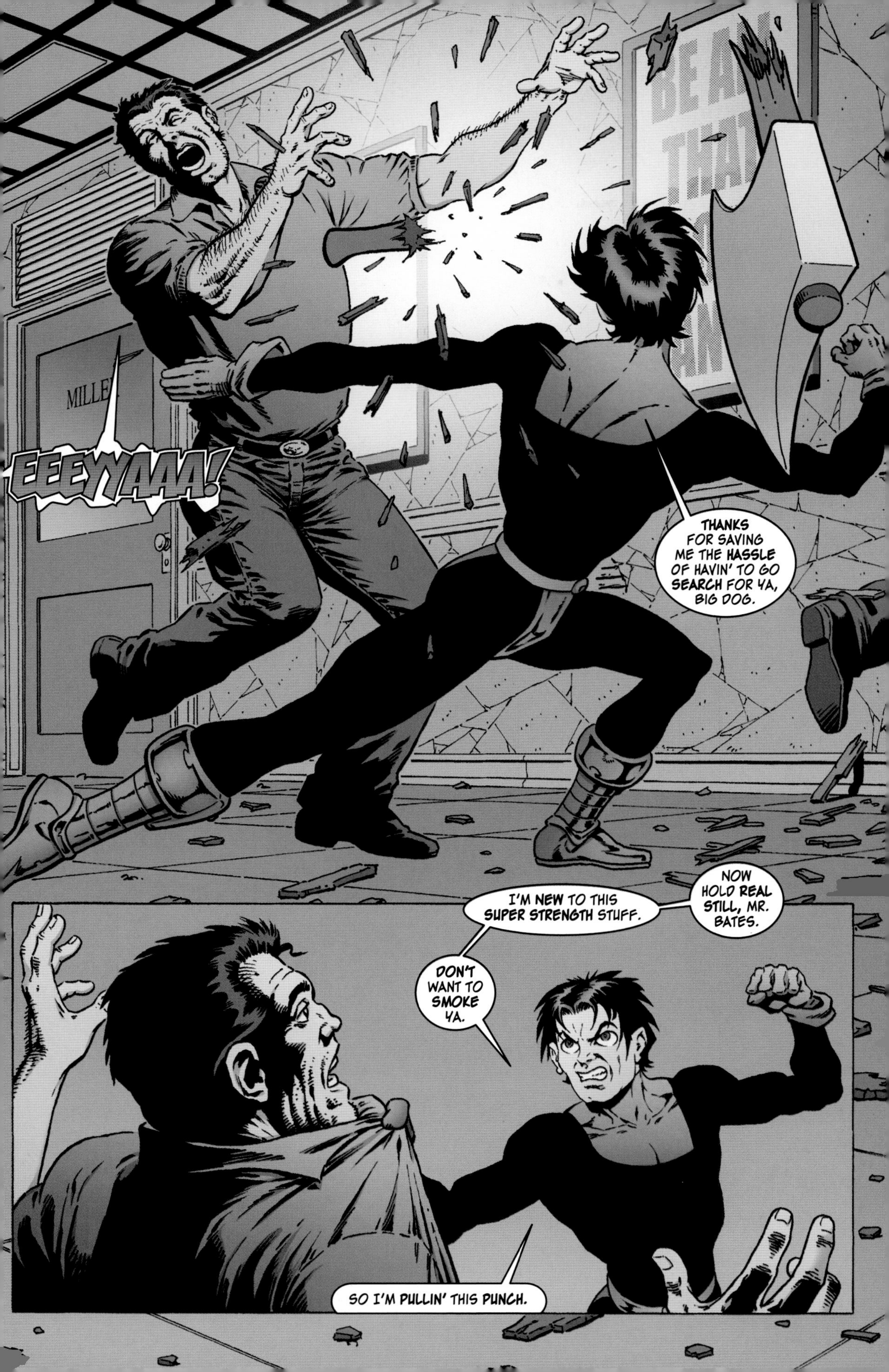
MILLE
EEEYYAAA!
THANKS FOR SAVING ME THE HASSLE OF HAVIN' TO GO SEARCH FOR YA, BIG DOG.
I'M NEW TO THIS SUPER STRENGTH STUFF.
NOW HOLD REAL STILL, MR. BATES.
DON'T WANT TO SMOKE YA.
SO I'M PULLIN' THIS PUNCH.

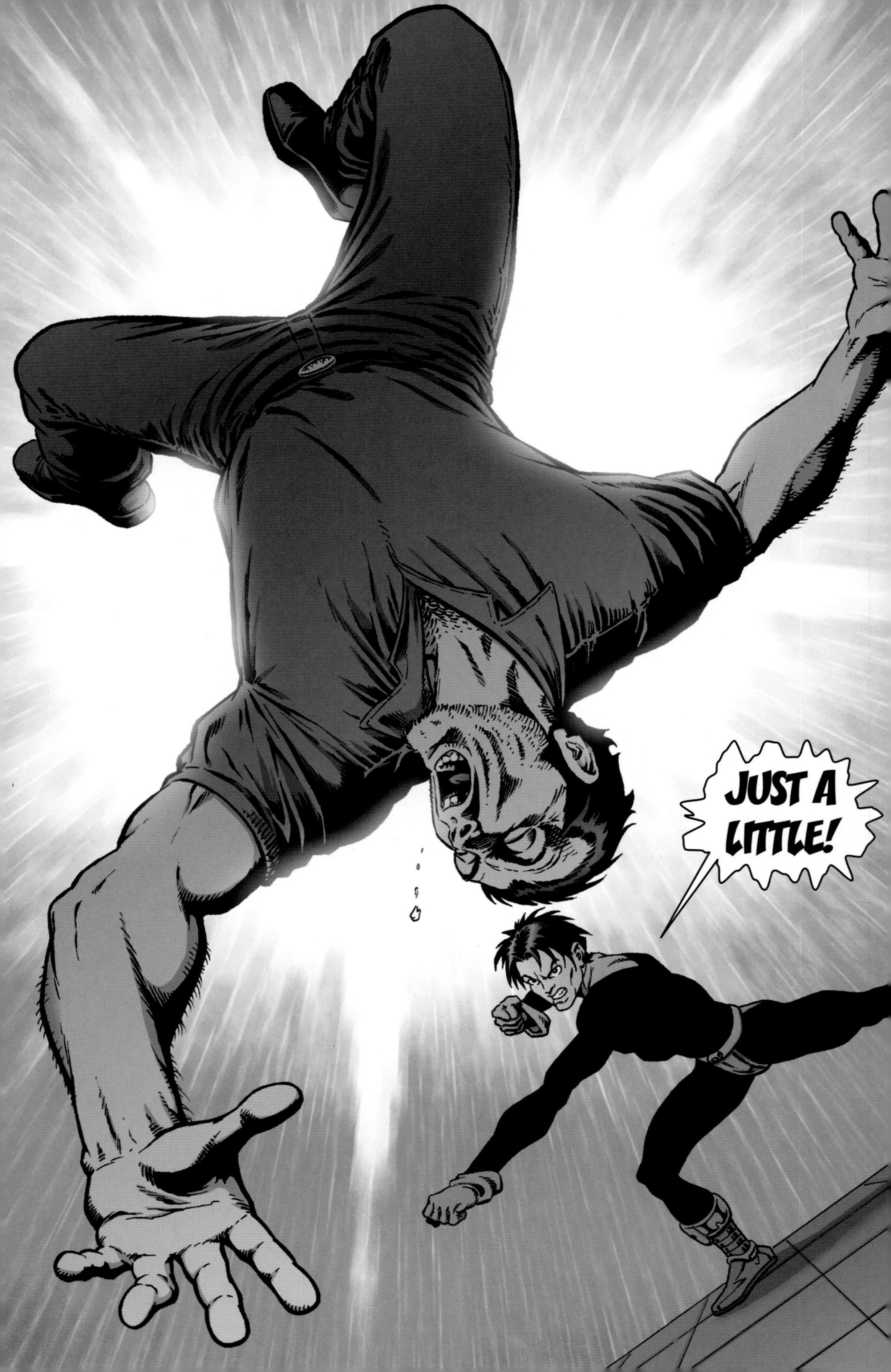
JUST A LITTLE!

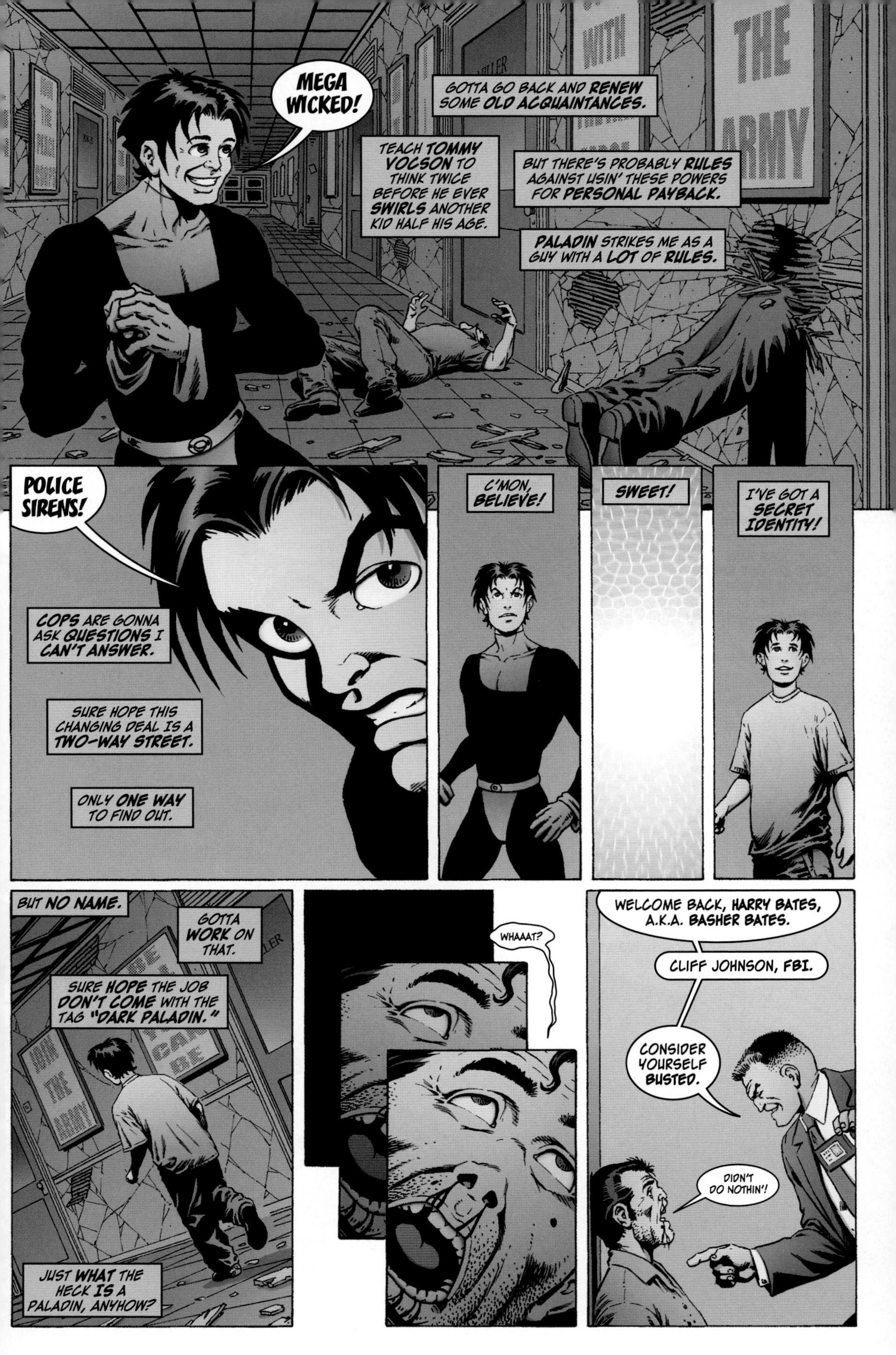
MEGA WICKED!
GOTTA GO BACK AND RENEW SOME OLD ACQUAINTANCES.
TEACH TOMMY VOCSON TO THINK TWICE BEFORE HE EVER SWIRLS ANOTHER KID HALF HIS AGE.
BUT THERE'S PROBABLY RULES AGAINST USIN' THESE POWERS FOR PERSONAL PAYBACK.
PALADIN STRIKES ME AS A GUY WITH A LOT OF RULES.
THE ARMY
POLICE SIRENS!
COPS ARE GONNA ASK QUESTIONS I CAN'T ANSWER.
SURE HOPE THIS CHANGING DEAL IS A TWO-WAY STREET.
ONLY ONE WAY TO FIND OUT.
C'MON, BELIEVE!
SWEET!
I'VE GOT A SECRET IDENTITY!
BUT NO NAME.
GOTTA WORK ON THAT.
SURE HOPE THE JOB DON'T COME WITH THE TAG "DARK PALADIN."
JUST WHAT THE HECK IS A PALADIN, ANYHOW?
WHAAAT?
WELCOME BACK, HARRY BATES, A.K.A. BASHER BATES.
CLIFF JOHNSON, FBI.
CONSIDER YOURSELF BUSTED.
DIDN'T DO NOTHIN'!

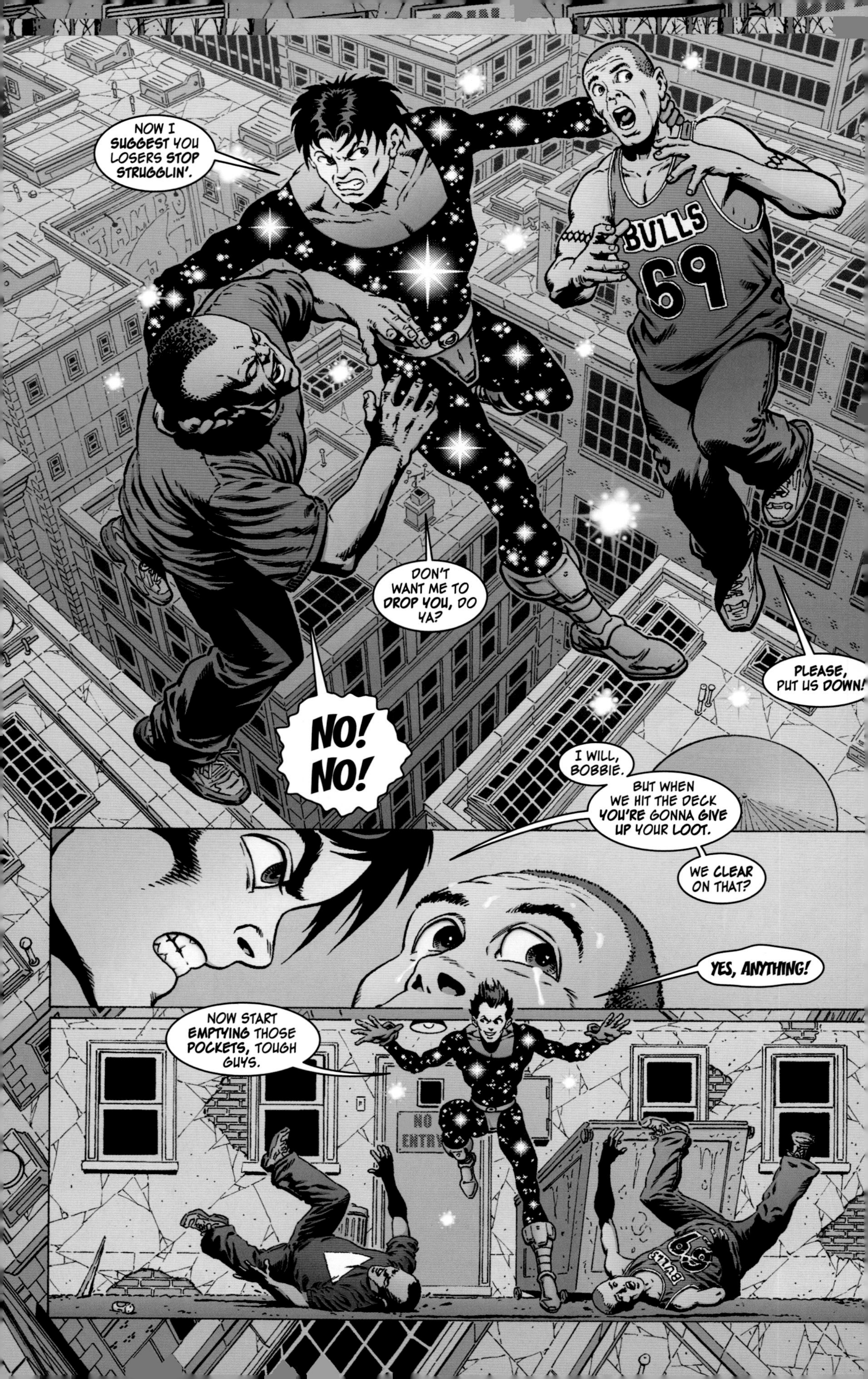
NOW I SUGGEST YOU LOSERS STOP STRUGGLIN'.
DON'T WANT ME TO DROP YOU, DO YA?
PLEASE, PUT US DOWN!
NO! NO!
I WILL, BOBBIE.
BUT WHEN WE HIT THE DECK YOU'RE GONNA GIVE UP YOUR LOOT.
WE CLEAR ON THAT?
YES, ANYTHING!
NOW START EMPTYING THOSE POCKETS, TOUGH GUYS.
NO ENTRY

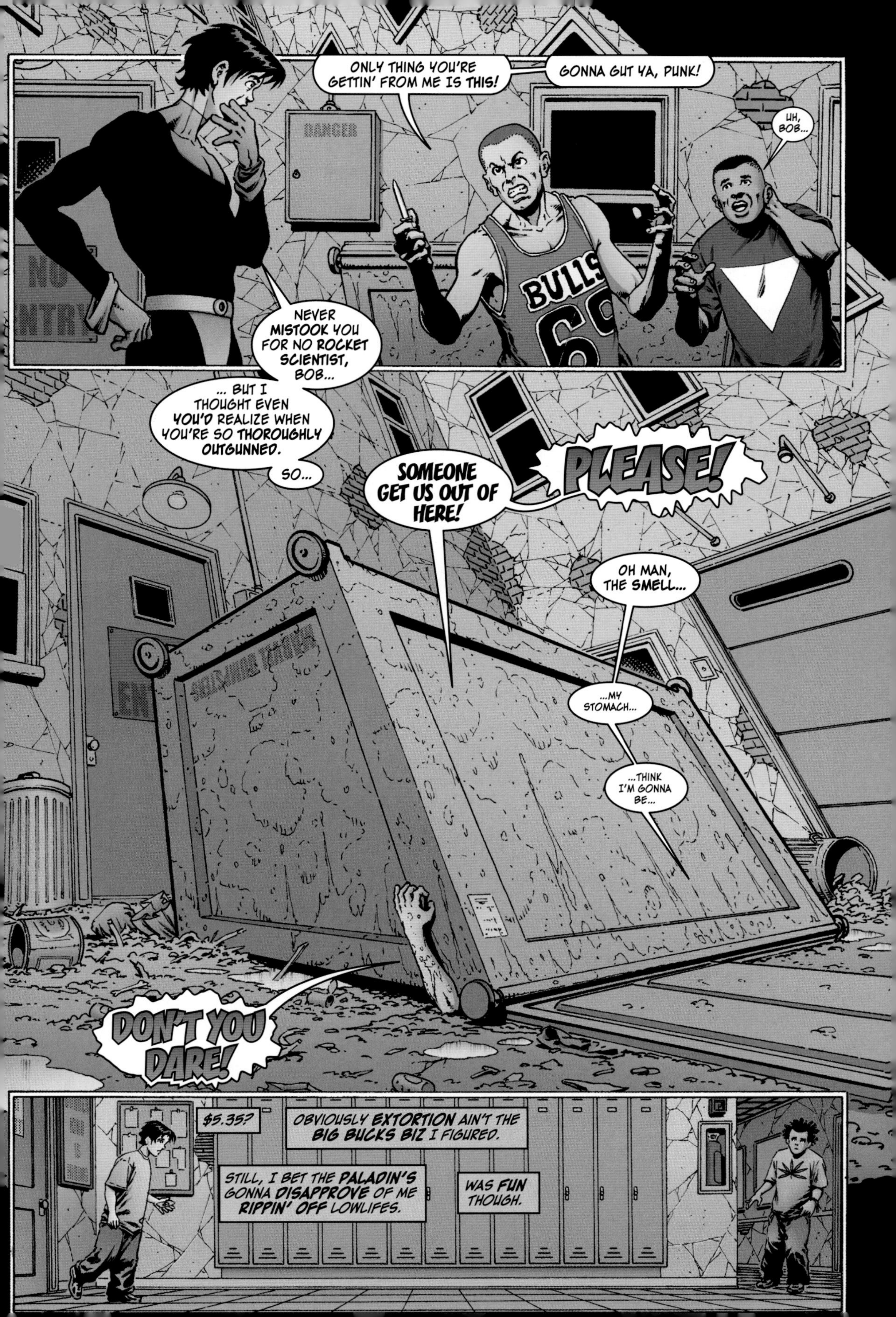

ONLY THING YOU'RE GETTIN' FROM ME IS THIS!
GONNA GUT YA, PUNK!
UH, BOB...
DANGER
NO ENTRY
NEVER MISTOOK YOU FOR NO ROCKET SCIENTIST, BOB...
... BUT I THOUGHT EVEN YOU'D REALIZE WHEN YOU'RE SO THOROUGHLY OUTGUNNED.
SO...
SOMEONE GET US OUT OF HERE!
PLEASE!
OH MAN, THE SMELL...
...MY STOMACH...
...THINK I'M GONNA BE...
DON'T YOU DARE!
$5.35?
OBVIOUSLY EXTORTION AIN'T THE BIG BUCKS BIZ I FIGURED.
STILL, I BET THE PALADIN'S GONNA DISAPPROVE OF ME RIPPIN' OFF LOWLIFES.
WAS FUN THOUGH.

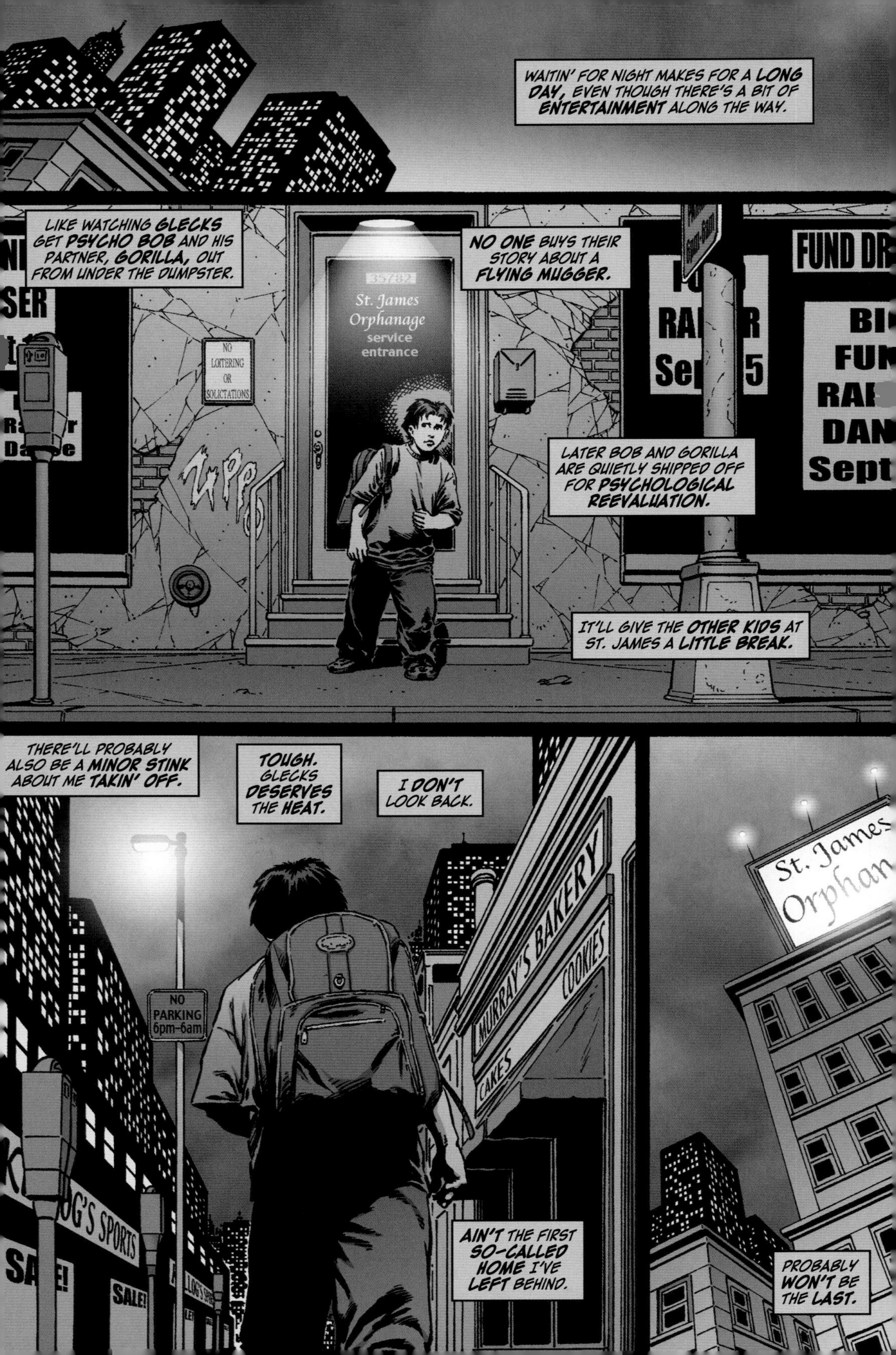
WAITIN' FOR NIGHT MAKES FOR A LONG DAY, EVEN THOUGH THERE'S A BIT OF ENTERTAINMENT ALONG THE WAY.
LIKE WATCHING GLECKS GET PSYCHO BOB AND HIS PARTNER, GORILLA, OUT FROM UNDER THE DUMPSTER.
St. James Orphanage service entrance
NO LOITERING OR SOLICTATIONS
NO ONE BUYS THEIR STORY ABOUT A FLYING MUGGER.
LATER BOB AND GORILLA ARE QUIETLY SHIPPED OFF FOR PSYCHOLOGICAL REEVALUATION.
IT'LL GIVE THE OTHER KIDS AT ST. JAMES A LITTLE BREAK.
THERE'LL PROBABLY ALSO BE A MINOR STINK ABOUT ME TAKIN' OFF.
TOUGH. GLECKS DESERVES THE HEAT.
I DON'T LOOK BACK.
NO PARKING 6pm–6am
MURRAY'S BAKERY
CAKES
COOKIES
AIN'T THE FIRST SO-CALLED HOME I'VE LEFT BEHIND.
PROBABLY WON'T BE THE LAST.

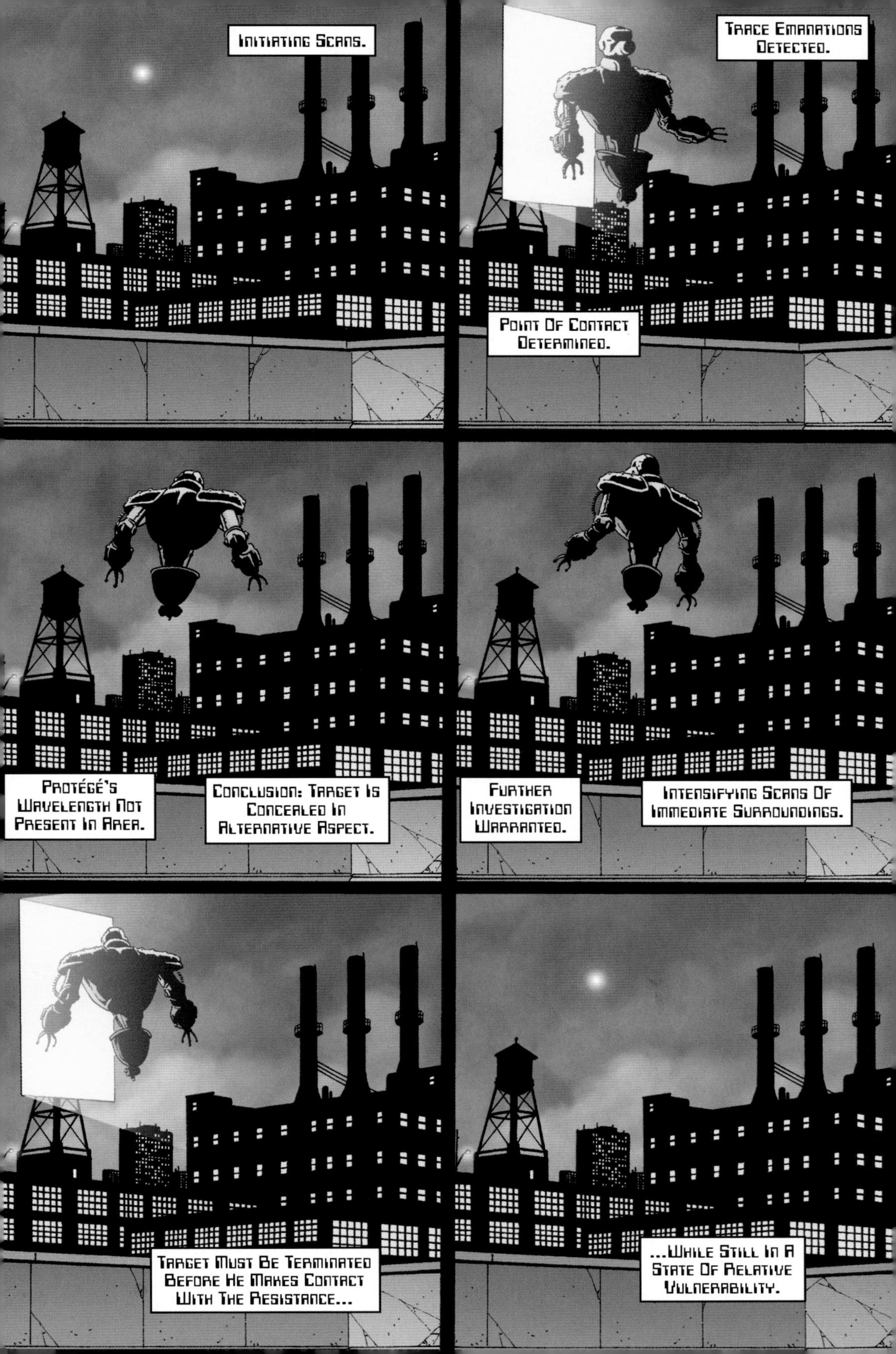
Initiating Scans.
Trace Emanations Detected.
Point Of Contact Determined.
Protégé's Wavelength Not Present In Area.
Conclusion: Target Is Concealed In Alternative Aspect.
Further Investigation Warranted.
Intensifying Scans Of Immediate Surroundings.
Target Must Be Terminated Before He Makes Contact With The Resistance...
...While Still In A State Of Relative Vulnerability.

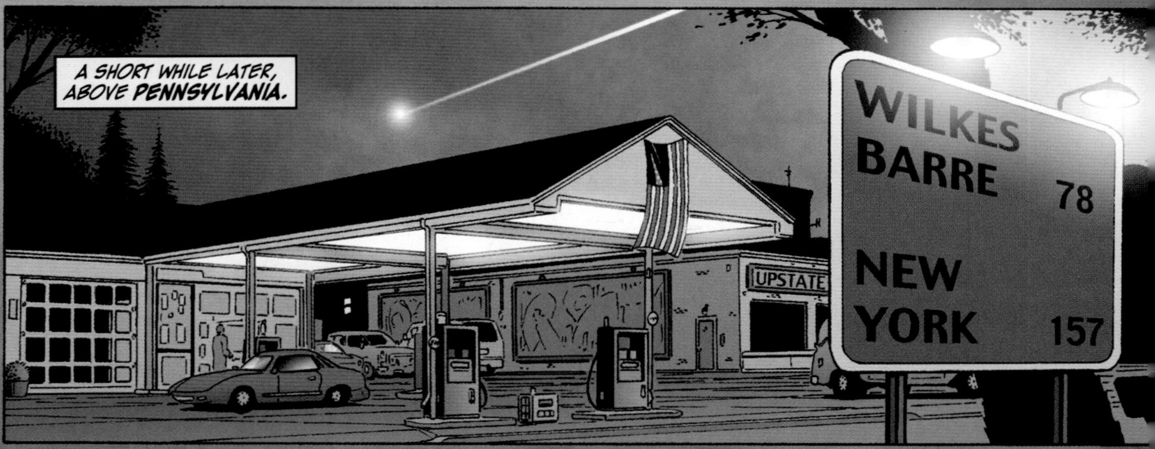
A SHORT WHILE LATER, ABOVE PENNSYLVANIA.
UPSTATE
WILKES BARRE 78
NEW YORK 157

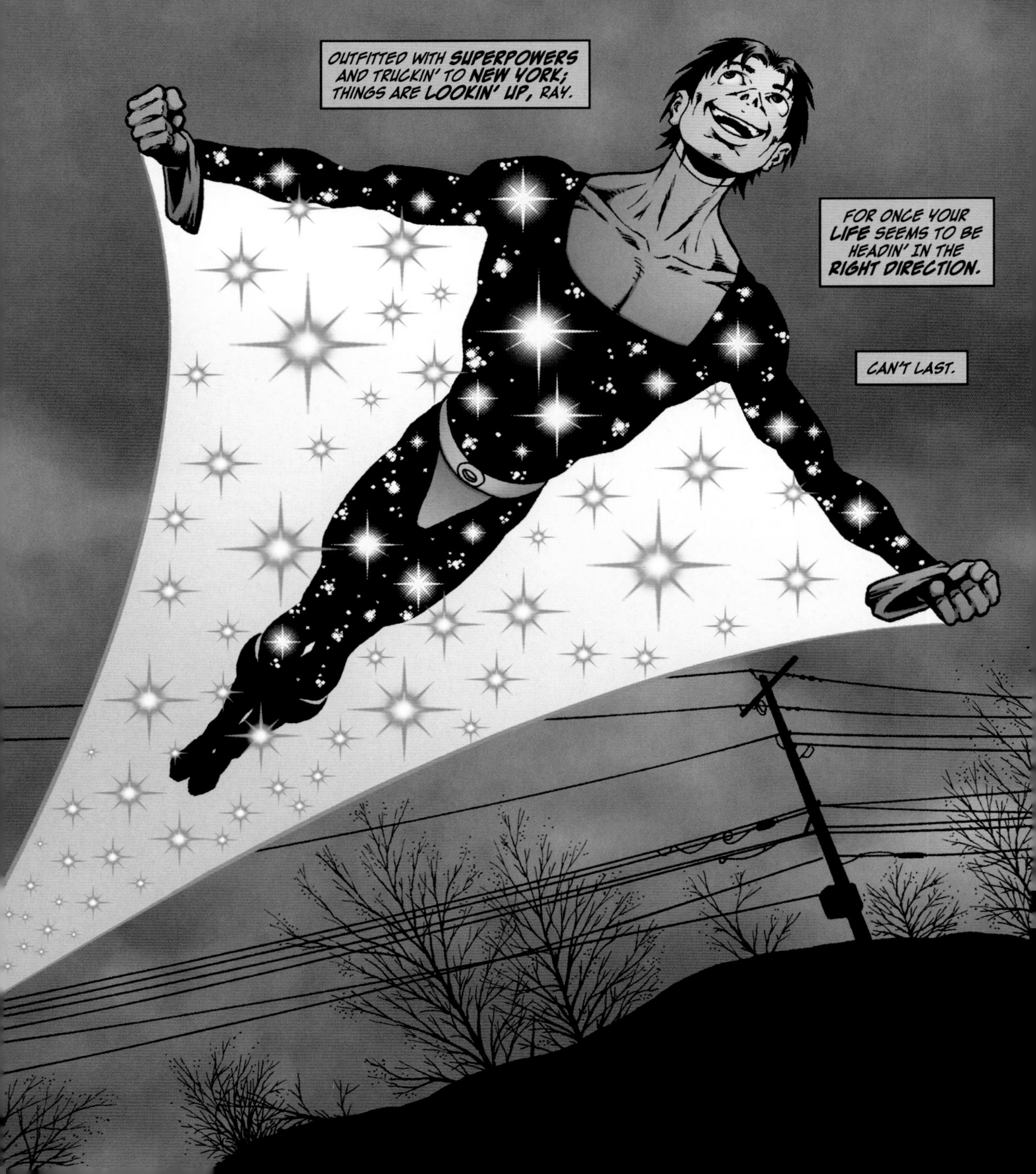
OUTFITTED WITH SUPERPOWERS AND TRUCKIN' TO NEW YORK; THINGS ARE LOOKIN' UP, RAY.
FOR ONCE YOUR LIFE SEEMS TO BE HEADIN' IN THE RIGHT DIRECTION.
CAN'T LAST.

NYC TRIP

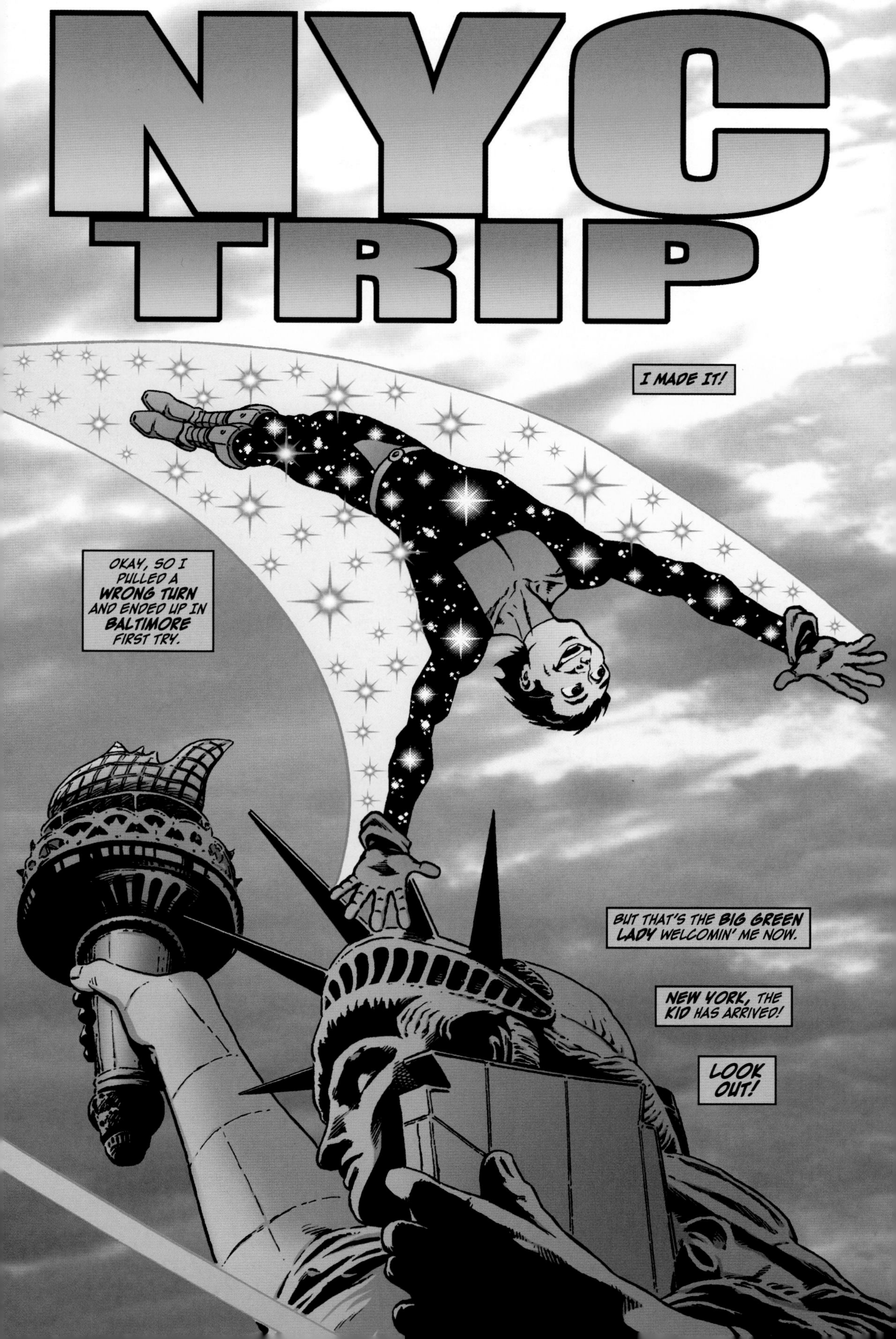

I MADE IT!
OKAY, SO I PULLED A WRONG TURN AND ENDED UP IN BALTIMORE FIRST TRY.
BUT THAT'S THE BIG GREEN LADY WELCOMIN' ME NOW.
NEW YORK, THE KID HAS ARRIVED!
LOOK OUT!

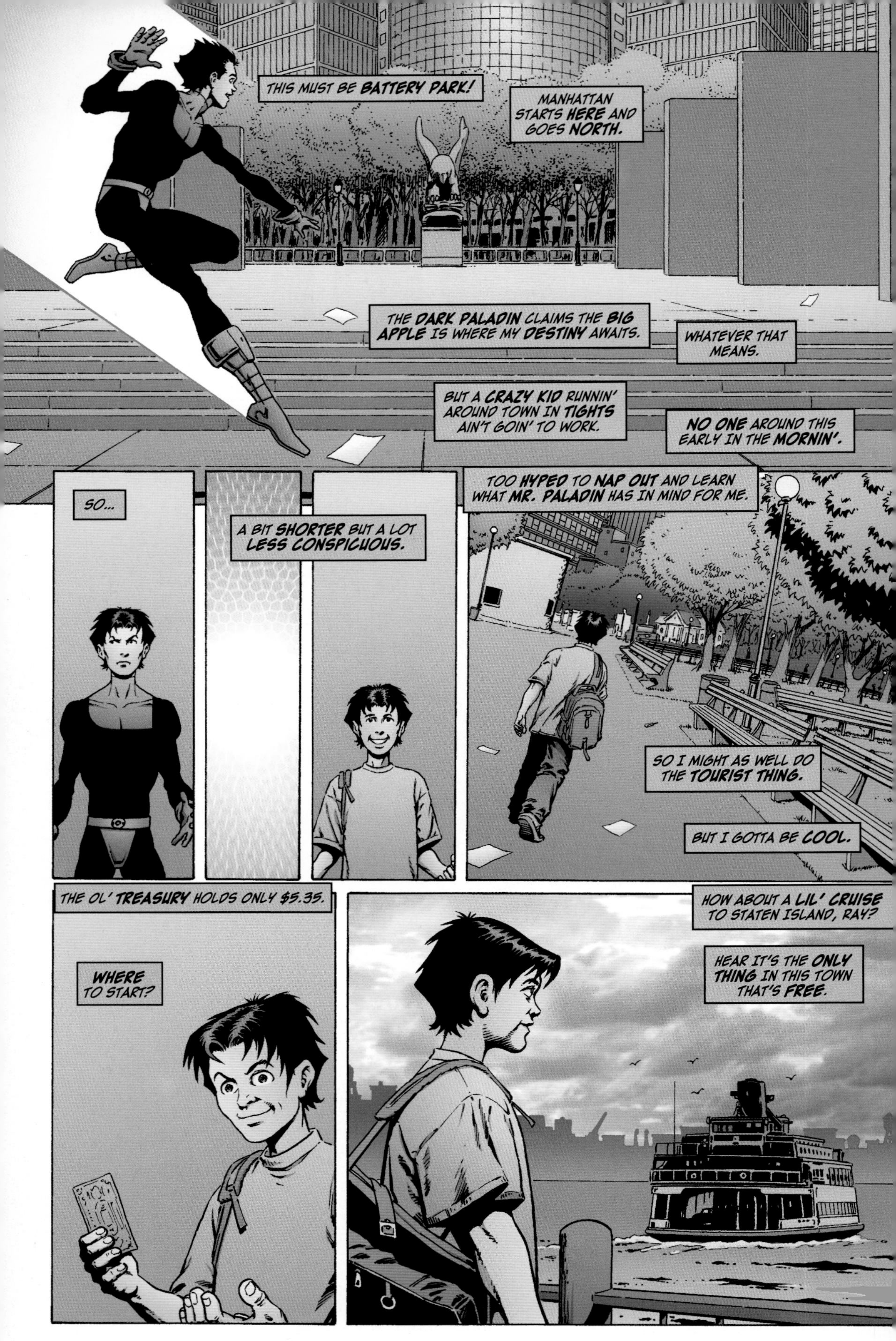
THIS MUST BE BATTERY PARK!
MANHATTAN STARTS HERE AND GOES NORTH.
THE DARK PALADIN CLAIMS THE BIG APPLE IS WHERE MY DESTINY AWAITS.
WHATEVER THAT MEANS.
BUT A CRAZY KID RUNNIN' AROUND TOWN IN TIGHTS AIN'T GOIN' TO WORK.
NO ONE AROUND THIS EARLY IN THE MORNIN'.
SO...
A BIT SHORTER BUT A LOT LESS CONSPICUOUS.
TOO HYPED TO NAP OUT AND LEARN WHAT MR. PALADIN HAS IN MIND FOR ME.
SO I MIGHT AS WELL DO THE TOURIST THING.
BUT I GOTTA BE COOL.
THE OL' TREASURY HOLDS ONLY $5.35.
WHERE TO START?
HOW ABOUT A LIL' CRUISE TO STATEN ISLAND, RAY?
HEAR IT'S THE ONLY THING IN THIS TOWN THAT'S FREE.

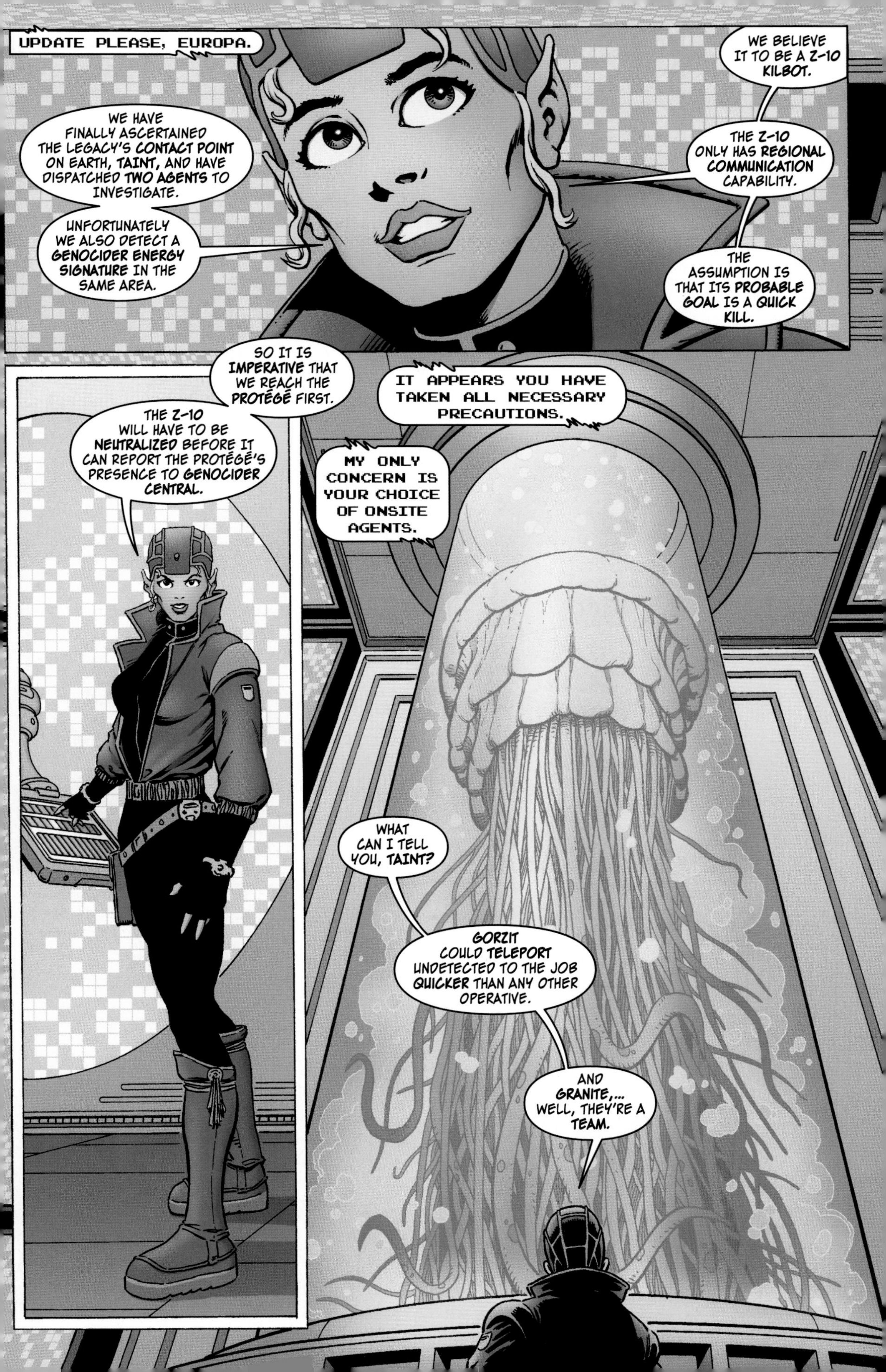

UPDATE PLEASE, EUROPA.
WE HAVE FINALLY ASCERTAINED THE LEGACY'S CONTACT POINT ON EARTH, TAINT, AND HAVE DISPATCHED TWO AGENTS TO INVESTIGATE.
UNFORTUNATELY WE ALSO DETECT A GENOCIDER ENERGY SIGNATURE IN THE SAME AREA.
WE BELIEVE IT TO BE A Z-10 KILBOT.
THE Z-10 ONLY HAS REGIONAL COMMUNICATION CAPABILITY.
THE ASSUMPTION IS THAT ITS PROBABLE GOAL IS A QUICK KILL.
SO IT IS IMPERATIVE THAT WE REACH THE PROTÉGÉ FIRST.
THE Z-10 WILL HAVE TO BE NEUTRALIZED BEFORE IT CAN REPORT THE PROTÉGÉ'S PRESENCE TO GENOCIDER CENTRAL.
IT APPEARS YOU HAVE TAKEN ALL NECESSARY PRECAUTIONS.
MY ONLY CONCERN IS YOUR CHOICE OF ONSITE AGENTS.
WHAT CAN I TELL YOU, TAINT?
GORZIT COULD TELEPORT UNDETECTED TO THE JOB QUICKER THAN ANY OTHER OPERATIVE.
AND GRANITE,... WELL, THEY'RE A TEAM.

IT IS NO EASY MATTER, **LEAVING** AN **OLD LIFE** BEHIND.

SOME **THREADS** SEVER **MORE EASILY** THAN OTHERS.

OLD BUSINESS #1.

St. Ja... Orphanage

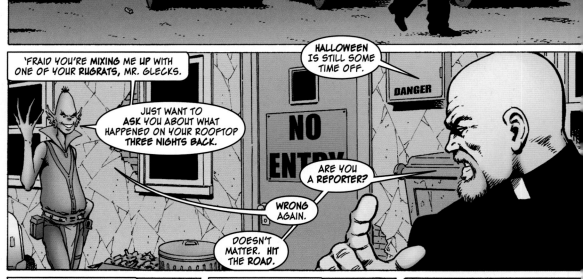

HEY, PADRE, CAN I HAVE A **WORD** WITH YOU?

HUH? OH. SHOULDN'T YOU BE IN CLASS?

AND THAT OUTFIT.

'FRAID YOU'RE MIXING ME UP WITH ONE OF YOUR **RUGRATS**, MR. GLECKS.

HALLOWEEN IS STILL SOME TIME OFF.

DANGER

NO ENTRY

JUST WANT TO ASK YOU ABOUT WHAT HAPPENED ON YOUR ROOFTOP THREE NIGHTS BACK.

ARE YOU A REPORTER?

WRONG AGAIN.

DOESN'T MATTER. HIT THE ROAD.

EVERYTHING THAT HAPPENS INSIDE ST. JAMES ORPHANAGE IS STRICTLY CONFIDENTIAL.

C'MON. YOU CAN TRUST ME.

DO I LOOK LIKE A BLABBERMOUTH?

NO, YOU LOOK **CRAZY**.

OKAY, I TRIED TO BE NICE ABOUT THIS.

GUESS I'M JUST NOT THE PERSUASIVE TYPE.

BUT MAYBE YOU'LL TALK TO GRANITE.

GRANITE?

YEAH, HE'S GOT PEOPLE SKILLS.

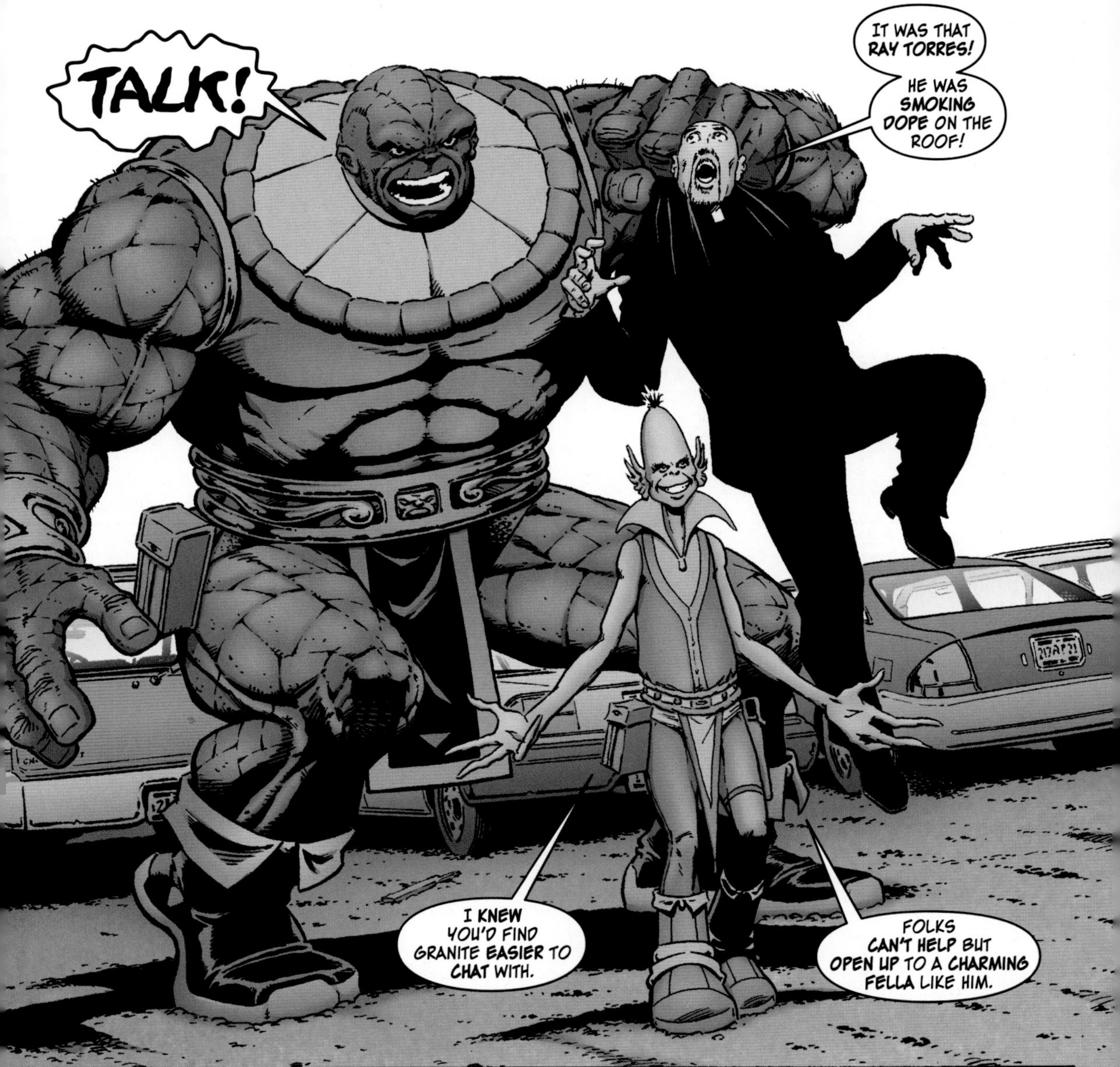
TALK!
IT WAS THAT RAY TORRES!
HE WAS SMOKING DOPE ON THE ROOF!
I KNEW YOU'D FIND GRANITE EASIER TO CHAT WITH.
FOLKS CAN'T HELP BUT OPEN UP TO A CHARMING FELLA LIKE HIM.

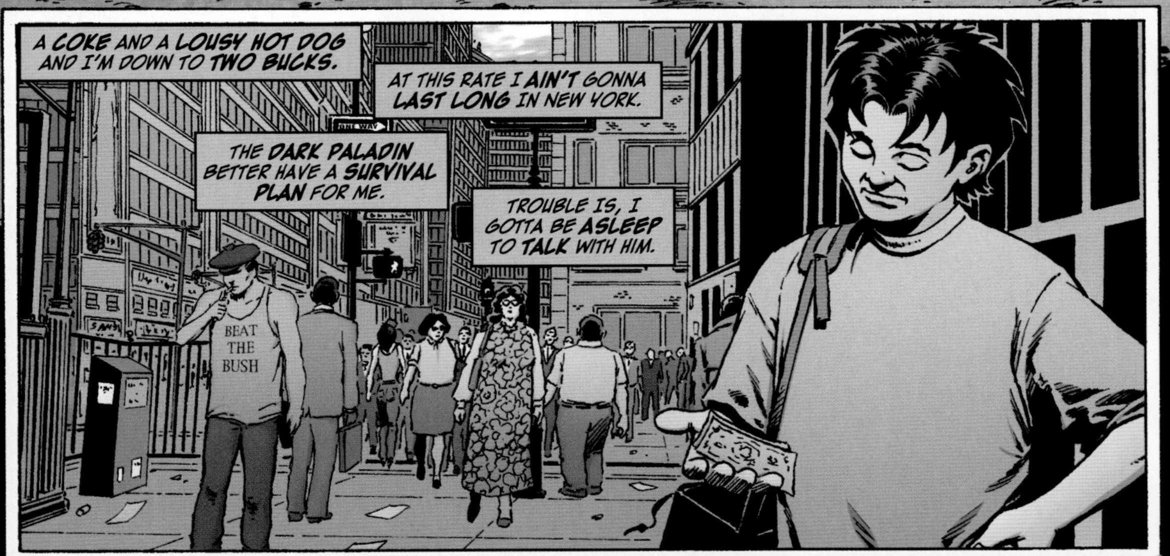
A COKE AND A LOUSY HOT DOG AND I'M DOWN TO TWO BUCKS.
AT THIS RATE I AIN'T GONNA LAST LONG IN NEW YORK.
THE DARK PALADIN BETTER HAVE A SURVIVAL PLAN FOR ME.
TROUBLE IS, I GOTTA BE ASLEEP TO TALK WITH HIM.
ONE WAY
BEAT THE BUSH

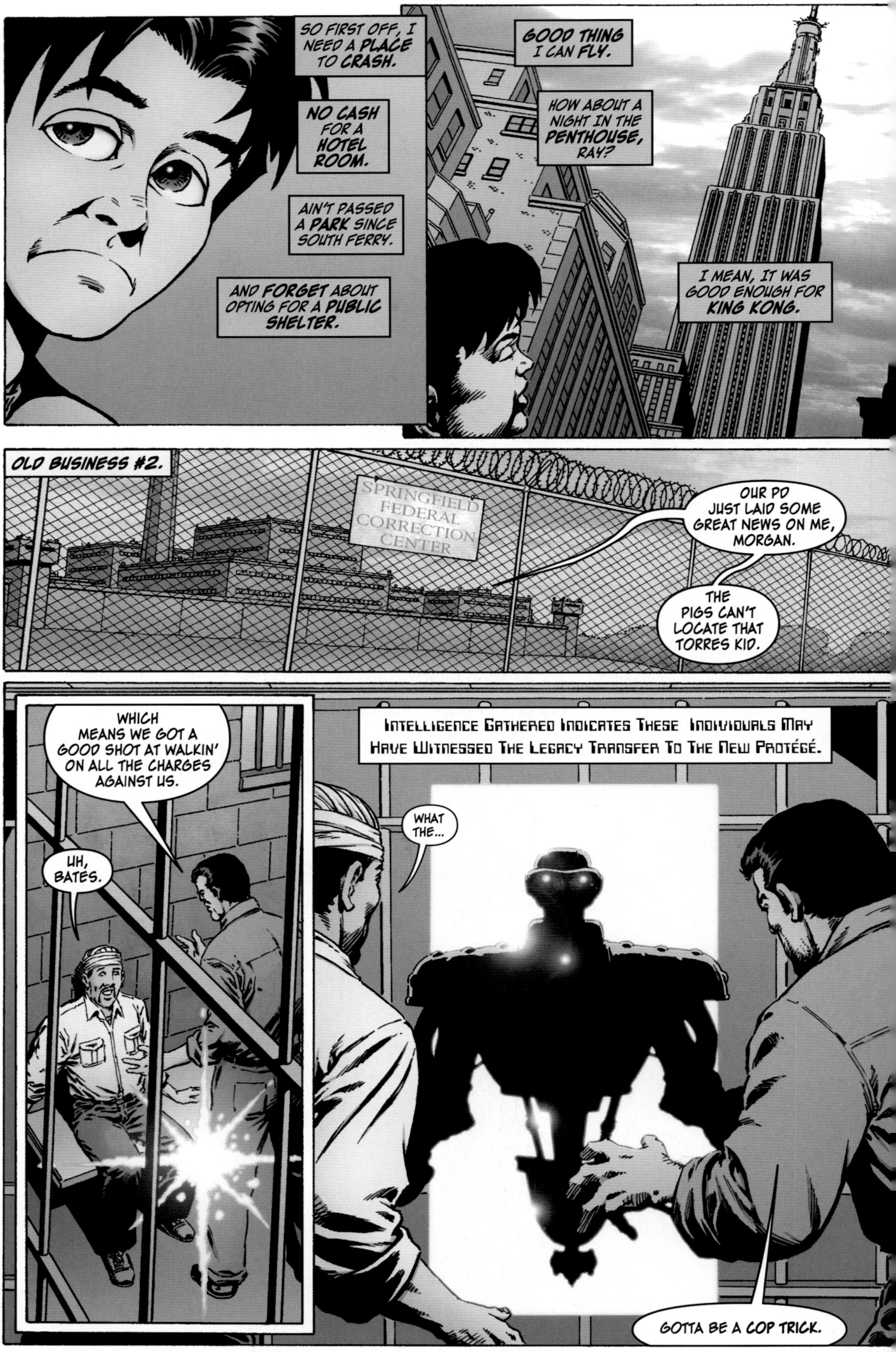
SO FIRST OFF, I NEED A PLACE TO CRASH.
NO CASH FOR A HOTEL ROOM.
AIN'T PASSED A PARK SINCE SOUTH FERRY.
AND FORGET ABOUT OPTING FOR A PUBLIC SHELTER.
GOOD THING I CAN FLY.
HOW ABOUT A NIGHT IN THE PENTHOUSE, RAY?
I MEAN, IT WAS GOOD ENOUGH FOR KING KONG.
OLD BUSINESS #2.
SPRINGFIELD FEDERAL CORRECTION CENTER
OUR PD JUST LAID SOME GREAT NEWS ON ME, MORGAN.
THE PIGS CAN'T LOCATE THAT TORRES KID.
WHICH MEANS WE GOT A GOOD SHOT AT WALKIN' ON ALL THE CHARGES AGAINST US.
UH, BATES.
INTELLIGENCE GATHERED INDICATES THESE INDIVIDUALS MAY HAVE WITNESSED THE LEGACY TRANSFER TO THE NEW PROTÉGÉ.
WHAT THE...
GOTTA BE A COP TRICK.

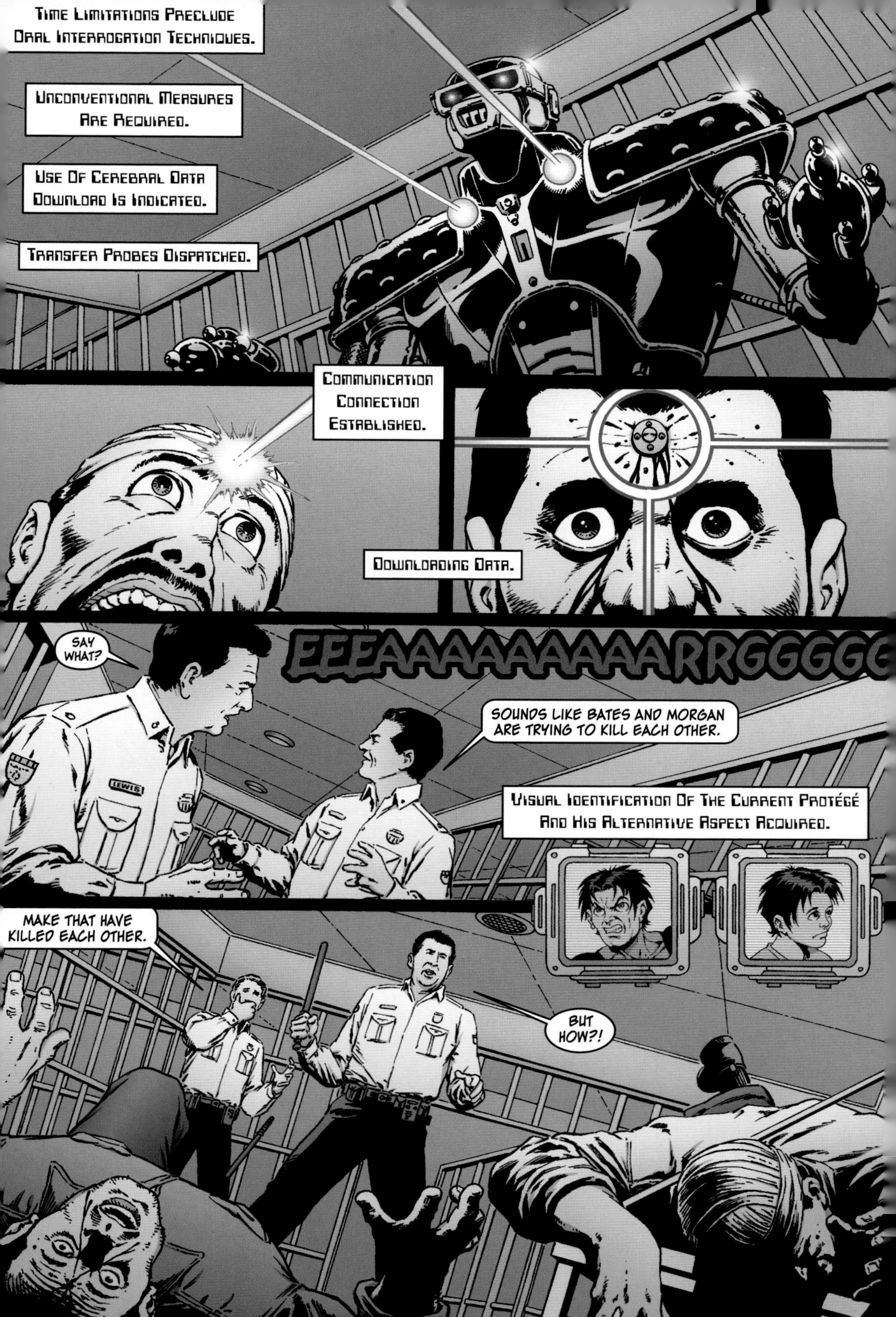

Time Limitations Preclude Oral Interrogation Techniques.
Unconventional Measures Are Required.
Use Of Cerebral Data Download Is Indicated.
Transfer Probes Dispatched.
Communication Connection Established.
Downloading Data.
SAY WHAT?
EEEAAAAAAAAARRGGGGG
SOUNDS LIKE BATES AND MORGAN ARE TRYING TO KILL EACH OTHER.
LEWIS
Visual Identification Of The Current Protégé And His Alternative Aspect Acquired.
MAKE THAT HAVE KILLED EACH OTHER.
BUT HOW?!

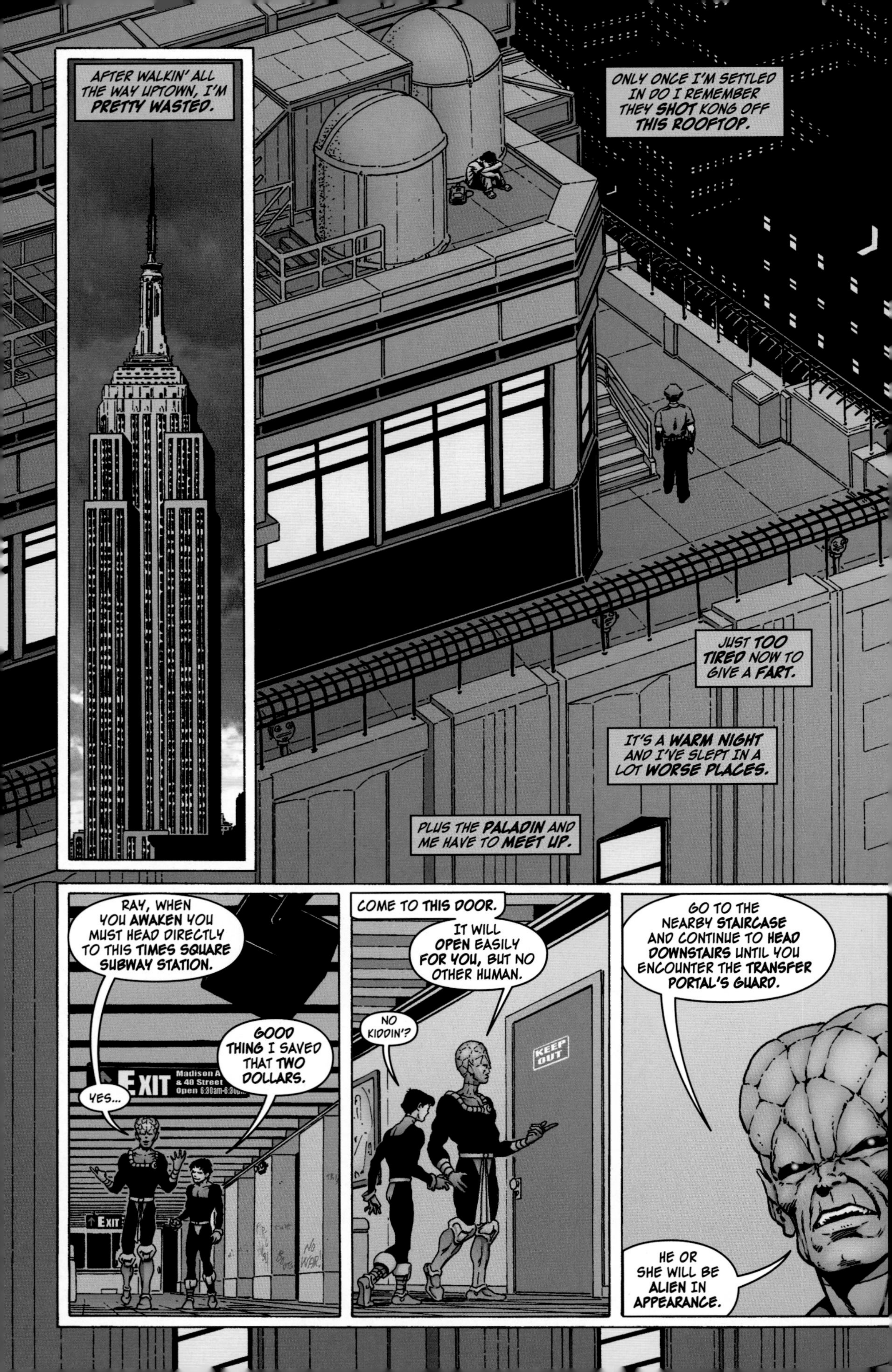

AFTER WALKIN' ALL THE WAY UPTOWN, I'M **PRETTY WASTED.**

ONLY ONCE I'M SETTLED IN DO I REMEMBER THEY **SHOT KONG** OFF **THIS ROOFTOP.**

JUST **TOO TIRED** NOW TO GIVE A **FART.**

IT'S A **WARM NIGHT** AND I'VE SLEPT IN A LOT **WORSE PLACES.**

PLUS THE **PALADIN** AND ME HAVE TO **MEET UP.**

RAY, WHEN YOU AWAKEN YOU MUST HEAD DIRECTLY TO THIS TIMES SQUARE SUBWAY STATION.

GOOD THING I SAVED THAT TWO DOLLARS.

YES...

E XIT

Madison A & 40 Street Open 6:00am-6:30p

EXIT

COME TO THIS DOOR.

IT WILL OPEN EASILY FOR YOU, BUT NO OTHER HUMAN.

NO KIDDIN'?

KEEP OUT

GO TO THE NEARBY STAIRCASE AND CONTINUE TO HEAD DOWNSTAIRS UNTIL YOU ENCOUNTER THE TRANSFER PORTAL'S GUARD.

HE OR SHE WILL BE ALIEN IN APPEARANCE.

TRUST FULLY THIS SENTRY.

HE OR SHE WILL LEAD YOU TO SANCTUARY.

KEEP OUT

SANCTUARY?

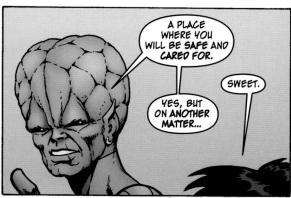

A PLACE WHERE YOU WILL BE SAFE AND CARED FOR.

SWEET.

YES, BUT ON ANOTHER MATTER...

MEMBERS OF THE COSMIC GUARD DO NOT THIEVE, EVEN FROM MISCREANTS!

DO I MAKE MYSELF CLEAR?

BUT WHAT'S A "MISCREANT"?

VERY.

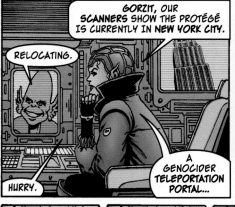

GORZIT, OUR SCANNERS SHOW THE PROTÉGÉ IS CURRENTLY IN NEW YORK CITY.

RELOCATING.

HURRY.

A GENOCIDER TELEPORTATION PORTAL...

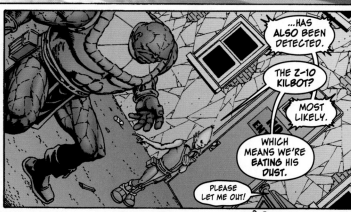

...HAS ALSO BEEN DETECTED.

THE Z-10 KILBOT?

MOST LIKELY.

WHICH MEANS WE'RE EATING HIS DUST.

PLEASE LET ME OUT!

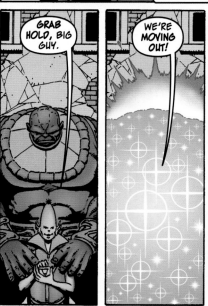

GRAB HOLD, BIG GUY.

WE'RE MOVING OUT!

UPDATE, GORZIT, SCANNERS INDICATE...

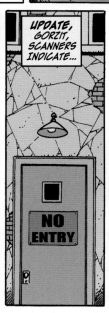

NO ENTRY

...THE PROTEGE IS ONCE AGAIN ON THE MOVE."

THIS EARLY, I'LL BE DUCKIN' THE RUSH HOUR CROWD.

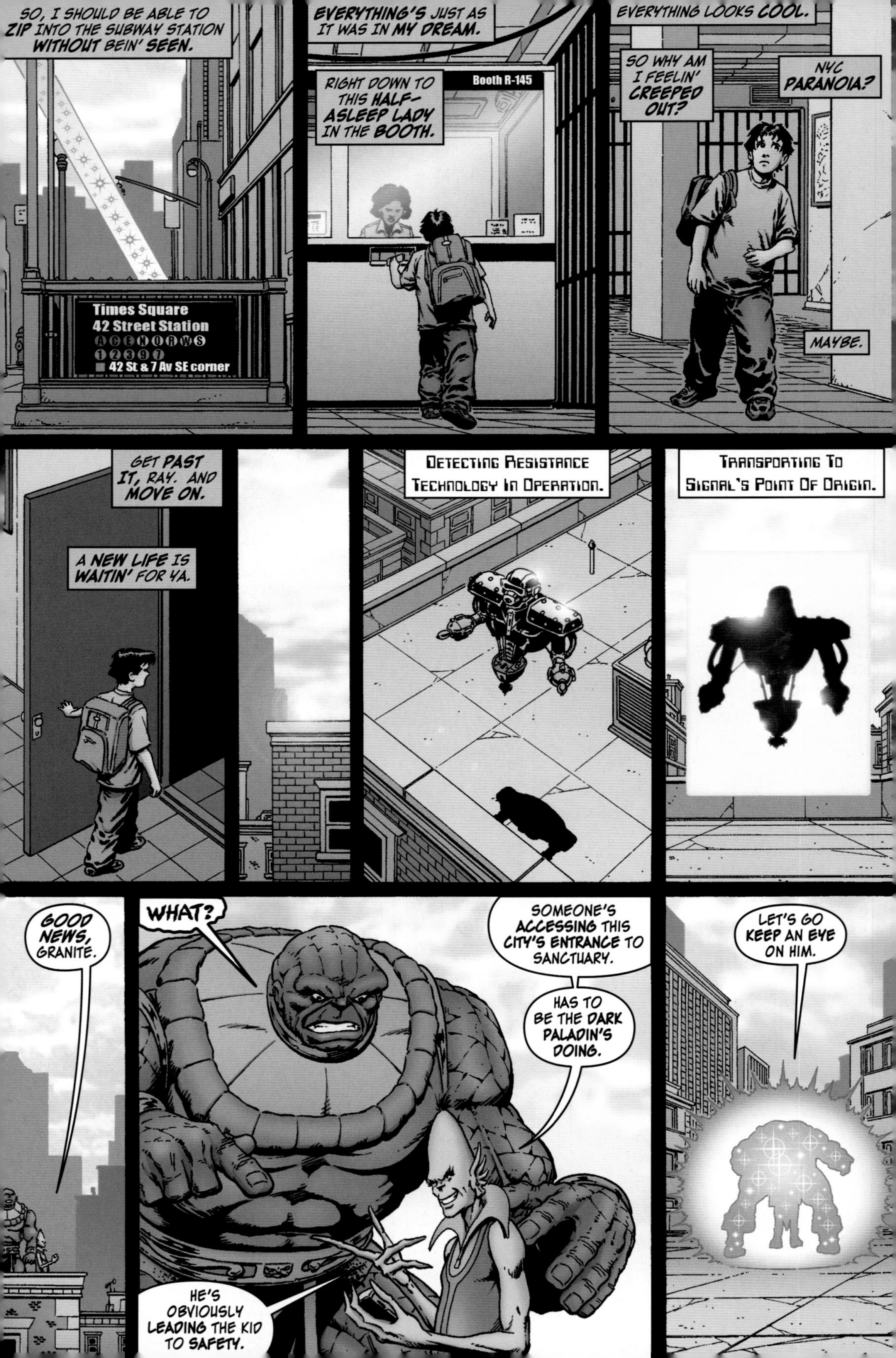
SO, I SHOULD BE ABLE TO ZIP INTO THE SUBWAY STATION WITHOUT BEIN' SEEN.
Times Square
42 Street Station
A C E N Q R W S
1 2 3 9 7
42 St & 7 Av SE corner
EVERYTHING'S JUST AS IT WAS IN MY DREAM.
RIGHT DOWN TO THIS HALF-ASLEEP LADY IN THE BOOTH.
Booth R-145
EVERYTHING LOOKS COOL.
SO WHY AM I FEELIN' CREEPED OUT?
NYC PARANOIA?
MAYBE.
GET PAST IT, RAY. AND MOVE ON.
A NEW LIFE IS WAITIN' FOR YA.
DETECTING RESISTANCE TECHNOLOGY IN OPERATION.
TRANSPORTING TO SIGNAL'S POINT OF ORIGIN.
GOOD NEWS, GRANITE.
WHAT?
SOMEONE'S ACCESSING THIS CITY'S ENTRANCE TO SANCTUARY.
HAS TO BE THE DARK PALADIN'S DOING.
HE'S OBVIOUSLY LEADING THE KID TO SAFETY.
LET'S GO KEEP AN EYE ON HIM.

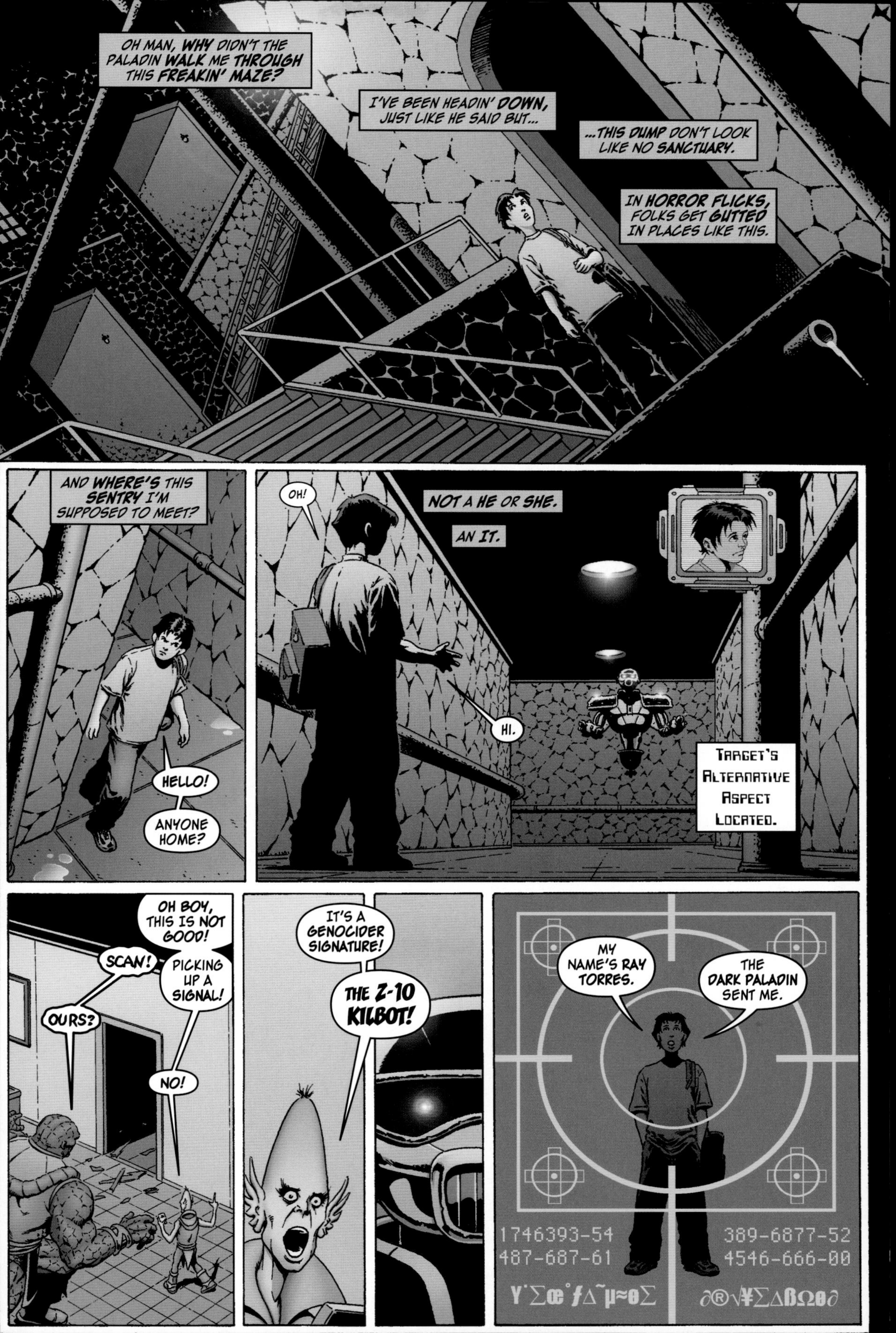
OH MAN, WHY DIDN'T THE PALADIN WALK ME THROUGH THIS FREAKIN' MAZE?
I'VE BEEN HEADIN' DOWN, JUST LIKE HE SAID BUT...
...THIS DUMP DON'T LOOK LIKE NO SANCTUARY.
IN HORROR FLICKS, FOLKS GET GUTTED IN PLACES LIKE THIS.
AND WHERE'S THIS SENTRY I'M SUPPOSED TO MEET?
HELLO!
ANYONE HOME?
OH!
NOT A HE OR SHE.
AN IT.
HI.
TARGET'S ALTERNATIVE ASPECT LOCATED.
OH BOY, THIS IS NOT GOOD!
SCAN!
PICKING UP A SIGNAL!
OURS?
NO!
IT'S A GENOCIDER SIGNATURE!
THE Z-10 KILBOT!
MY NAME'S RAY TORRES.
THE DARK PALADIN SENT ME.
1746393-54
487-687-61
389-6877-52
4546-666-00

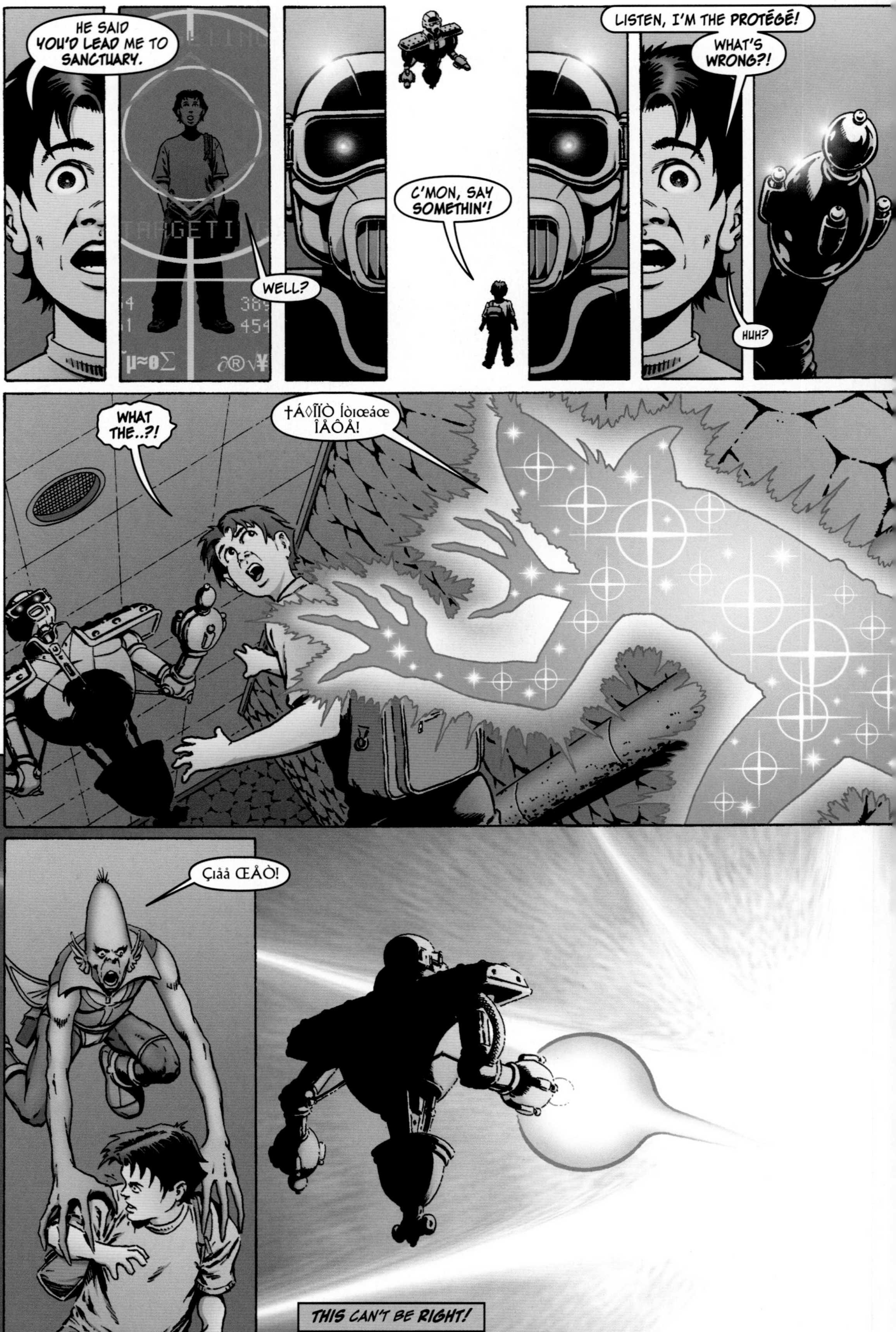

HE SAID YOU'D LEAD ME TO SANCTUARY.
TARGETING
WELL?
C'MON, SAY SOMETHIN'!
LISTEN, I'M THE PROTÉGÉ!
WHAT'S WRONG?!
HUH?
WHAT THE..?!
†Á◊ÎÏÒ Íòıœáœ ÎÅÔÅ!
Çiåå ŒÅÒ!
THIS CAN'T BE RIGHT!

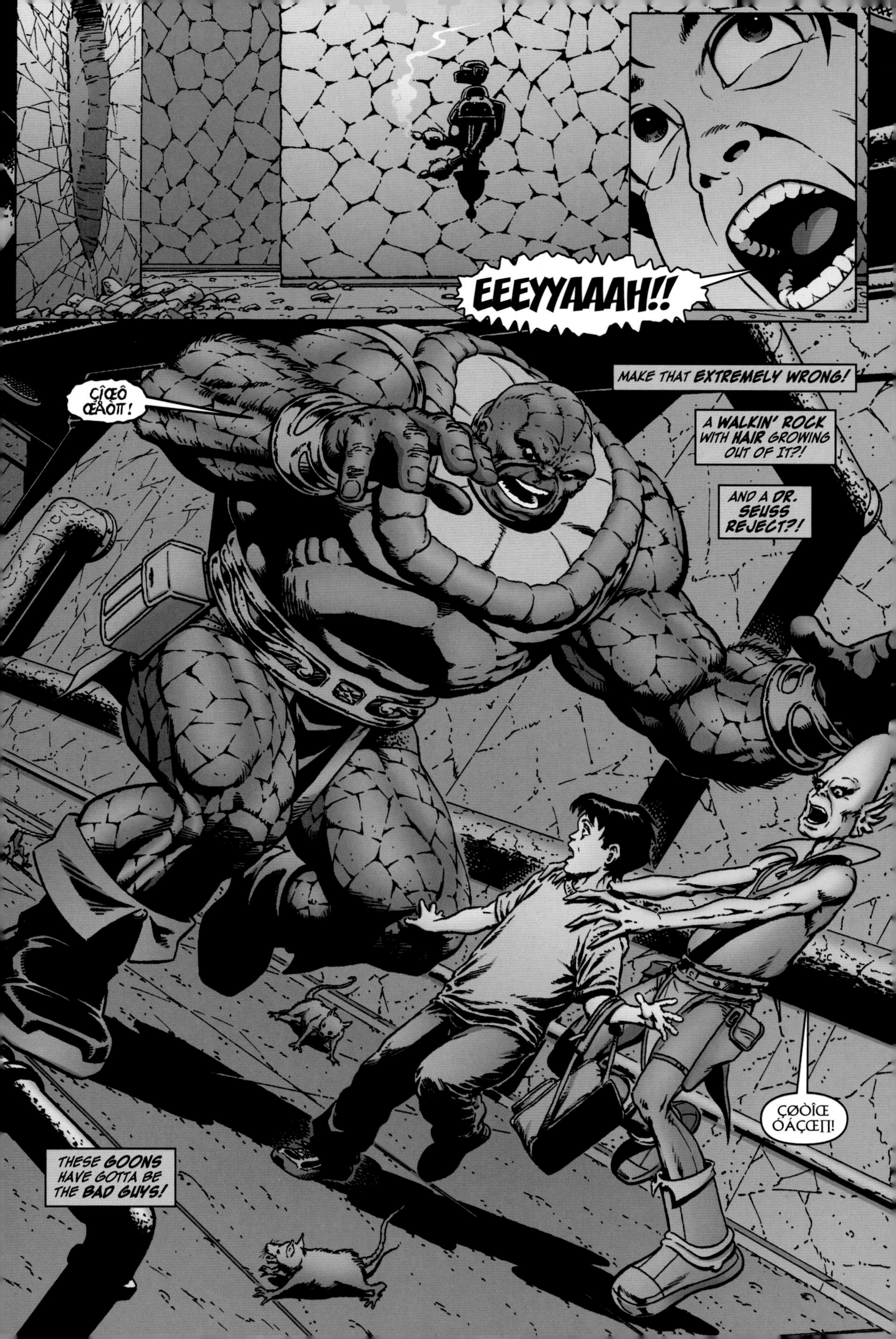
EEEYYAAAH!!
MAKE THAT EXTREMELY WRONG!
ÇÎŒÔ ŒÅÒΠ!
A WALKIN' ROCK WITH HAIR GROWING OUT OF IT?!
AND A DR. SEUSS REJECT?!
THESE GOONS HAVE GOTTA BE THE BAD GUYS!
ÇØÒÎŒ ÓÁÇŒΠ!

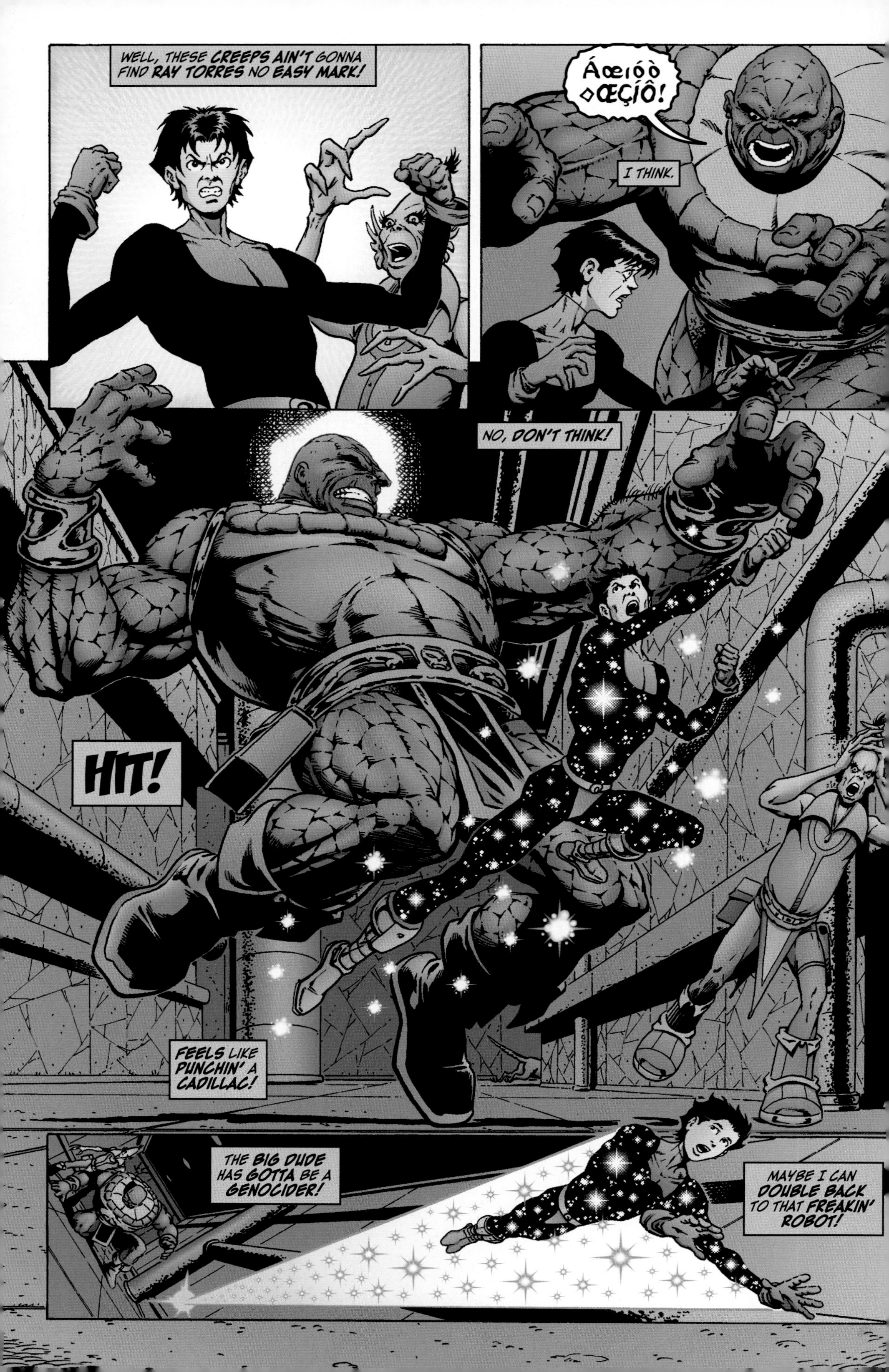

WELL, THESE CREEPS AIN'T GONNA FIND RAY TORRES NO EASY MARK!
Áœιóò ◊ŒÇÍÔ!
I THINK.
NO, DON'T THINK!
HIT!
FEELS LIKE PUNCHIN' A CADILLAC!
THE BIG DUDE HAS GOTTA BE A GENOCIDER!
MAYBE I CAN DOUBLE BACK TO THAT FREAKIN' ROBOT!

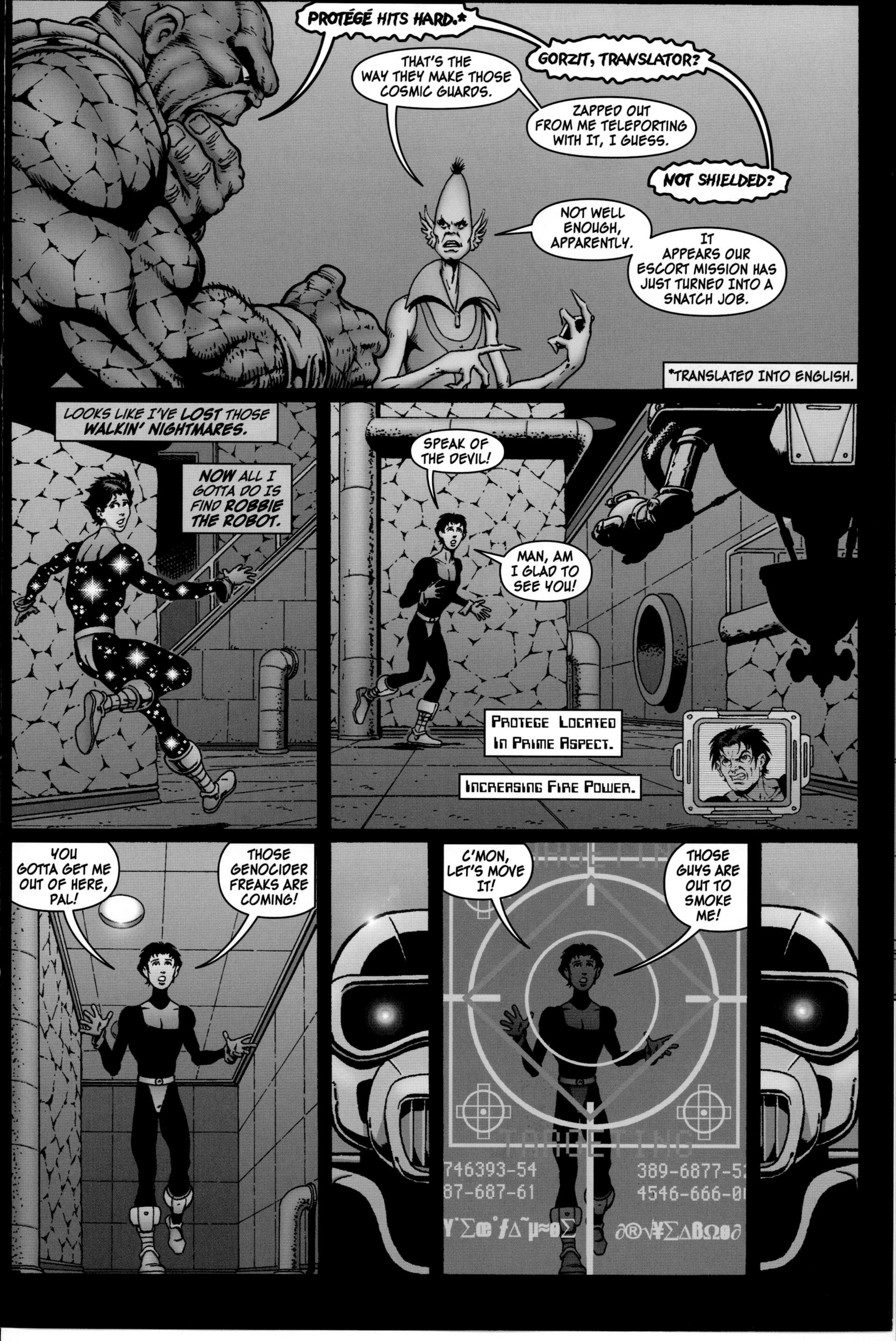
PROTÉGÉ HITS HARD.*
THAT'S THE WAY THEY MAKE THOSE COSMIC GUARDS.
GORZIT, TRANSLATOR?
ZAPPED OUT FROM ME TELEPORTING WITH IT, I GUESS.
NOT SHIELDED?
NOT WELL ENOUGH, APPARENTLY.
IT APPEARS OUR ESCORT MISSION HAS JUST TURNED INTO A SNATCH JOB.
*TRANSLATED INTO ENGLISH.
LOOKS LIKE I'VE LOST THOSE WALKIN' NIGHTMARES.
NOW ALL I GOTTA DO IS FIND ROBBIE THE ROBOT.
SPEAK OF THE DEVIL!
MAN, AM I GLAD TO SEE YOU!
PROTEGE LOCATED IN PRIME ASPECT.
INCREASING FIRE POWER.
YOU GOTTA GET ME OUT OF HERE, PAL!
THOSE GENOCIDER FREAKS ARE COMING!
C'MON, LET'S MOVE IT!
THOSE GUYS ARE OUT TO SMOKE ME!

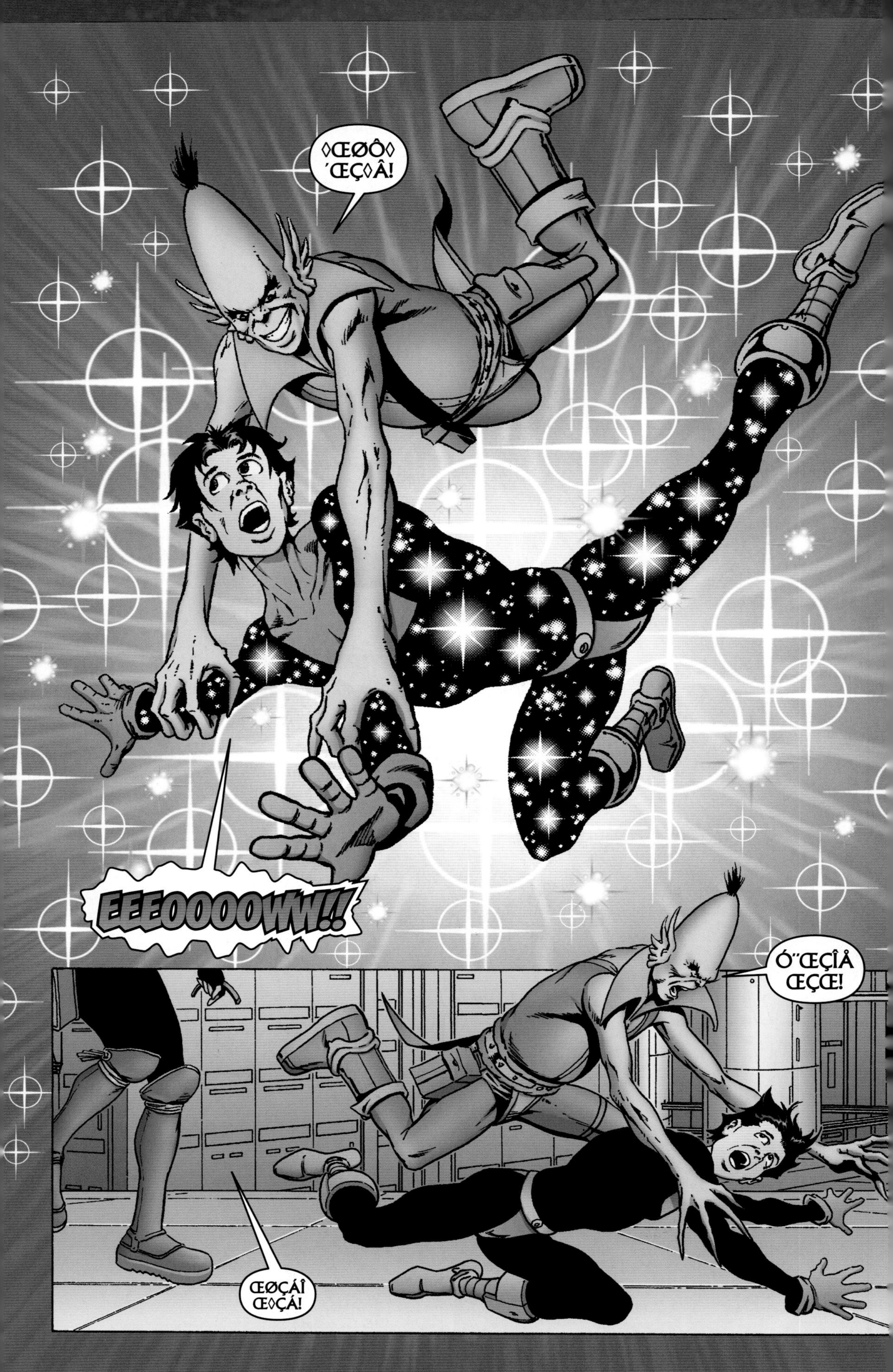
◊ŒØÔ◊ ´ŒÇ◊Â!
EEEOOOOOWW!!
Ó˝ŒÇÎÅ ŒÇŒ!
ŒØÇÁÎ Œ◊ÇÁ!

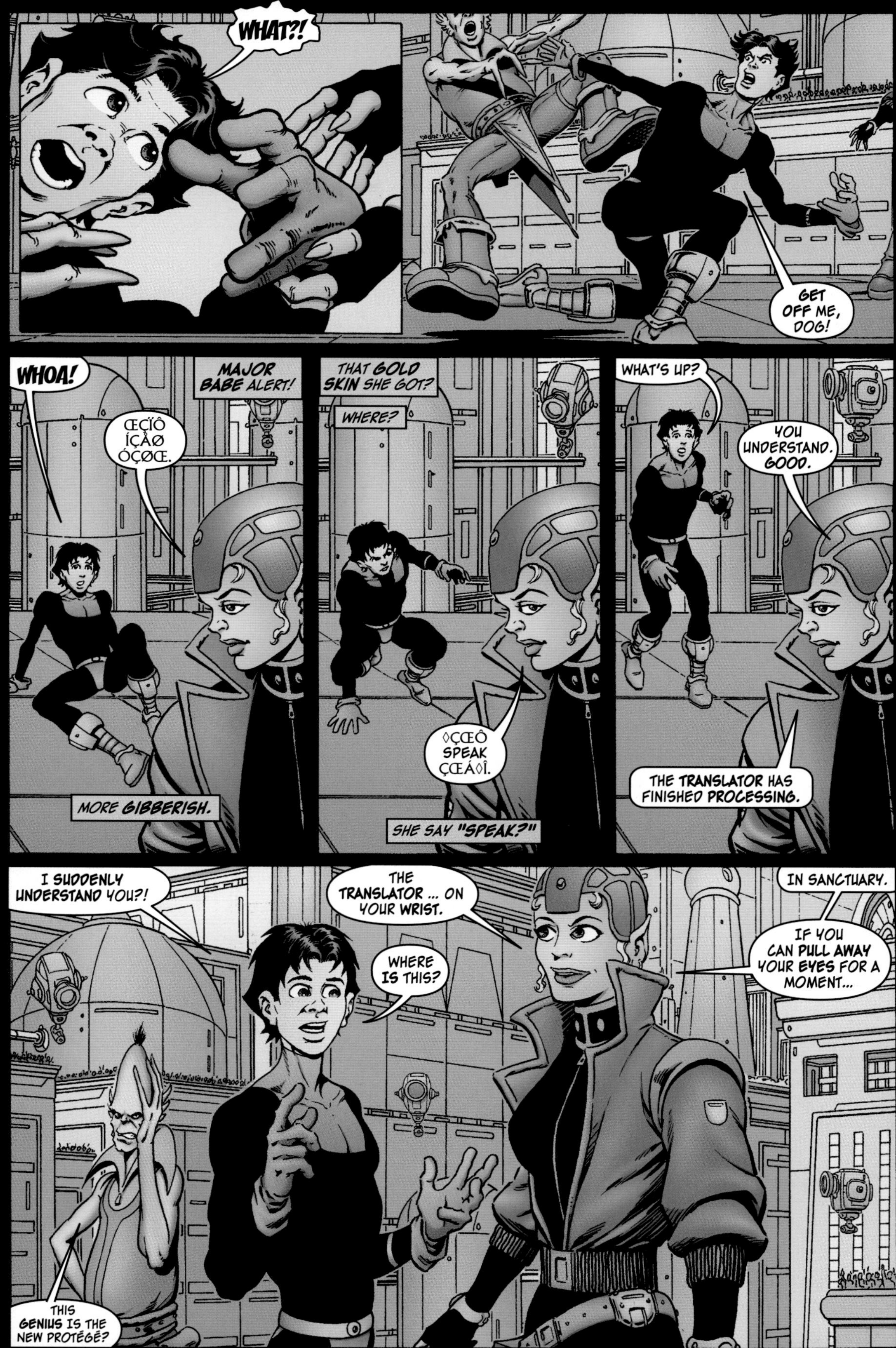

WHAT?!
GET OFF ME, DOG!
WHOA!
MAJOR BABE ALERT!
ŒÇÏÔ ÍÇÅØ ÓÇØŒ.
MORE GIBBERISH.
THAT GOLD SKIN SHE GOT?
WHERE?
◊ÇŒÔ SPEAK ÇŒÁ◊Î.
SHE SAY "SPEAK?"
WHAT'S UP?
YOU UNDERSTAND. GOOD.
THE TRANSLATOR HAS FINISHED PROCESSING.
I SUDDENLY UNDERSTAND YOU?!
THE TRANSLATOR ... ON YOUR WRIST.
WHERE IS THIS?
IN SANCTUARY.
IF YOU CAN PULL AWAY YOUR EYES FOR A MOMENT...
THIS GENIUS IS THE NEW PROTÉGÉ?

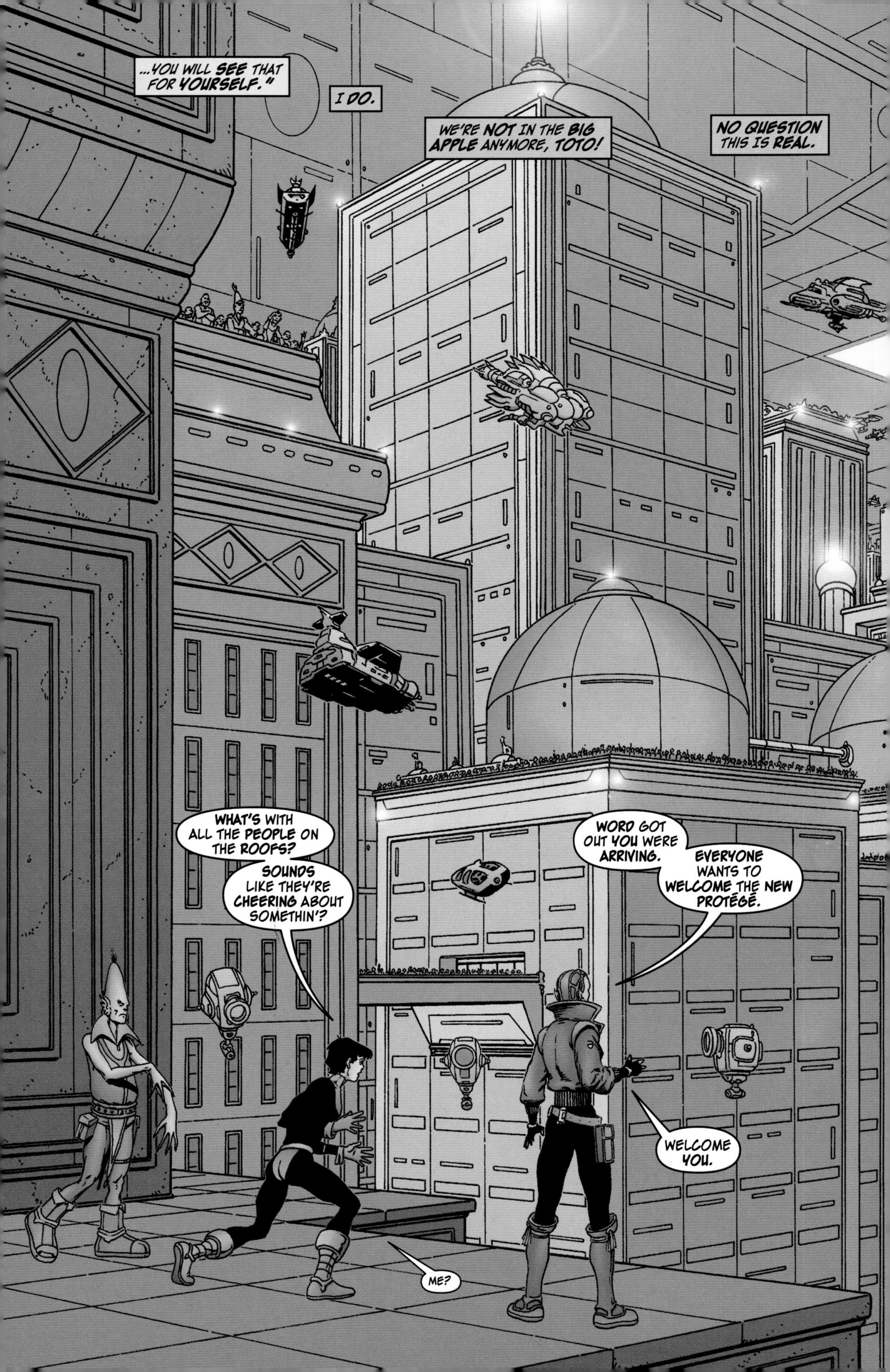
...YOU WILL SEE THAT FOR YOURSELF."
I DO.
WE'RE NOT IN THE BIG APPLE ANYMORE, TOTO!
NO QUESTION THIS IS REAL.
WHAT'S WITH ALL THE PEOPLE ON THE ROOFS?
SOUNDS LIKE THEY'RE CHEERING ABOUT SOMETHIN'?
WORD GOT OUT YOU WERE ARRIVING.
EVERYONE WANTS TO WELCOME THE NEW PROTÉGÉ.
WELCOME YOU.
ME?

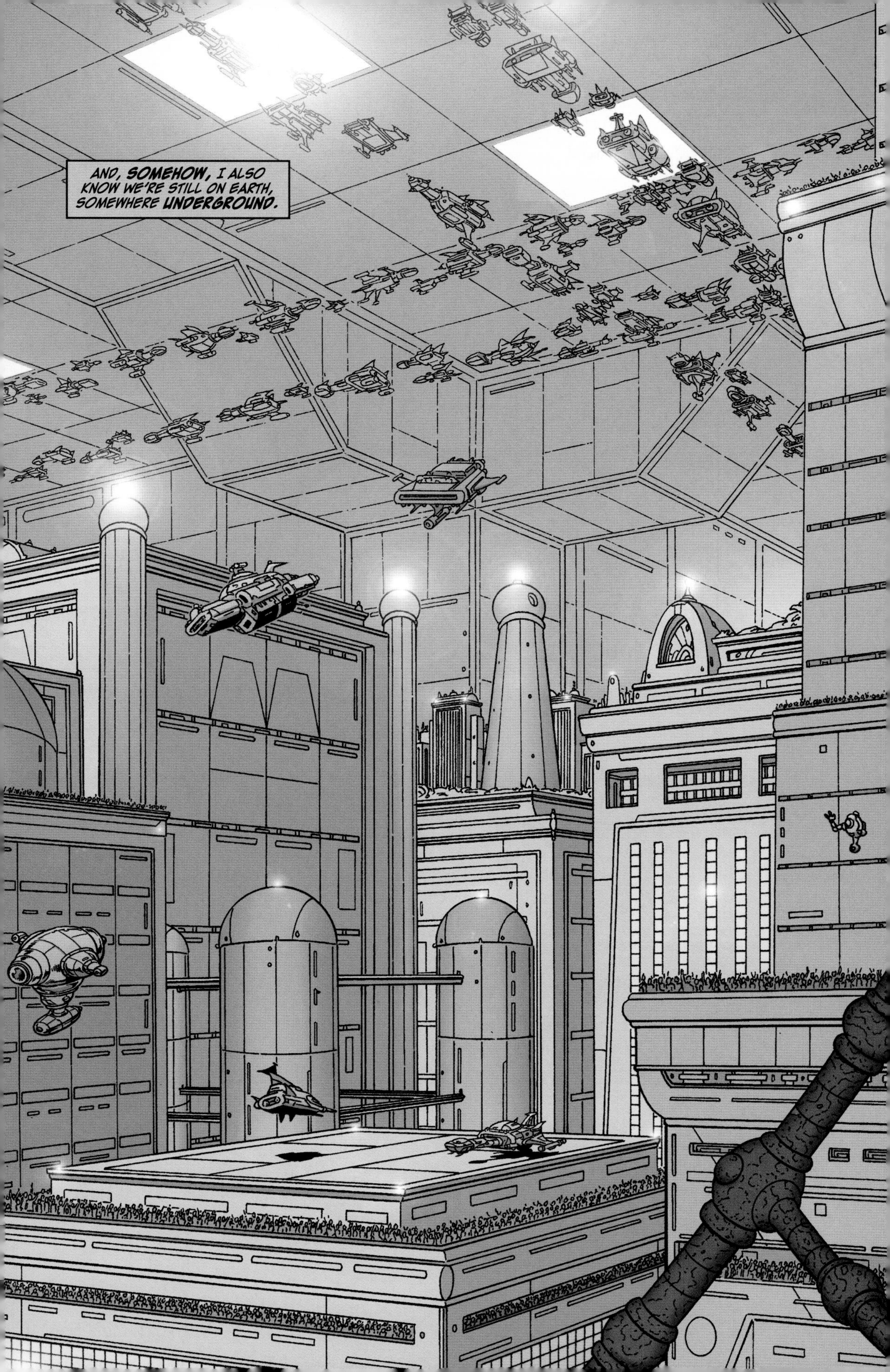
AND, **SOMEHOW,** I ALSO KNOW WE'RE STILL ON EARTH, SOMEWHERE **UNDERGROUND.**

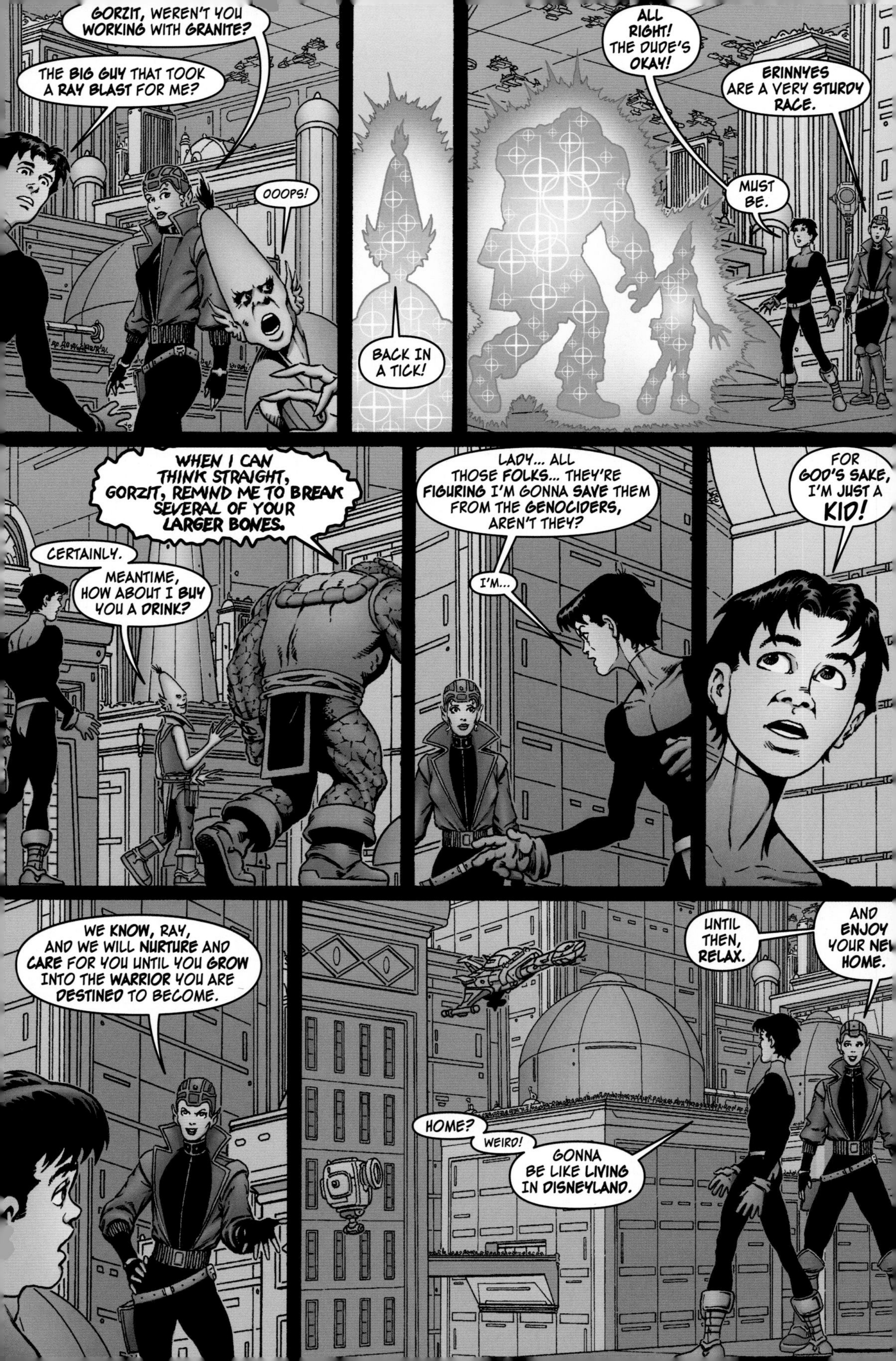
GORZIT, WEREN'T YOU WORKING WITH GRANITE?
THE BIG GUY THAT TOOK A RAY BLAST FOR ME?
OOOPS!
BACK IN A TICK!
ALL RIGHT! THE DUDE'S OKAY!
ERINNYES ARE A VERY STURDY RACE.
MUST BE.
WHEN I CAN THINK STRAIGHT, GORZIT, REMIND ME TO BREAK SEVERAL OF YOUR LARGER BONES.
CERTAINLY.
MEANTIME, HOW ABOUT I BUY YOU A DRINK?
LADY... ALL THOSE FOLKS... THEY'RE FIGURING I'M GONNA SAVE THEM FROM THE GENOCIDERS, AREN'T THEY?
I'M...
FOR GOD'S SAKE, I'M JUST A KID!
WE KNOW, RAY, AND WE WILL NURTURE AND CARE FOR YOU UNTIL YOU GROW INTO THE WARRIOR YOU ARE DESTINED TO BECOME.
UNTIL THEN, RELAX.
AND ENJOY YOUR NEW HOME.
HOME?
WEIRD!
GONNA BE LIKE LIVING IN DISNEYLAND.

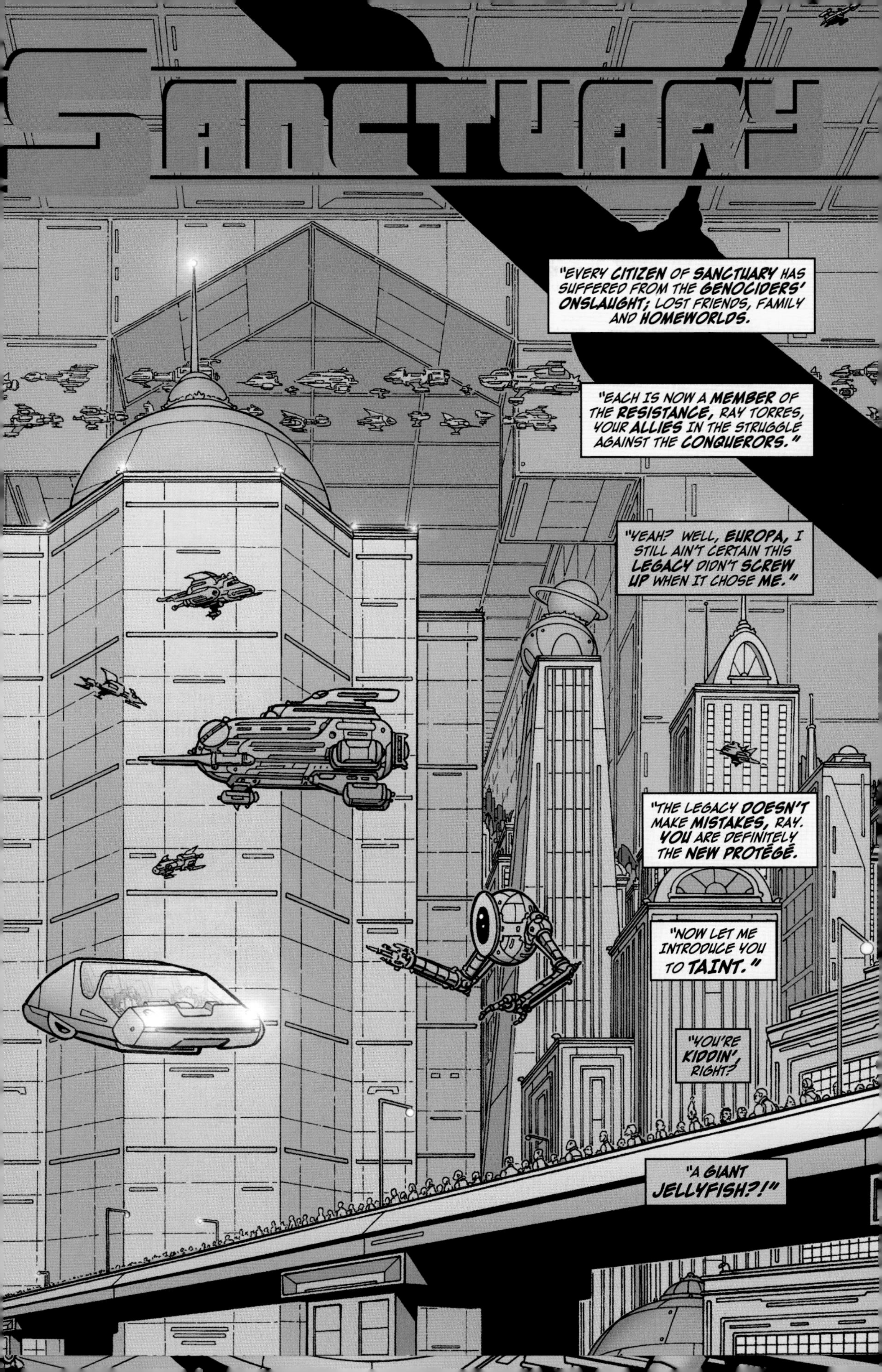
SANCTUARY
"EVERY CITIZEN OF SANCTUARY HAS SUFFERED FROM THE GENOCIDERS' ONSLAUGHT; LOST FRIENDS, FAMILY AND HOMEWORLDS.
"EACH IS NOW A MEMBER OF THE RESISTANCE, RAY TORRES, YOUR ALLIES IN THE STRUGGLE AGAINST THE CONQUERORS."
"YEAH? WELL, EUROPA, I STILL AIN'T CERTAIN THIS LEGACY DIDN'T SCREW UP WHEN IT CHOSE ME."
"THE LEGACY DOESN'T MAKE MISTAKES, RAY. YOU ARE DEFINITELY THE NEW PROTÉGÉ.
"NOW LET ME INTRODUCE YOU TO TAINT."
"YOU'RE KIDDIN', RIGHT?
"A GIANT JELLYFISH?!"

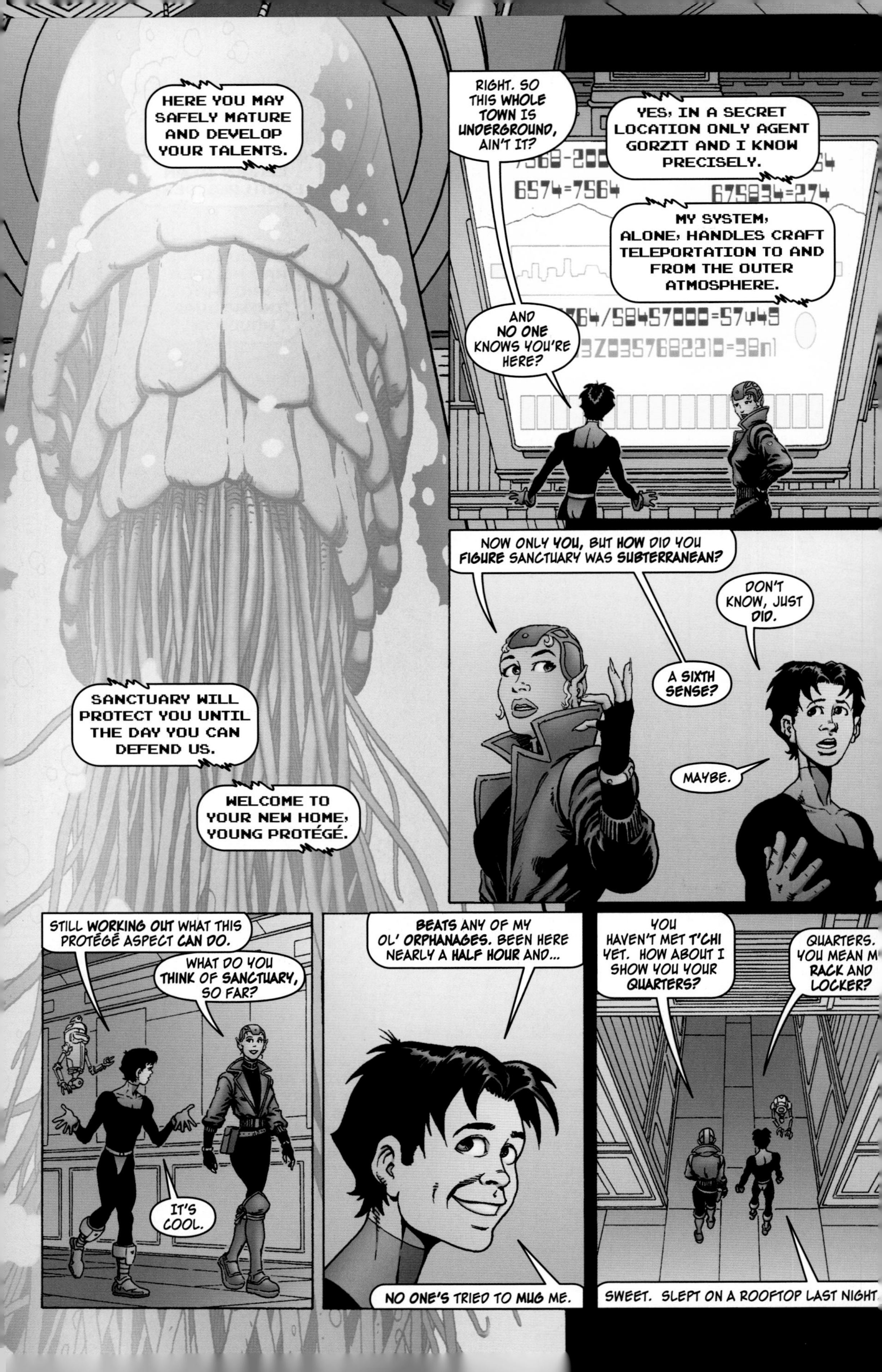
HERE YOU MAY SAFELY MATURE AND DEVELOP YOUR TALENTS.
SANCTUARY WILL PROTECT YOU UNTIL THE DAY YOU CAN DEFEND US.
WELCOME TO YOUR NEW HOME, YOUNG PROTÉGÉ.
RIGHT. SO THIS WHOLE TOWN IS UNDERGROUND, AIN'T IT?
YES, IN A SECRET LOCATION ONLY AGENT GORZIT AND I KNOW PRECISELY.
MY SYSTEM, ALONE, HANDLES CRAFT TELEPORTATION TO AND FROM THE OUTER ATMOSPHERE.
AND NO ONE KNOWS YOU'RE HERE?
NOW ONLY YOU, BUT HOW DID YOU FIGURE SANCTUARY WAS SUBTERRANEAN?
DON'T KNOW, JUST DID.
A SIXTH SENSE?
MAYBE.
STILL WORKING OUT WHAT THIS PROTÉGÉ ASPECT CAN DO.
WHAT DO YOU THINK OF SANCTUARY, SO FAR?
IT'S COOL.
BEATS ANY OF MY OL' ORPHANAGES. BEEN HERE NEARLY A HALF HOUR AND...
NO ONE'S TRIED TO MUG ME.
YOU HAVEN'T MET T'CHI YET. HOW ABOUT I SHOW YOU YOUR QUARTERS?
QUARTERS. YOU MEAN M RACK AND LOCKER?
SWEET. SLEPT ON A ROOFTOP LAST NIGHT

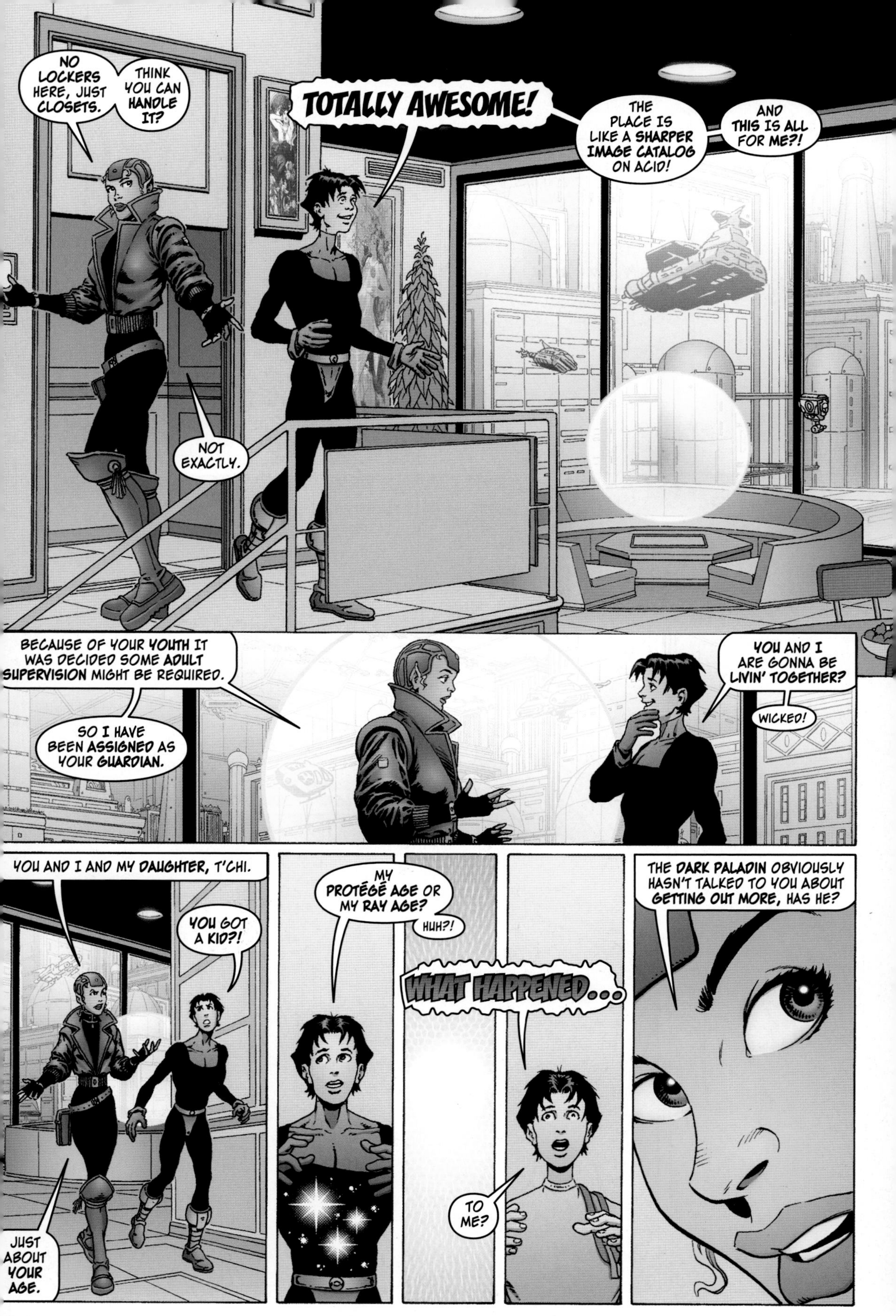
NO LOCKERS HERE, JUST CLOSETS.
THINK YOU CAN HANDLE IT?
TOTALLY AWESOME!
THE PLACE IS LIKE A SHARPER IMAGE CATALOG ON ACID!
AND THIS IS ALL FOR ME?!
NOT EXACTLY.
BECAUSE OF YOUR YOUTH IT WAS DECIDED SOME ADULT SUPERVISION MIGHT BE REQUIRED.
SO I HAVE BEEN ASSIGNED AS YOUR GUARDIAN.
YOU AND I ARE GONNA BE LIVIN' TOGETHER?
WICKED!
YOU AND I AND MY DAUGHTER, T'CHI.
YOU GOT A KID?!
JUST ABOUT YOUR AGE.
MY PROTÉGÉ AGE OR MY RAY AGE?
HUH?!
WHAT HAPPENED...
TO ME?
THE DARK PALADIN OBVIOUSLY HASN'T TALKED TO YOU ABOUT GETTING OUT MORE, HAS HE?

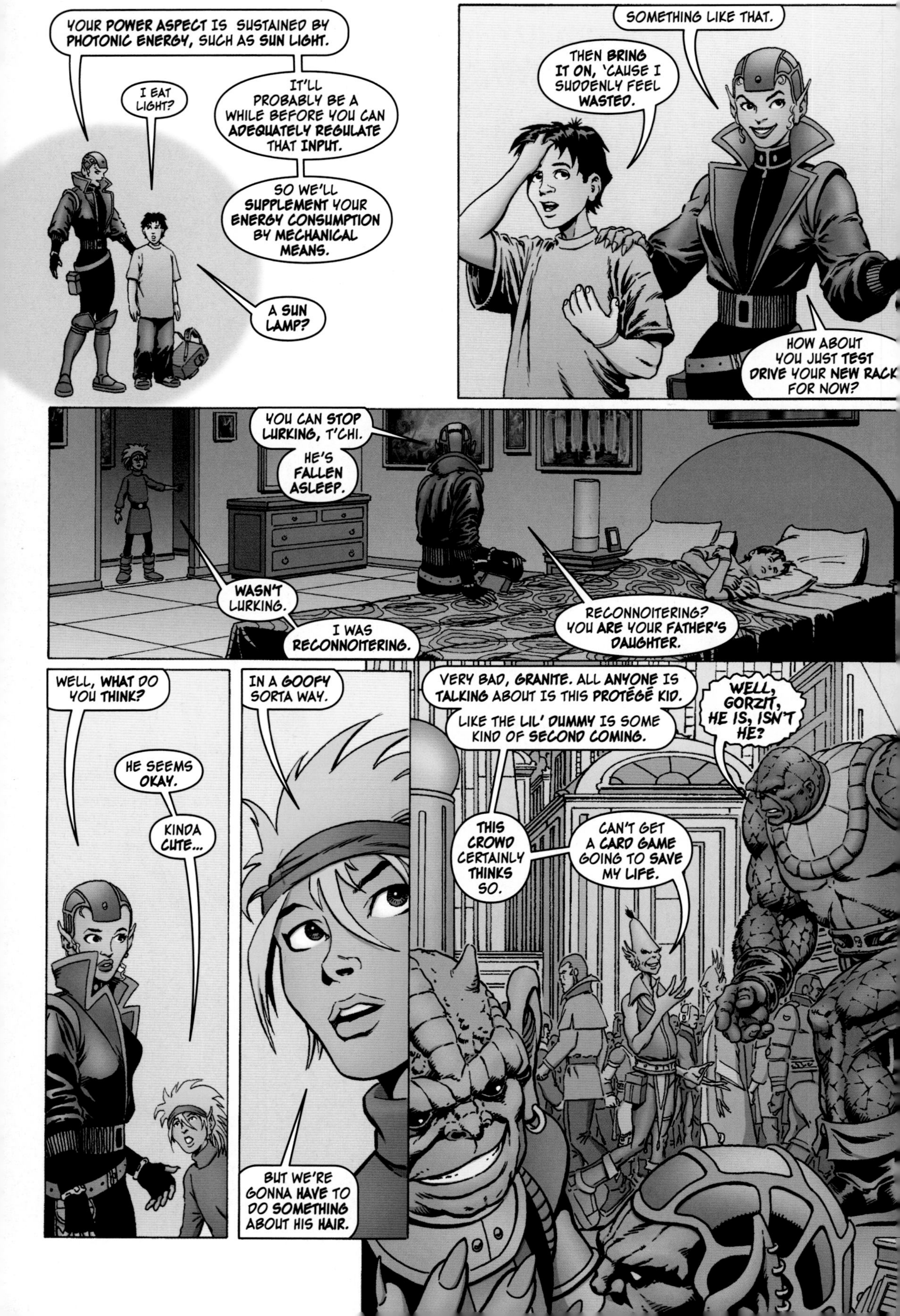
YOUR POWER ASPECT IS SUSTAINED BY PHOTONIC ENERGY, SUCH AS SUN LIGHT.
I EAT LIGHT?
IT'LL PROBABLY BE A WHILE BEFORE YOU CAN ADEQUATELY REGULATE THAT INPUT.
SO WE'LL SUPPLEMENT YOUR ENERGY CONSUMPTION BY MECHANICAL MEANS.
A SUN LAMP?
SOMETHING LIKE THAT.
THEN BRING IT ON, 'CAUSE I SUDDENLY FEEL WASTED.
HOW ABOUT YOU JUST TEST DRIVE YOUR NEW RACK FOR NOW?
YOU CAN STOP LURKING, T'CHI.
HE'S FALLEN ASLEEP.
WASN'T LURKING.
I WAS RECONNOITERING.
RECONNOITERING? YOU ARE YOUR FATHER'S DAUGHTER.
WELL, WHAT DO YOU THINK?
HE SEEMS OKAY.
KINDA CUTE...
IN A GOOFY SORTA WAY.
BUT WE'RE GONNA HAVE TO DO SOMETHING ABOUT HIS HAIR.
VERY BAD, GRANITE. ALL ANYONE IS TALKING ABOUT IS THIS PROTÉGÉ KID.
LIKE THE LIL' DUMMY IS SOME KIND OF SECOND COMING.
WELL, GORZIT, HE IS, ISN'T HE?
THIS CROWD CERTAINLY THINKS SO.
CAN'T GET A CARD GAME GOING TO SAVE MY LIFE.

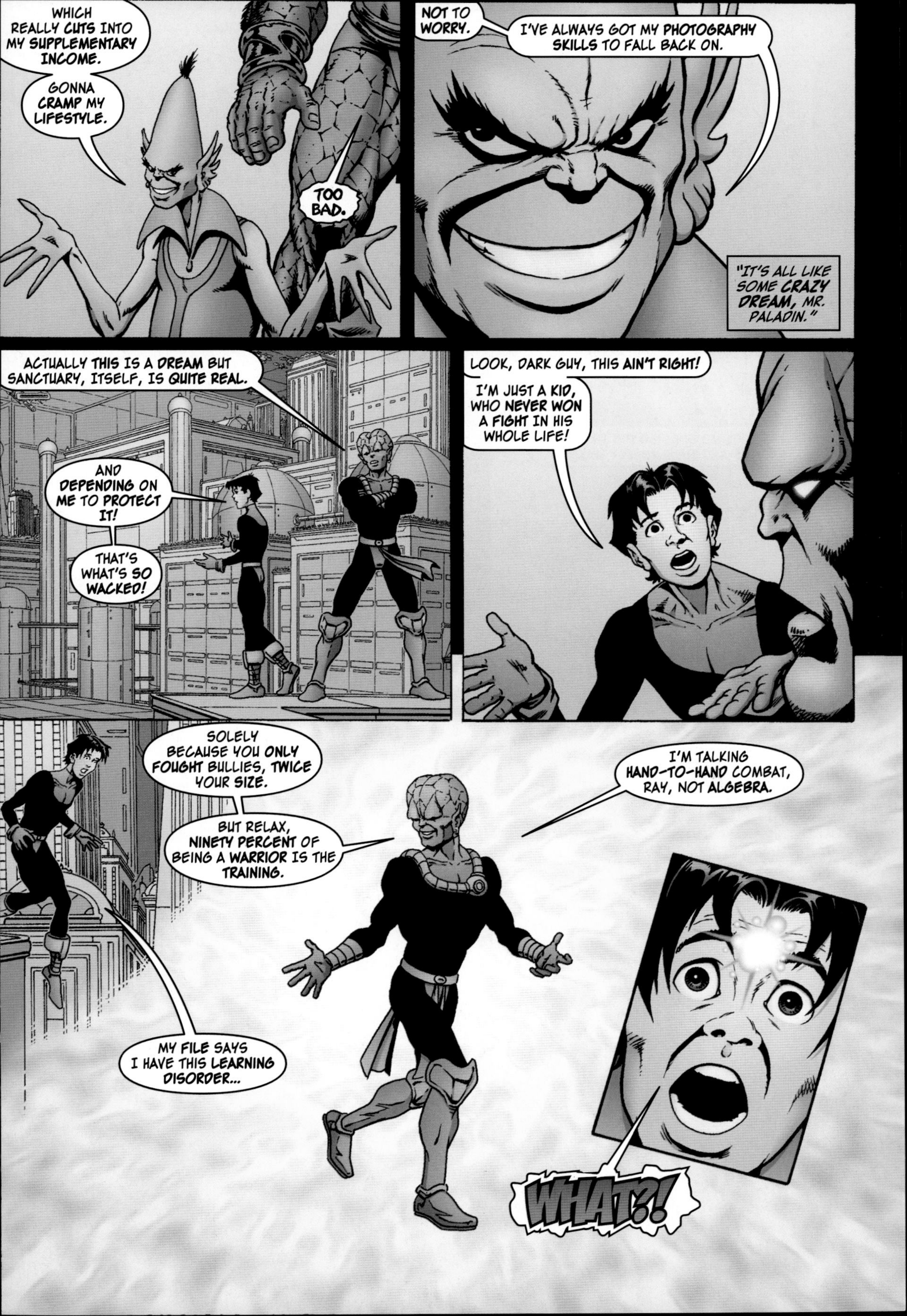

WHICH REALLY CUTS INTO MY SUPPLEMENTARY INCOME.
GONNA CRAMP MY LIFESTYLE.
TOO BAD.
NOT TO WORRY.
I'VE ALWAYS GOT MY PHOTOGRAPHY SKILLS TO FALL BACK ON.
"IT'S ALL LIKE SOME CRAZY DREAM, MR. PALADIN."
ACTUALLY THIS IS A DREAM BUT SANCTUARY, ITSELF, IS QUITE REAL.
AND DEPENDING ON ME TO PROTECT IT!
THAT'S WHAT'S SO WACKED!
LOOK, DARK GUY, THIS AIN'T RIGHT!
I'M JUST A KID, WHO NEVER WON A FIGHT IN HIS WHOLE LIFE!
SOLELY BECAUSE YOU ONLY FOUGHT BULLIES, TWICE YOUR SIZE.
BUT RELAX, NINETY PERCENT OF BEING A WARRIOR IS THE TRAINING.
MY FILE SAYS I HAVE THIS LEARNING DISORDER...
I'M TALKING HAND-TO-HAND COMBAT, RAY, NOT ALGEBRA.
WHAT?!

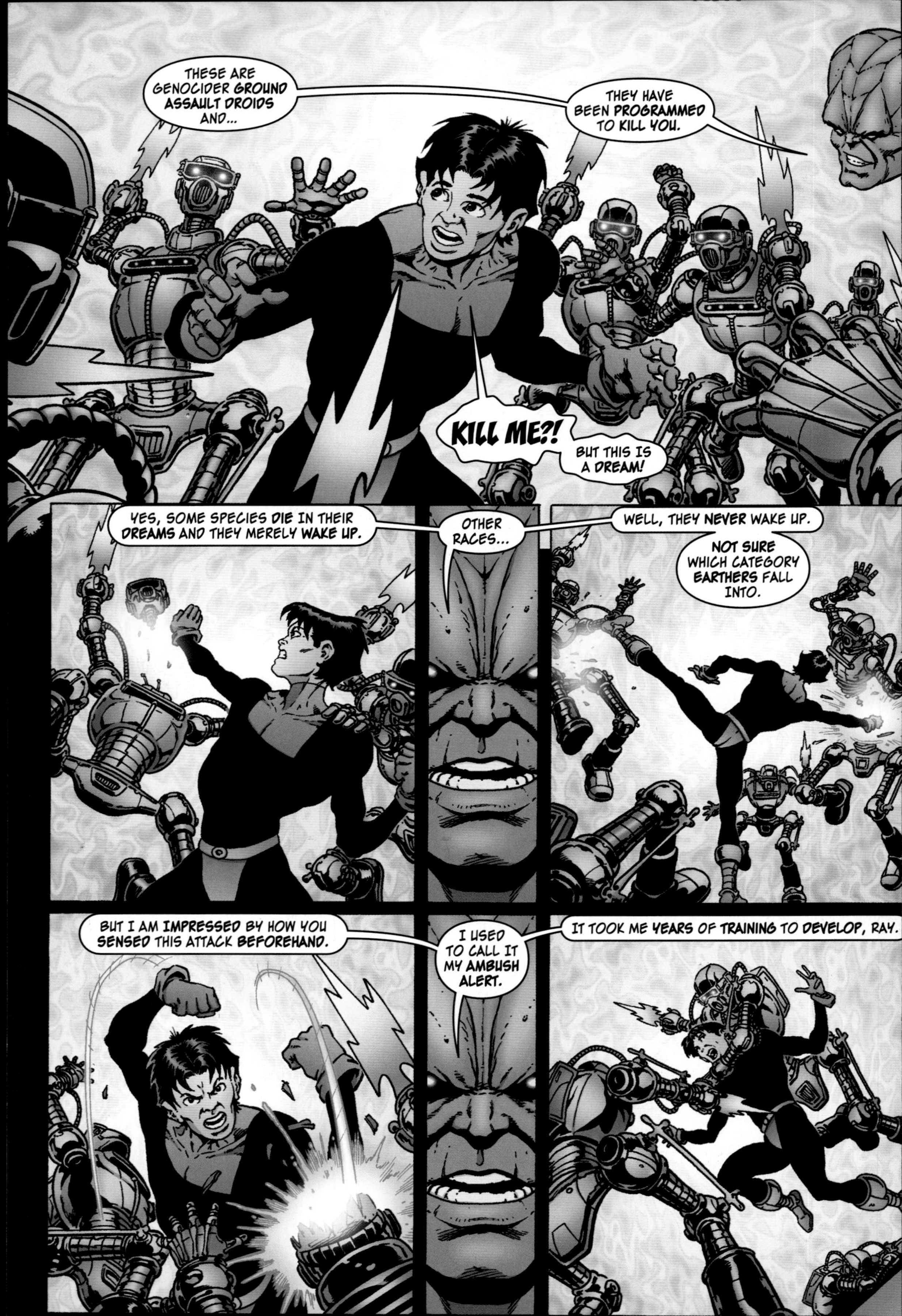
THESE ARE GENOCIDER GROUND ASSAULT DROIDS AND...
THEY HAVE BEEN PROGRAMMED TO KILL YOU.
KILL ME?!
BUT THIS IS A DREAM!
YES, SOME SPECIES DIE IN THEIR DREAMS AND THEY MERELY WAKE UP.
OTHER RACES...
WELL, THEY NEVER WAKE UP.
NOT SURE WHICH CATEGORY EARTHERS FALL INTO.
BUT I AM IMPRESSED BY HOW YOU SENSED THIS ATTACK BEFOREHAND.
I USED TO CALL IT MY AMBUSH ALERT.
IT TOOK ME YEARS OF TRAINING TO DEVELOP, RAY.

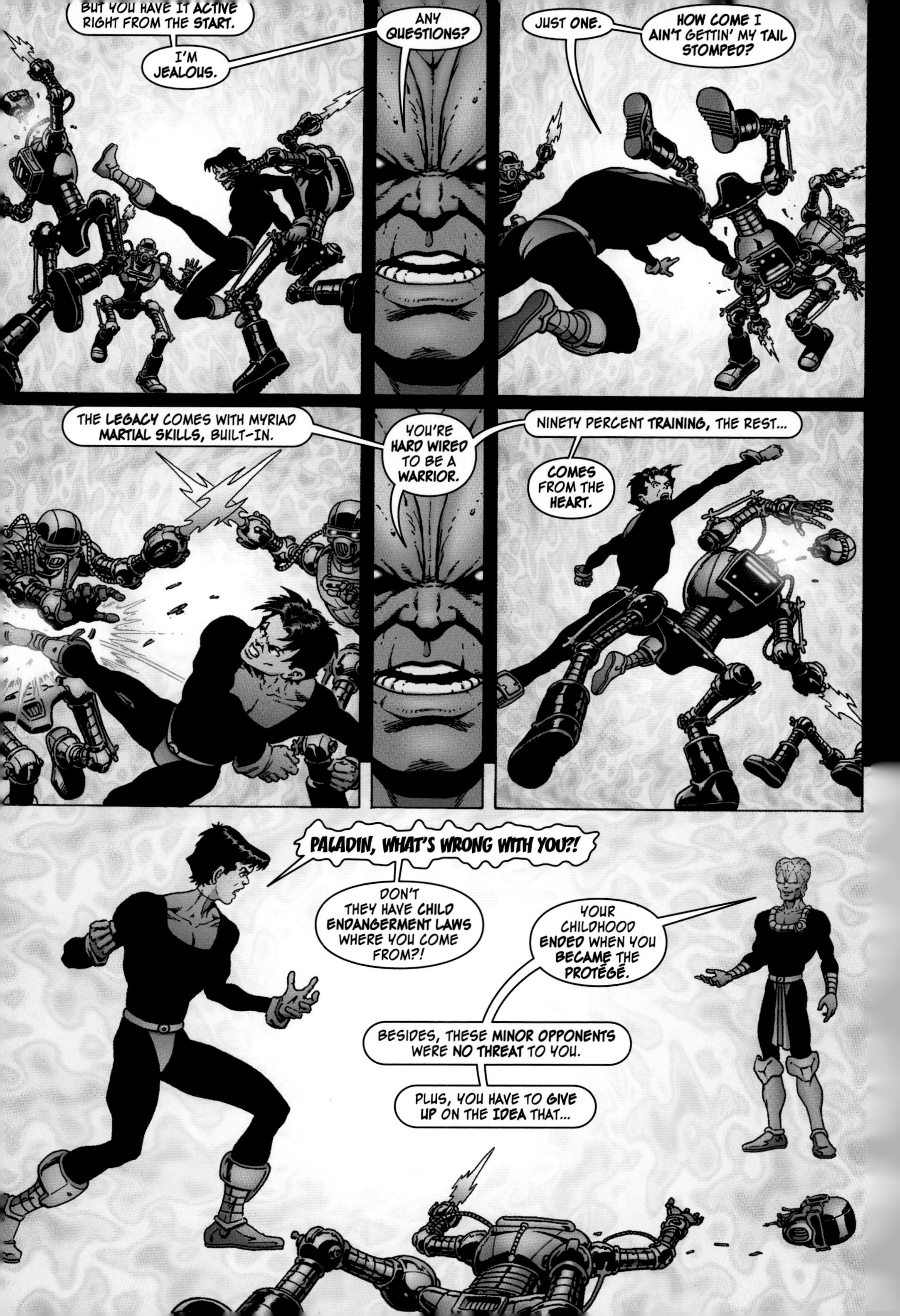

BUT YOU HAVE IT ACTIVE RIGHT FROM THE START.
I'M JEALOUS.
ANY QUESTIONS?
JUST ONE.
HOW COME I AIN'T GETTIN' MY TAIL STOMPED?
THE LEGACY COMES WITH MYRIAD MARTIAL SKILLS, BUILT-IN.
YOU'RE HARD WIRED TO BE A WARRIOR.
NINETY PERCENT TRAINING, THE REST...
COMES FROM THE HEART.
PALADIN, WHAT'S WRONG WITH YOU?!
DON'T THEY HAVE CHILD ENDANGERMENT LAWS WHERE YOU COME FROM?!
YOUR CHILDHOOD ENDED WHEN YOU BECAME THE PROTÉGÉ.
BESIDES, THESE MINOR OPPONENTS WERE NO THREAT TO YOU.
PLUS, YOU HAVE TO GIVE UP ON THE IDEA THAT...

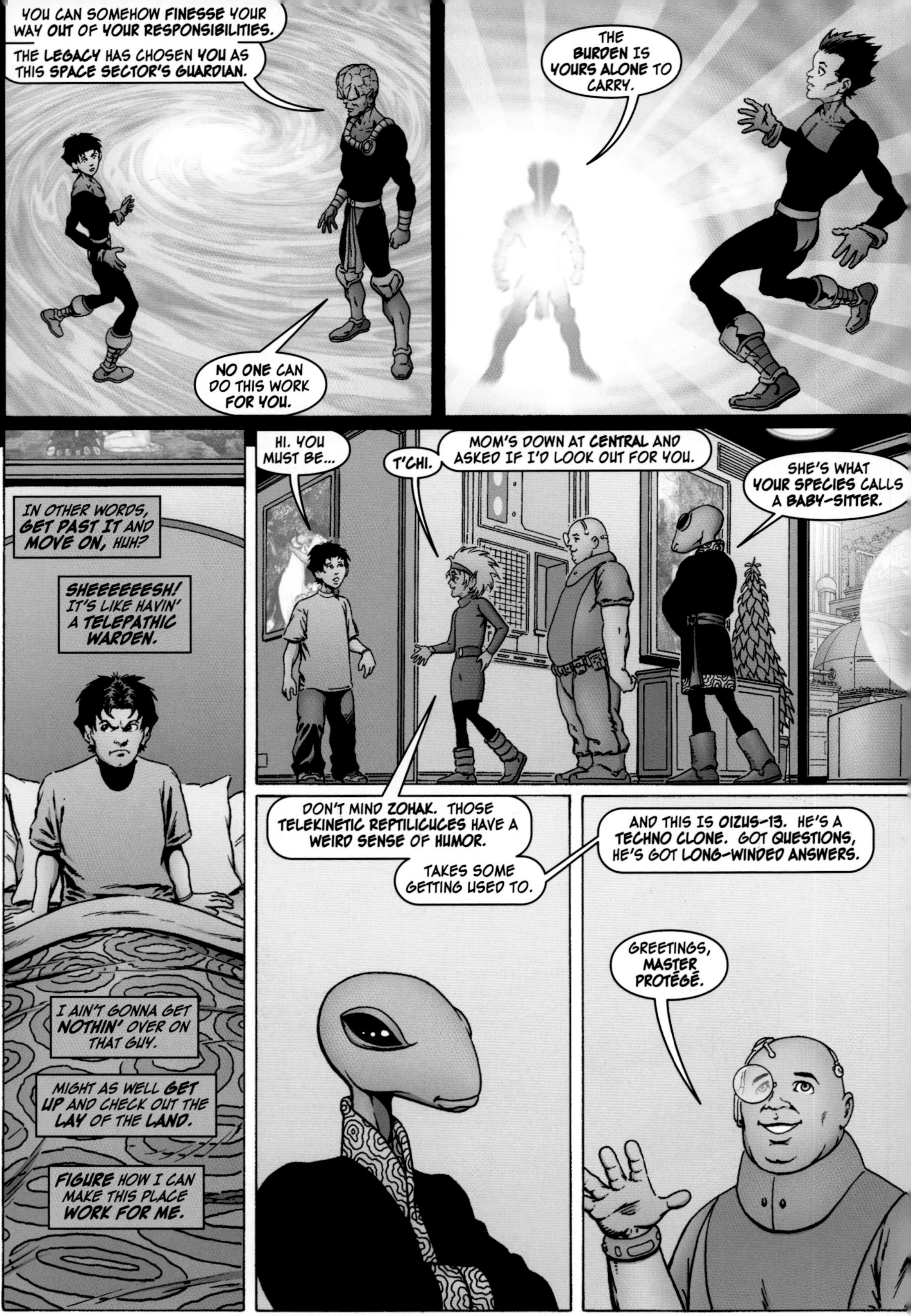

YOU CAN SOMEHOW FINESSE YOUR WAY OUT OF YOUR RESPONSIBILITIES.
THE LEGACY HAS CHOSEN YOU AS THIS SPACE SECTOR'S GUARDIAN.
NO ONE CAN DO THIS WORK FOR YOU.
THE BURDEN IS YOURS ALONE TO CARRY.
IN OTHER WORDS, GET PAST IT AND MOVE ON, HUH?
SHEEEEEEESH! IT'S LIKE HAVIN' A TELEPATHIC WARDEN.
I AIN'T GONNA GET NOTHIN' OVER ON THAT GUY.
MIGHT AS WELL GET UP AND CHECK OUT THE LAY OF THE LAND.
FIGURE HOW I CAN MAKE THIS PLACE WORK FOR ME.
HI. YOU MUST BE...
T'CHI.
MOM'S DOWN AT CENTRAL AND ASKED IF I'D LOOK OUT FOR YOU.
SHE'S WHAT YOUR SPECIES CALLS A BABY-SITTER.
DON'T MIND ZOHAK. THOSE TELEKINETIC REPTILICUCES HAVE A WEIRD SENSE OF HUMOR.
TAKES SOME GETTING USED TO.
AND THIS IS OIZUS-13. HE'S A TECHNO CLONE. GOT QUESTIONS, HE'S GOT LONG-WINDED ANSWERS.
GREETINGS, MASTER PROTÉGÉ.

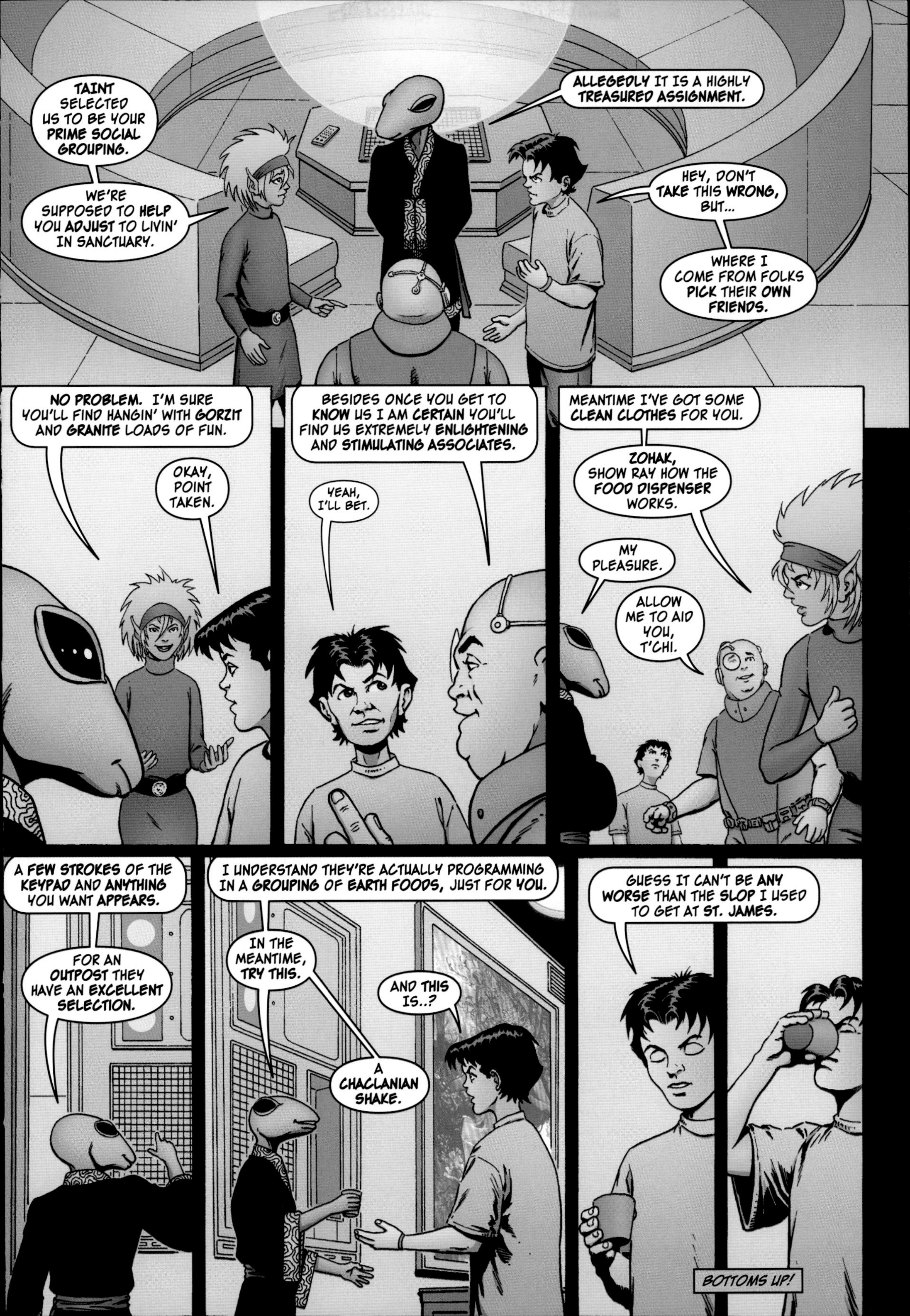
TAINT SELECTED US TO BE YOUR PRIME SOCIAL GROUPING.
ALLEGEDLY IT IS A HIGHLY TREASURED ASSIGNMENT.
WE'RE SUPPOSED TO HELP YOU ADJUST TO LIVIN' IN SANCTUARY.
HEY, DON'T TAKE THIS WRONG, BUT...
WHERE I COME FROM FOLKS PICK THEIR OWN FRIENDS.
NO PROBLEM. I'M SURE YOU'LL FIND HANGIN' WITH GORZIT AND GRANITE LOADS OF FUN.
OKAY, POINT TAKEN.
BESIDES ONCE YOU GET TO KNOW US I AM CERTAIN YOU'LL FIND US EXTREMELY ENLIGHTENING AND STIMULATING ASSOCIATES.
YEAH, I'LL BET.
MEANTIME I'VE GOT SOME CLEAN CLOTHES FOR YOU.
ZOHAK, SHOW RAY HOW THE FOOD DISPENSER WORKS.
MY PLEASURE.
ALLOW ME TO AID YOU, T'CHI.
A FEW STROKES OF THE KEYPAD AND ANYTHING YOU WANT APPEARS.
FOR AN OUTPOST THEY HAVE AN EXCELLENT SELECTION.
I UNDERSTAND THEY'RE ACTUALLY PROGRAMMING IN A GROUPING OF EARTH FOODS, JUST FOR YOU.
IN THE MEANTIME, TRY THIS.
AND THIS IS..?
A CHACLANIAN SHAKE.
GUESS IT CAN'T BE ANY WORSE THAN THE SLOP I USED TO GET AT ST. JAMES.
BOTTOMS UP!

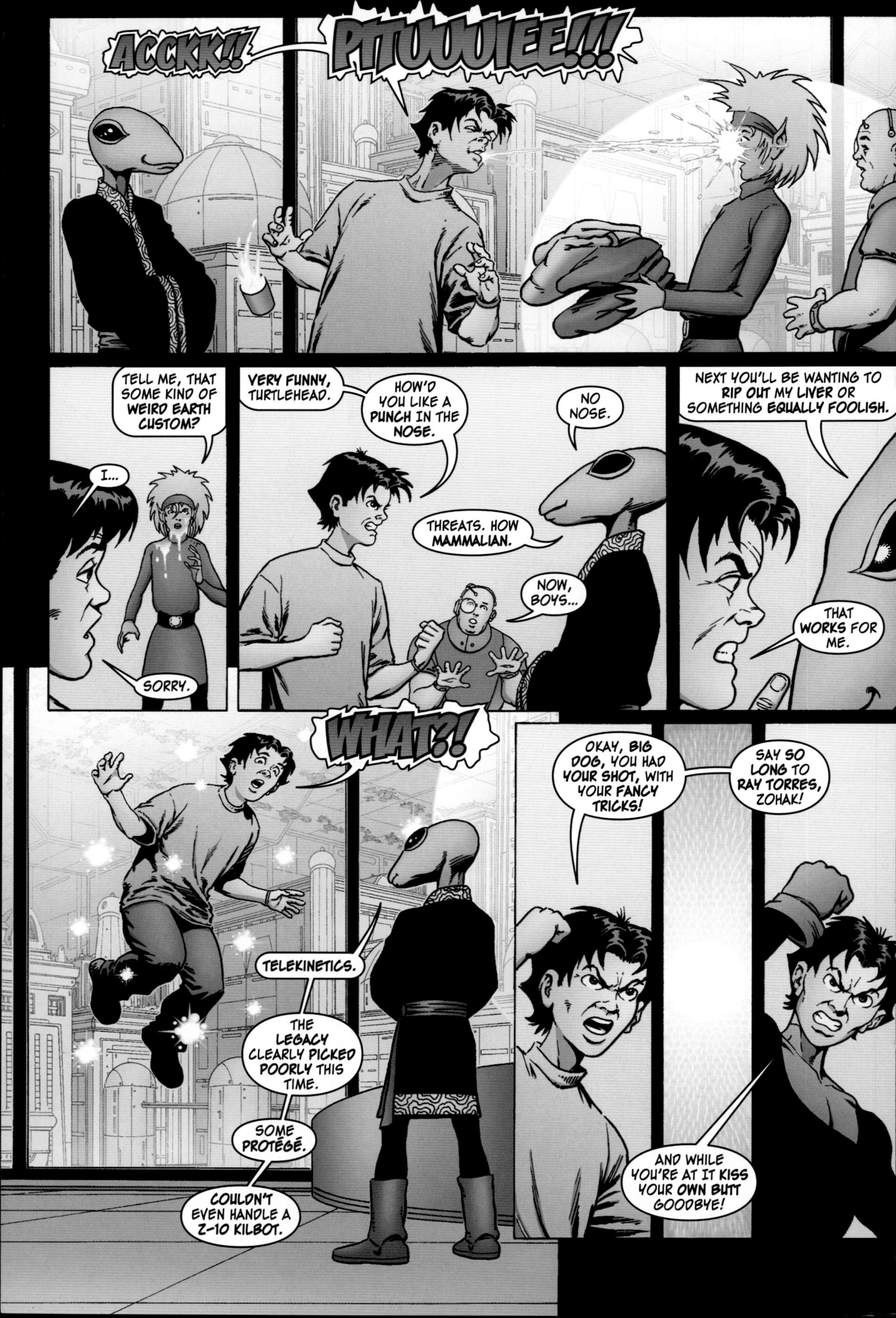
ACCKK!!
PITUUUIEE!!!
TELL ME, THAT SOME KIND OF WEIRD EARTH CUSTOM?
I...
SORRY.
VERY FUNNY, TURTLEHEAD.
HOW'D YOU LIKE A PUNCH IN THE NOSE.
NO NOSE.
THREATS. HOW MAMMALIAN.
NOW, BOYS...
NEXT YOU'LL BE WANTING TO RIP OUT MY LIVER OR SOMETHING EQUALLY FOOLISH.
THAT WORKS FOR ME.
WHAT?!
TELEKINETICS.
THE LEGACY CLEARLY PICKED POORLY THIS TIME.
SOME PROTÉGÉ.
COULDN'T EVEN HANDLE A Z-10 KILBOT.
OKAY, BIG DOG, YOU HAD YOUR SHOT, WITH YOUR FANCY TRICKS!
SAY SO LONG TO RAY TORRES, ZOHAK!
AND WHILE YOU'RE AT IT KISS YOUR OWN BUTT GOODBYE!

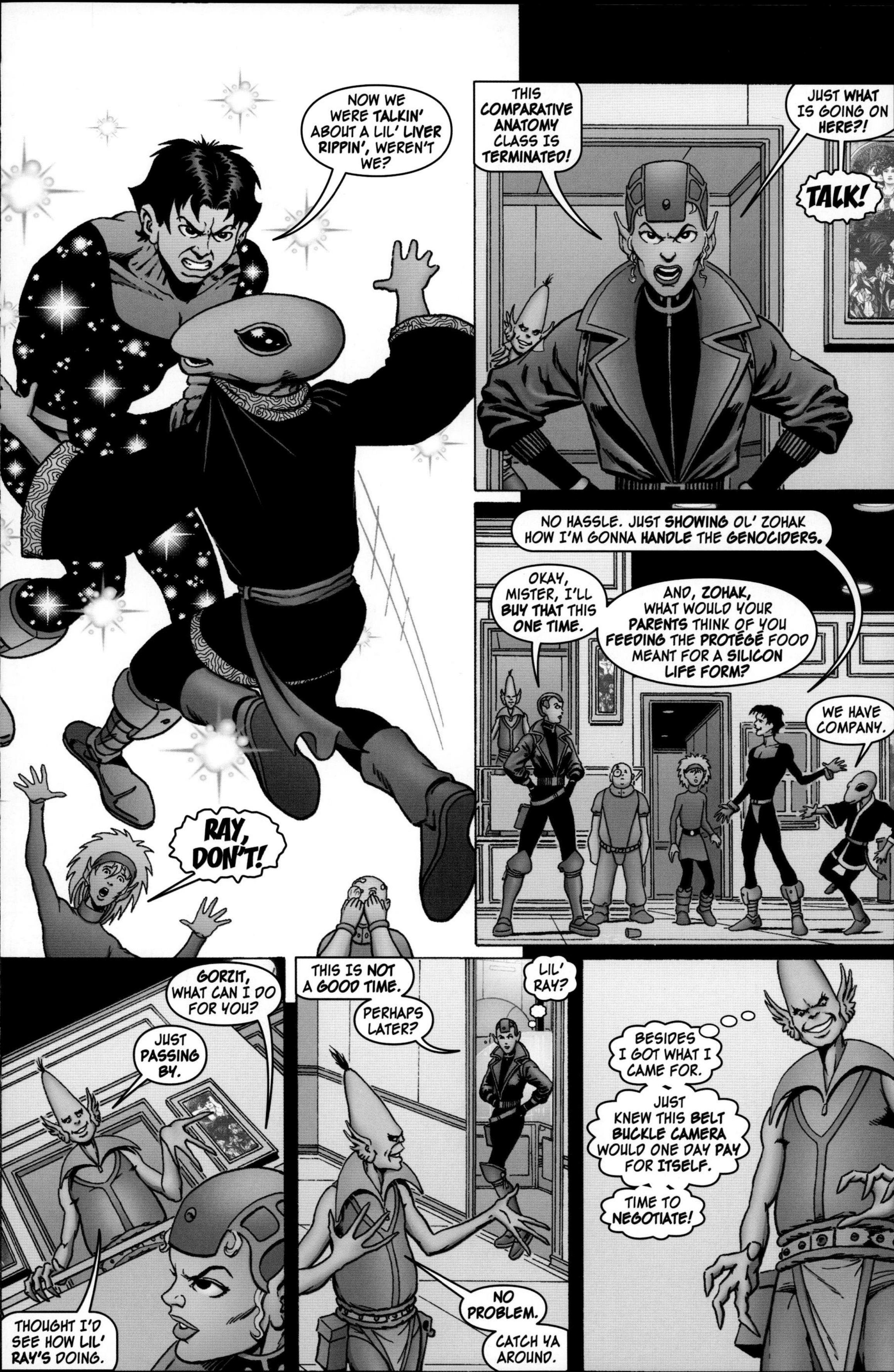
NOW WE WERE TALKIN' ABOUT A LIL' LIVER RIPPIN', WEREN'T WE?
RAY, DON'T!
THIS COMPARATIVE ANATOMY CLASS IS TERMINATED!
JUST WHAT IS GOING ON HERE?!
TALK!
NO HASSLE. JUST SHOWING OL' ZOHAK HOW I'M GONNA HANDLE THE GENOCIDERS.
OKAY, MISTER, I'LL BUY THAT THIS ONE TIME.
AND, ZOHAK, WHAT WOULD YOUR PARENTS THINK OF YOU FEEDING THE PROTÉGÉ FOOD MEANT FOR A SILICON LIFE FORM?
WE HAVE COMPANY.
GORZIT, WHAT CAN I DO FOR YOU?
JUST PASSING BY.
THOUGHT I'D SEE HOW LIL' RAY'S DOING.
THIS IS NOT A GOOD TIME.
PERHAPS LATER?
NO PROBLEM.
CATCH YA AROUND.
LIL' RAY?
BESIDES I GOT WHAT I CAME FOR.
JUST KNEW THIS BELT BUCKLE CAMERA WOULD ONE DAY PAY FOR ITSELF.
TIME TO NEGOTIATE!

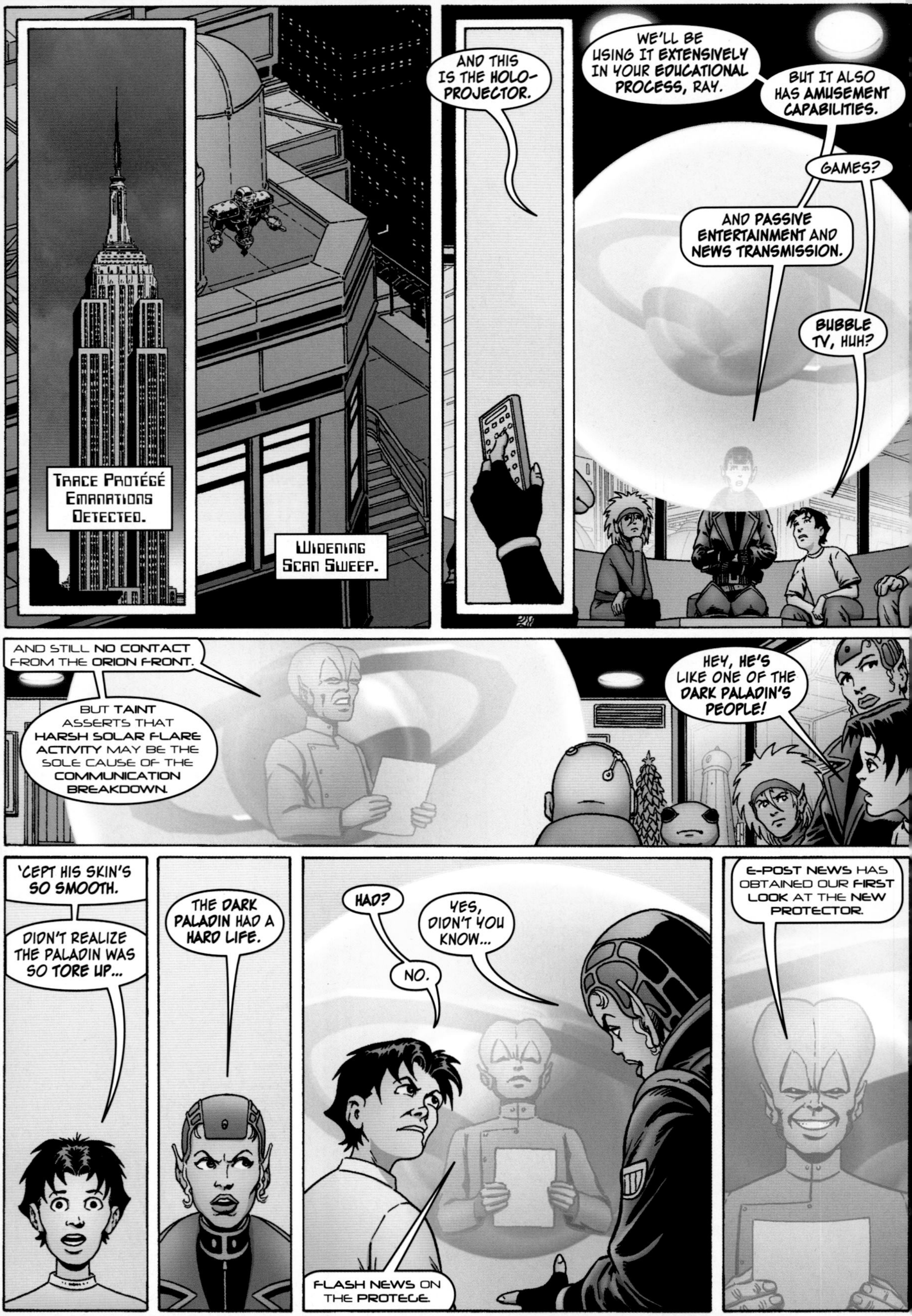
Trace Protégé Emanations Detected.
Widening Scan Sweep.
AND THIS IS THE HOLO-PROJECTOR.
WE'LL BE USING IT EXTENSIVELY IN YOUR EDUCATIONAL PROCESS, RAY.
BUT IT ALSO HAS AMUSEMENT CAPABILITIES.
GAMES?
AND PASSIVE ENTERTAINMENT AND NEWS TRANSMISSION.
BUBBLE TV, HUH?
AND STILL NO CONTACT FROM THE ORION FRONT.
BUT TAINT ASSERTS THAT HARSH SOLAR FLARE ACTIVITY MAY BE THE SOLE CAUSE OF THE COMMUNICATION BREAKDOWN.
HEY, HE'S LIKE ONE OF THE DARK PALADIN'S PEOPLE!
'CEPT HIS SKIN'S SO SMOOTH.
DIDN'T REALIZE THE PALADIN WAS SO TORE UP...
THE DARK PALADIN HAD A HARD LIFE.
HAD?
YES, DIDN'T YOU KNOW...
NO.
FLASH NEWS ON THE PROTEGE.
E-POST NEWS HAS OBTAINED OUR FIRST LOOK AT THE NEW PROTECTOR.

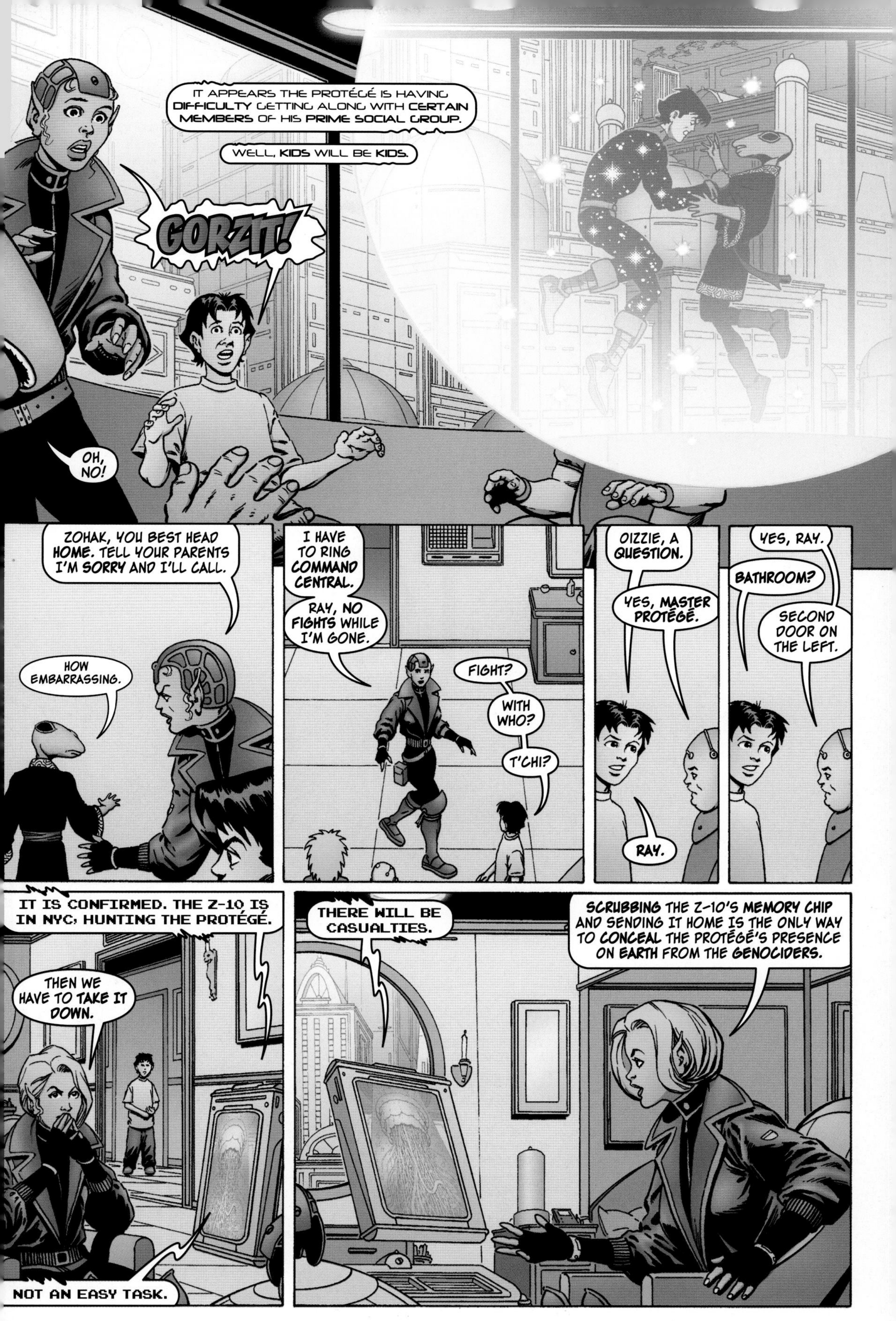
IT APPEARS THE PROTÉGÉ IS HAVING DIFFICULTY GETTING ALONG WITH CERTAIN MEMBERS OF HIS PRIME SOCIAL GROUP.
WELL, KIDS WILL BE KIDS.
GORZIT!
OH, NO!
ZOHAK, YOU BEST HEAD HOME. TELL YOUR PARENTS I'M SORRY AND I'LL CALL.
HOW EMBARRASSING.
I HAVE TO RING COMMAND CENTRAL.
RAY, NO FIGHTS WHILE I'M GONE.
FIGHT?
WITH WHO?
T'CHI?
OIZZIE, A QUESTION.
YES, MASTER PROTÉGÉ.
RAY.
YES, RAY.
BATHROOM?
SECOND DOOR ON THE LEFT.
IT IS CONFIRMED. THE Z-10 IS IN NYC; HUNTING THE PROTÉGÉ.
THEN WE HAVE TO TAKE IT DOWN.
NOT AN EASY TASK.
THERE WILL BE CASUALTIES.
SCRUBBING THE Z-10'S MEMORY CHIP AND SENDING IT HOME IS THE ONLY WAY TO CONCEAL THE PROTÉGÉ'S PRESENCE ON EARTH FROM THE GENOCIDERS.

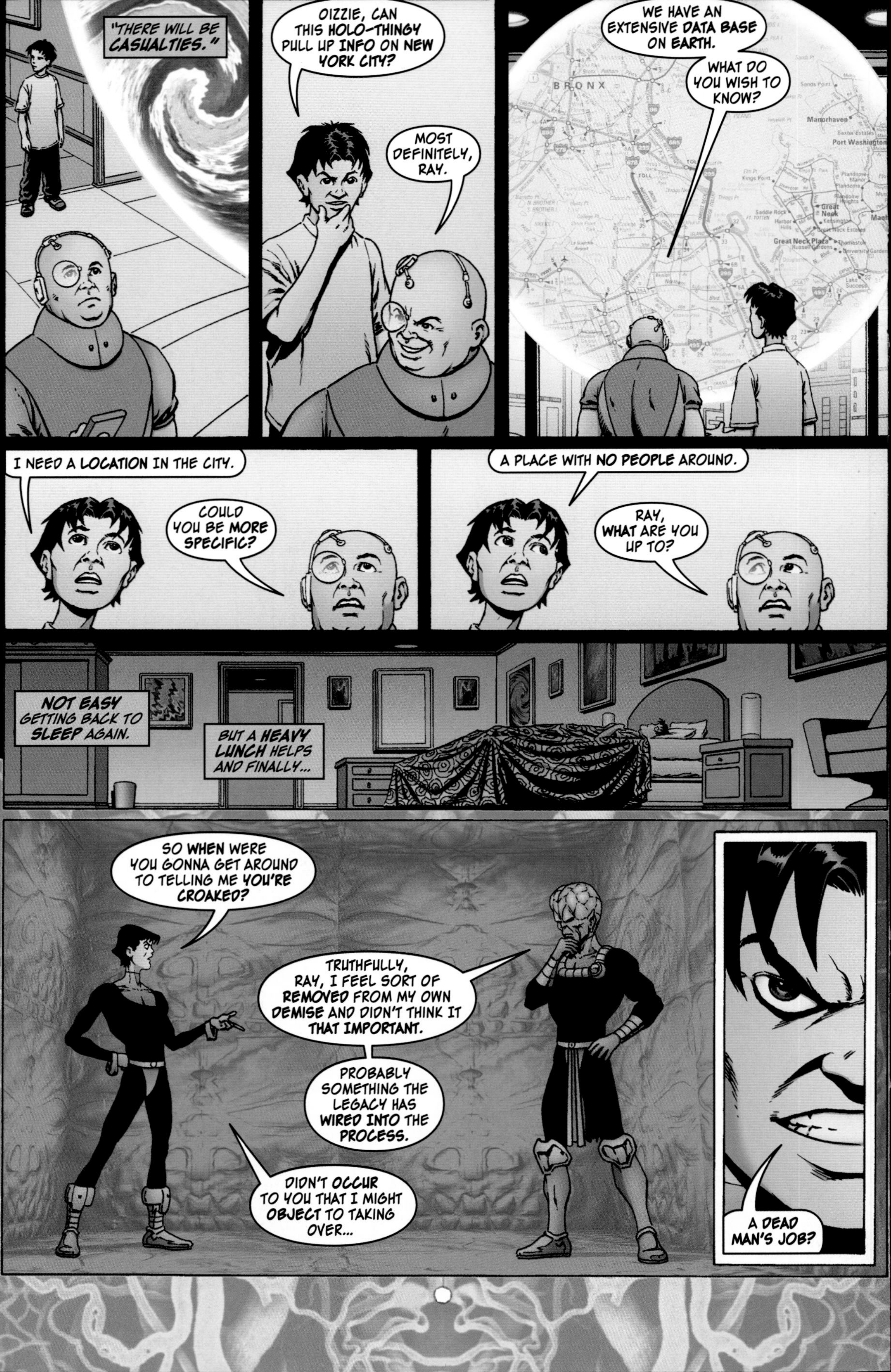

"THERE WILL BE CASUALTIES."
OIZZIE, CAN THIS HOLO-THINGY PULL UP INFO ON NEW YORK CITY?
MOST DEFINITELY, RAY.
WE HAVE AN EXTENSIVE DATA BASE ON EARTH.
WHAT DO YOU WISH TO KNOW?
I NEED A LOCATION IN THE CITY.
COULD YOU BE MORE SPECIFIC?
A PLACE WITH NO PEOPLE AROUND.
RAY, WHAT ARE YOU UP TO?
NOT EASY GETTING BACK TO SLEEP AGAIN.
BUT A HEAVY LUNCH HELPS AND FINALLY...
SO WHEN WERE YOU GONNA GET AROUND TO TELLING ME YOU'RE CROAKED?
TRUTHFULLY, RAY, I FEEL SORT OF REMOVED FROM MY OWN DEMISE AND DIDN'T THINK IT THAT IMPORTANT.
PROBABLY SOMETHING THE LEGACY HAS WIRED INTO THE PROCESS.
DIDN'T OCCUR TO YOU THAT I MIGHT OBJECT TO TAKING OVER...
A DEAD MAN'S JOB?

YOU'RE RIGHT, RAY.

I'M SORRY.

SO WHAT EXACTLY ARE YOU?

A GHOST?

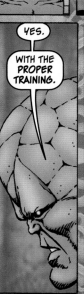

MORE LIKE A MEMORY OF ALL MY MEMORIES, SO THEY MAY BE PASSED ALONG TO YOU.

A RECORDING.

THAT'S THE BEST EXPLANATION I CAN GIVE YOU.

BUT THAT'S NOT WHAT YOU WANT TO DISCUSS.

NO.

EUROPA IS PLANNING ON BAGGIN' THE Z-10.

I PULL MY OWN WEIGHT.

CAN I TAKE OUT THIS ROBOT?

YES.

WITH THE PROPER TRAINING.

FIRST YOU NEED TO LEARN HOW TO USE THE FIST OF ASTRAL FIRE.

I CAN DO THAT?

SECONDLY, I'LL SHOW YOU A WEAK POINT ON THE Z-10'S BACK.

MY ONLY CONCERN IS THAT A BRUISED EGO IS NOT A VERY SOUND MOTIVATION.

"COULDN'T EVEN HANDLE A Z-10 KILBOT."

I'M DOING THIS BECAUSE I CAN'T GET OUT OF THIS FIGHT, SO I BETTER LEARN WHAT I CAN DO.

NOW THAT'S A MOTIVATION I CAN APPROVE.

LET US GET STARTED.

"I UNDERSTAND YOU ALREADY HAVE TRANSPORTATION ARRANGED."

"WILL HAVE, WITH ZOHAK'S HELP."

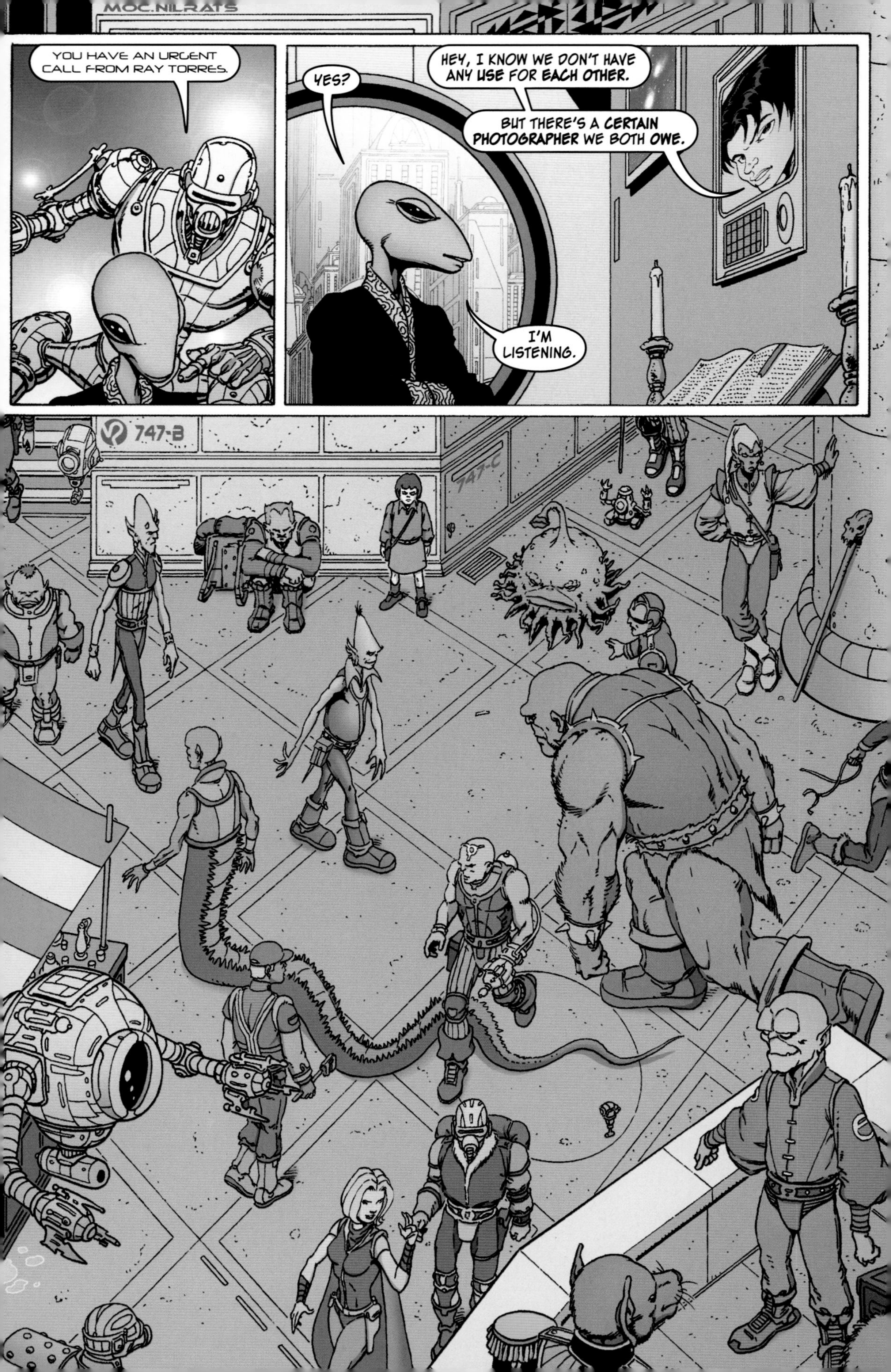
YOU HAVE AN URGENT CALL FROM RAY TORRES.
YES?
HEY, I KNOW WE DON'T HAVE ANY USE FOR EACH OTHER.
BUT THERE'S A CERTAIN PHOTOGRAPHER WE BOTH OWE.
I'M LISTENING.
747-B
747-C

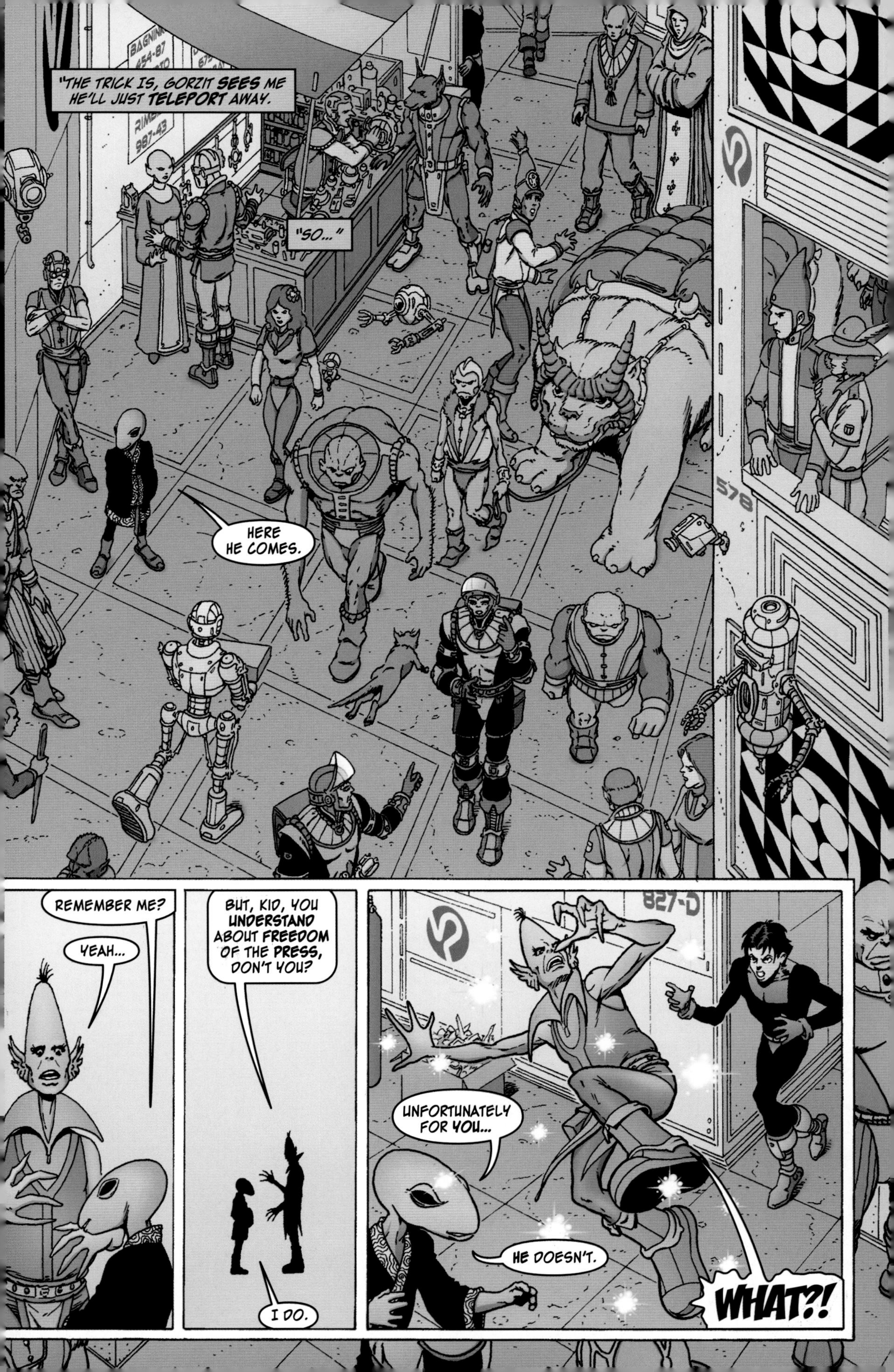
"THE TRICK IS, GORZIT **SEES** ME HE'LL JUST **TELEPORT** AWAY.
"SO..."
987-43
578
HERE HE COMES.
REMEMBER ME?
YEAH...
BUT, KID, YOU **UNDERSTAND** ABOUT **FREEDOM** OF THE **PRESS**, DON'T YOU?
I DO.
827-D
UNFORTUNATELY FOR **YOU**...
HE DOESN'T.
WHAT?!

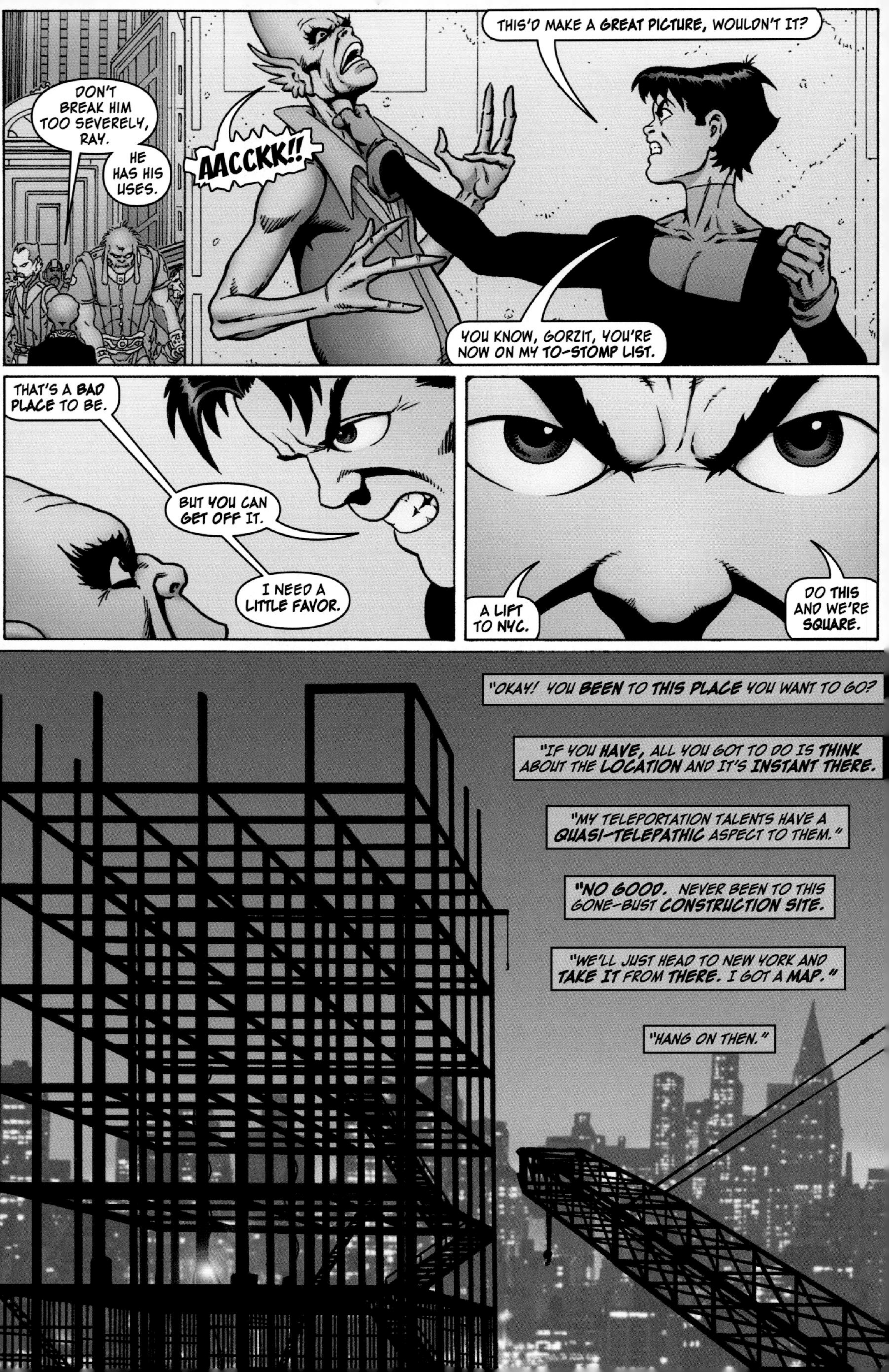
THIS'D MAKE A GREAT PICTURE, WOULDN'T IT?
DON'T BREAK HIM TOO SEVERELY, RAY.
HE HAS HIS USES.
AACCKK!!
YOU KNOW, GORZIT, YOU'RE NOW ON MY TO-STOMP LIST.
THAT'S A BAD PLACE TO BE.
BUT YOU CAN GET OFF IT.
I NEED A LITTLE FAVOR.
A LIFT TO NYC.
DO THIS AND WE'RE SQUARE.
"OKAY! YOU BEEN TO THIS PLACE YOU WANT TO GO?
"IF YOU HAVE, ALL YOU GOT TO DO IS THINK ABOUT THE LOCATION AND IT'S INSTANT THERE.
"MY TELEPORTATION TALENTS HAVE A QUASI-TELEPATHIC ASPECT TO THEM."
"NO GOOD. NEVER BEEN TO THIS GONE-BUST CONSTRUCTION SITE.
"WE'LL JUST HEAD TO NEW YORK AND TAKE IT FROM THERE. I GOT A MAP."
"HANG ON THEN."

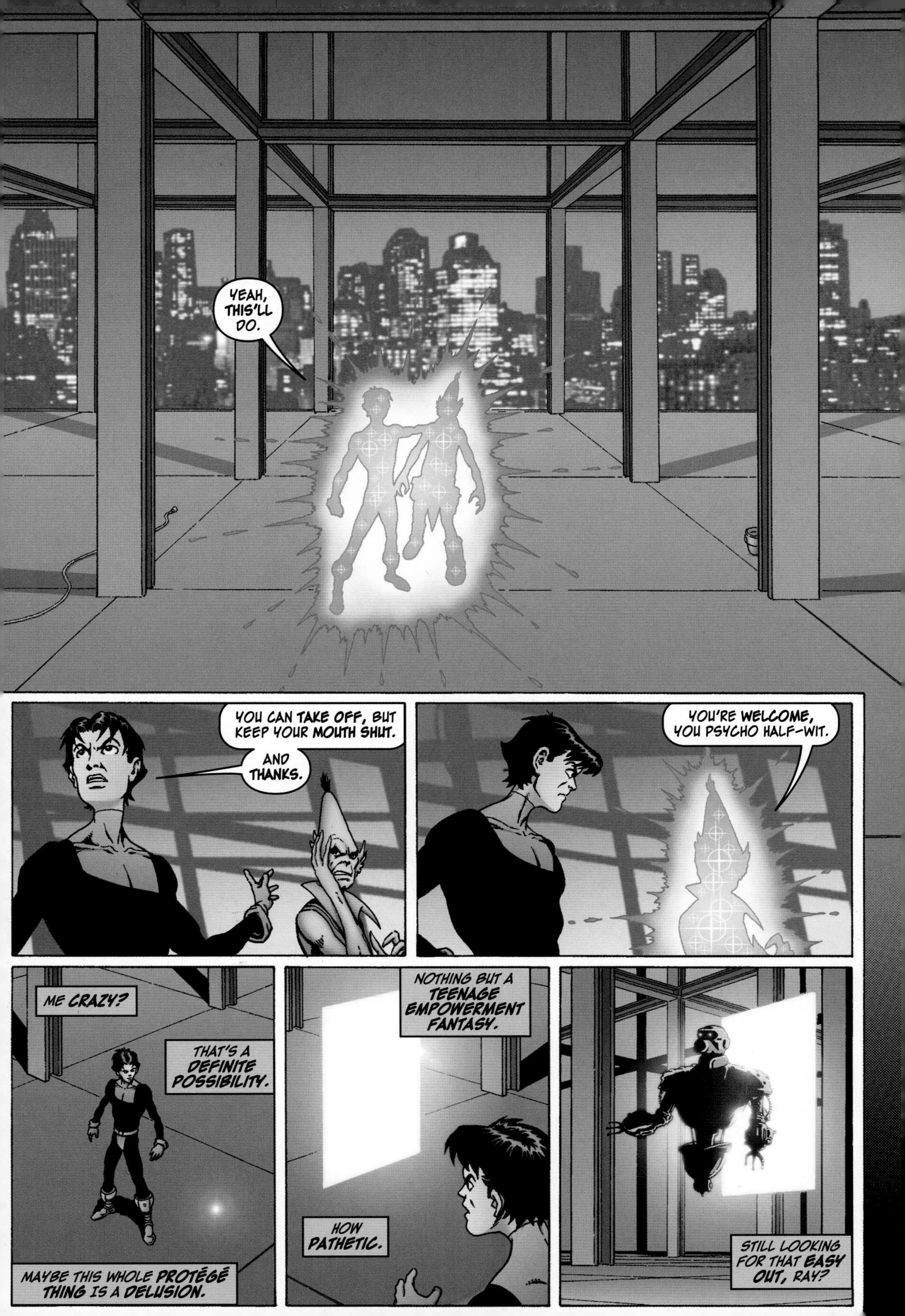
YEAH, THIS'LL DO.
YOU CAN TAKE OFF, BUT KEEP YOUR MOUTH SHUT.
AND THANKS.
YOU'RE WELCOME, YOU PSYCHO HALF-WIT.
ME CRAZY?
THAT'S A DEFINITE POSSIBILITY.
MAYBE THIS WHOLE PROTÉGÉ THING IS A DELUSION.
NOTHING BUT A TEENAGE EMPOWERMENT FANTASY.
HOW PATHETIC.
STILL LOOKING FOR THAT EASY OUT, RAY?

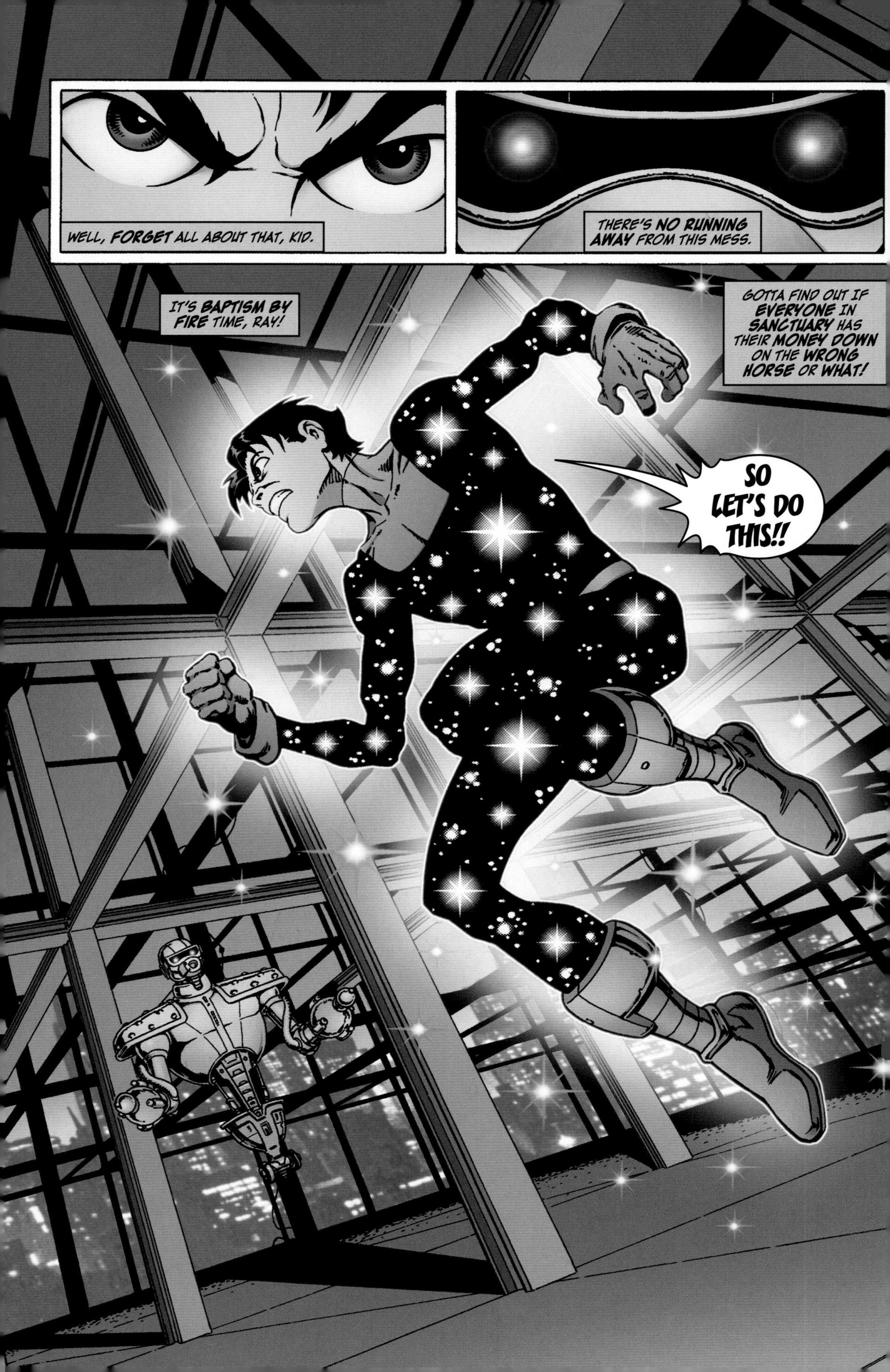
WELL, FORGET ALL ABOUT THAT, KID.
THERE'S NO RUNNING AWAY FROM THIS MESS.
IT'S BAPTISM BY FIRE TIME, RAY!
GOTTA FIND OUT IF EVERYONE IN SANCTUARY HAS THEIR MONEY DOWN ON THE WRONG HORSE OR WHAT!
SO LET'S DO THIS!!

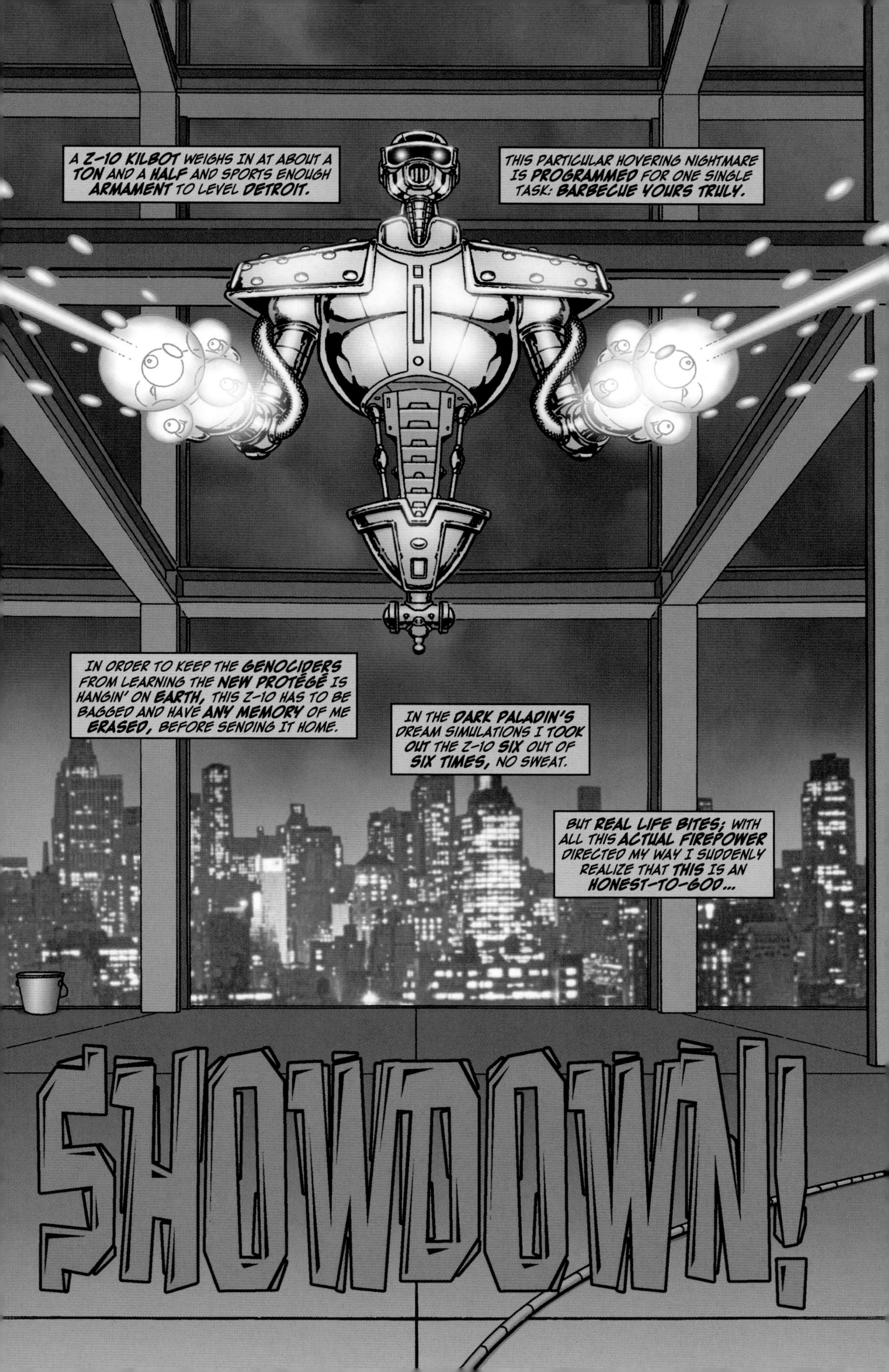
A Z-10 KILBOT WEIGHS IN AT ABOUT A TON AND A HALF AND SPORTS ENOUGH ARMAMENT TO LEVEL DETROIT.
THIS PARTICULAR HOVERING NIGHTMARE IS PROGRAMMED FOR ONE SINGLE TASK: BARBECUE YOURS TRULY.
IN ORDER TO KEEP THE GENOCIDERS FROM LEARNING THE NEW PROTÉGÉ IS HANGIN' ON EARTH, THIS Z-10 HAS TO BE BAGGED AND HAVE ANY MEMORY OF ME ERASED, BEFORE SENDING IT HOME.
IN THE DARK PALADIN'S DREAM SIMULATIONS I TOOK OUT THE Z-10 SIX OUT OF SIX TIMES, NO SWEAT.
BUT REAL LIFE BITES; WITH ALL THIS ACTUAL FIREPOWER DIRECTED MY WAY I SUDDENLY REALIZE THAT THIS IS AN HONEST-TO-GOD...
SHOWDOWN!

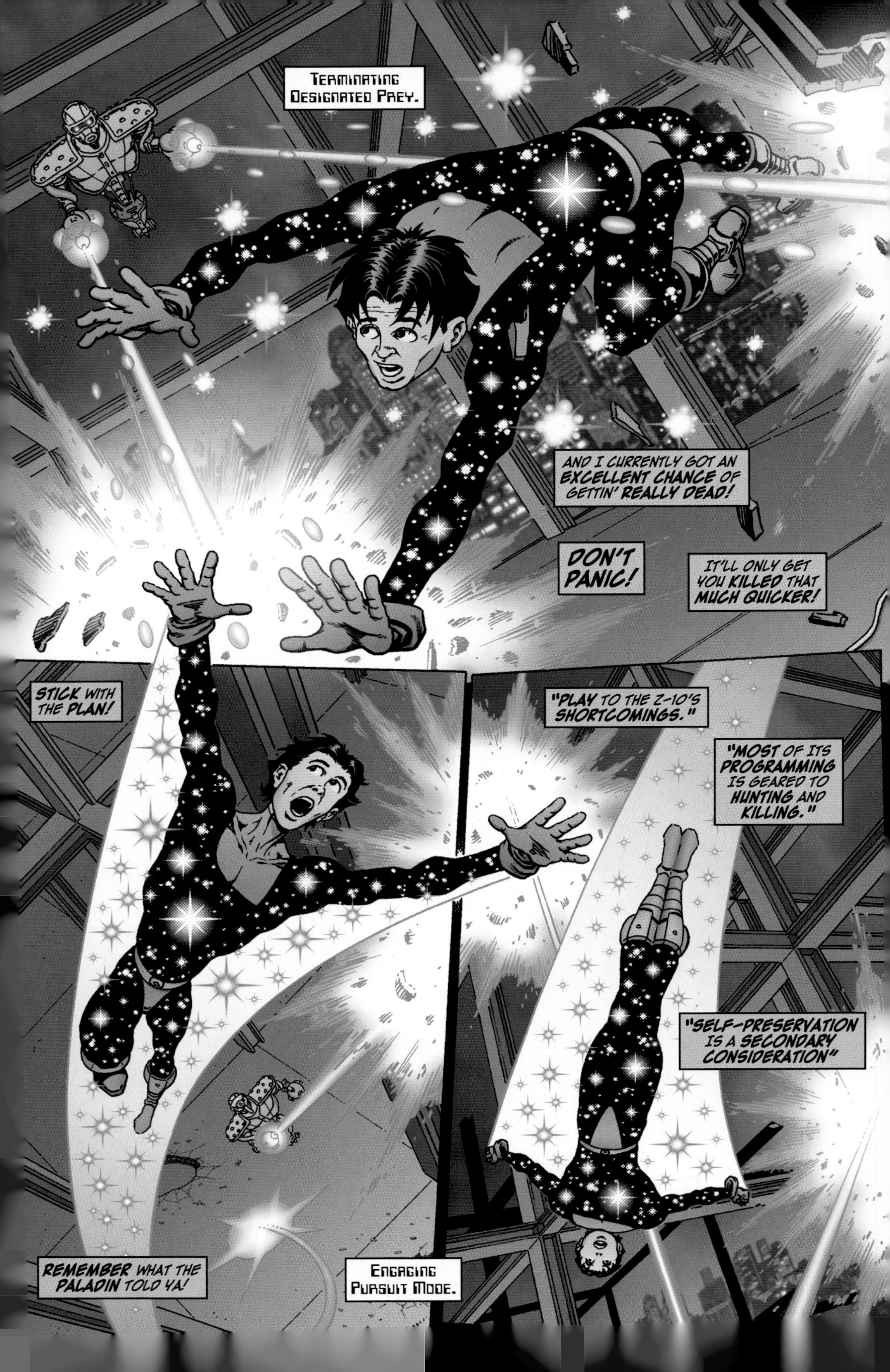
TERMINATING DESIGNATED PREY.
AND I CURRENTLY GOT AN EXCELLENT CHANCE OF GETTIN' REALLY DEAD!
DON'T PANIC!
IT'LL ONLY GET YOU KILLED THAT MUCH QUICKER!
STICK WITH THE PLAN!
REMEMBER WHAT THE PALADIN TOLD YA!
ENGAGING PURSUIT MODE.
"PLAY TO THE Z-10'S SHORTCOMINGS."
"MOST OF ITS PROGRAMMING IS GEARED TO HUNTING AND KILLING."
"SELF-PRESERVATION IS A SECONDARY CONSIDERATION"

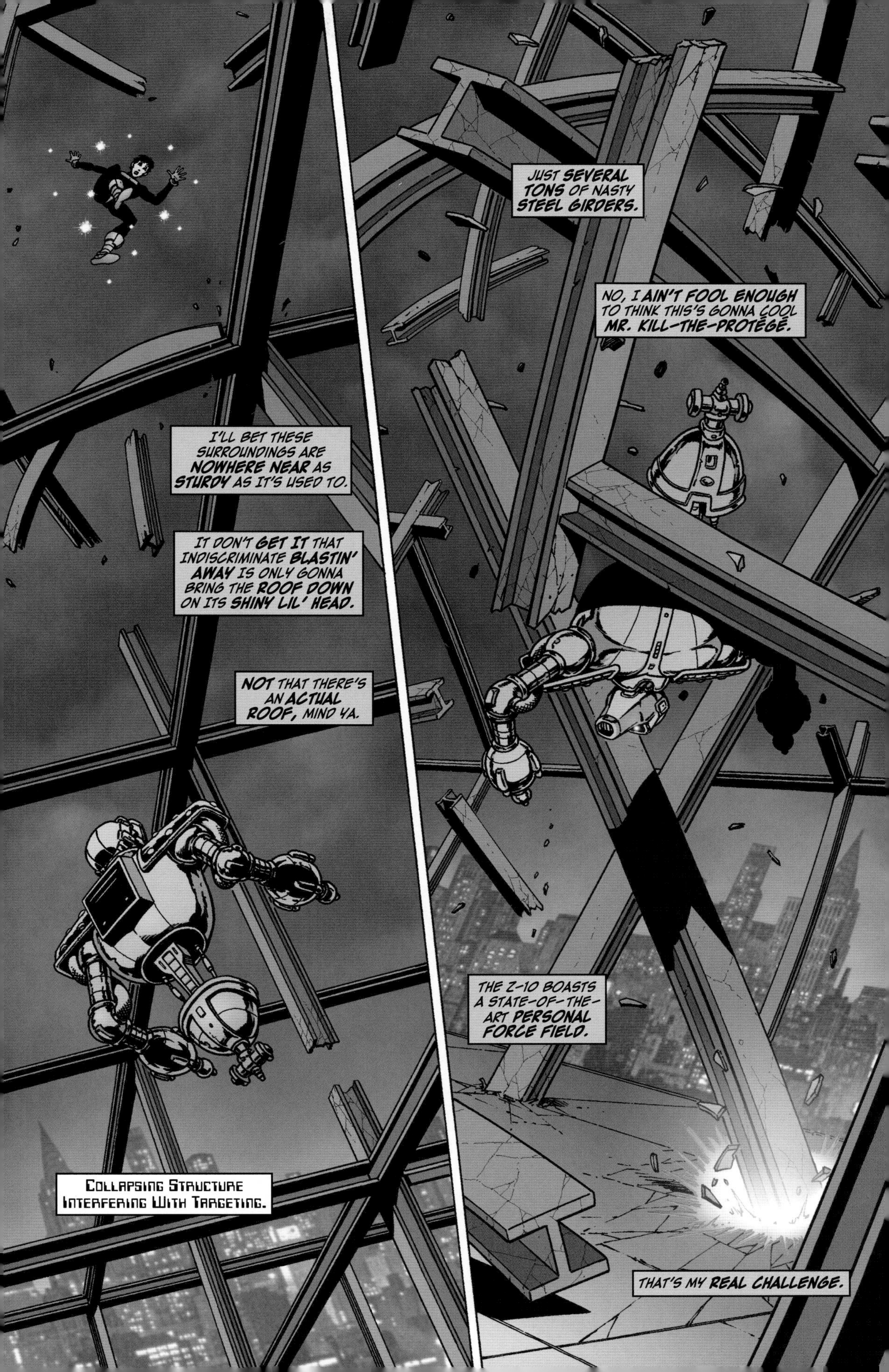

JUST SEVERAL TONS OF NASTY STEEL GIRDERS.
NO, I AIN'T FOOL ENOUGH TO THINK THIS'S GONNA COOL MR. KILL-THE-PROTEGE.
I'LL BET THESE SURROUNDINGS ARE NOWHERE NEAR AS STURDY AS IT'S USED TO.
IT DON'T GET IT THAT INDISCRIMINATE BLASTIN' AWAY IS ONLY GONNA BRING THE ROOF DOWN ON ITS SHINY LIL' HEAD.
NOT THAT THERE'S AN ACTUAL ROOF, MIND YA.
THE Z-10 BOASTS A STATE-OF-THE-ART PERSONAL FORCE FIELD.
COLLAPSING STRUCTURE INTERFERING WITH TARGETING.
THAT'S MY REAL CHALLENGE.

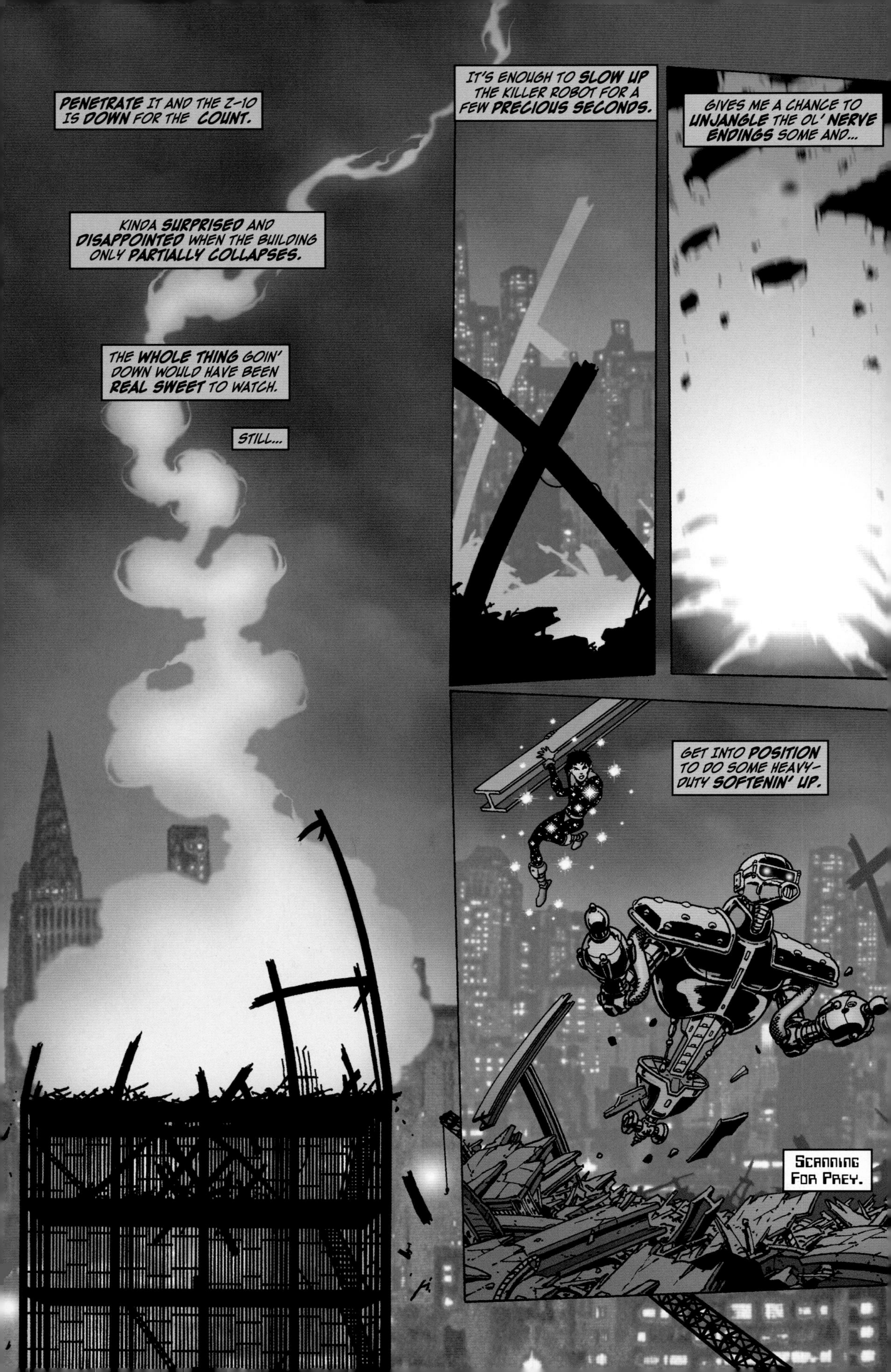
PENETRATE IT AND THE Z-10 IS DOWN FOR THE COUNT.
KINDA SURPRISED AND DISAPPOINTED WHEN THE BUILDING ONLY PARTIALLY COLLAPSES.
THE WHOLE THING GOIN' DOWN WOULD HAVE BEEN REAL SWEET TO WATCH.
STILL...
IT'S ENOUGH TO SLOW UP THE KILLER ROBOT FOR A FEW PRECIOUS SECONDS.
GIVES ME A CHANCE TO UNJANGLE THE OL' NERVE ENDINGS SOME AND...
GET INTO POSITION TO DO SOME HEAVY-DUTY SOFTENIN' UP.
SCANNING FOR PREY.

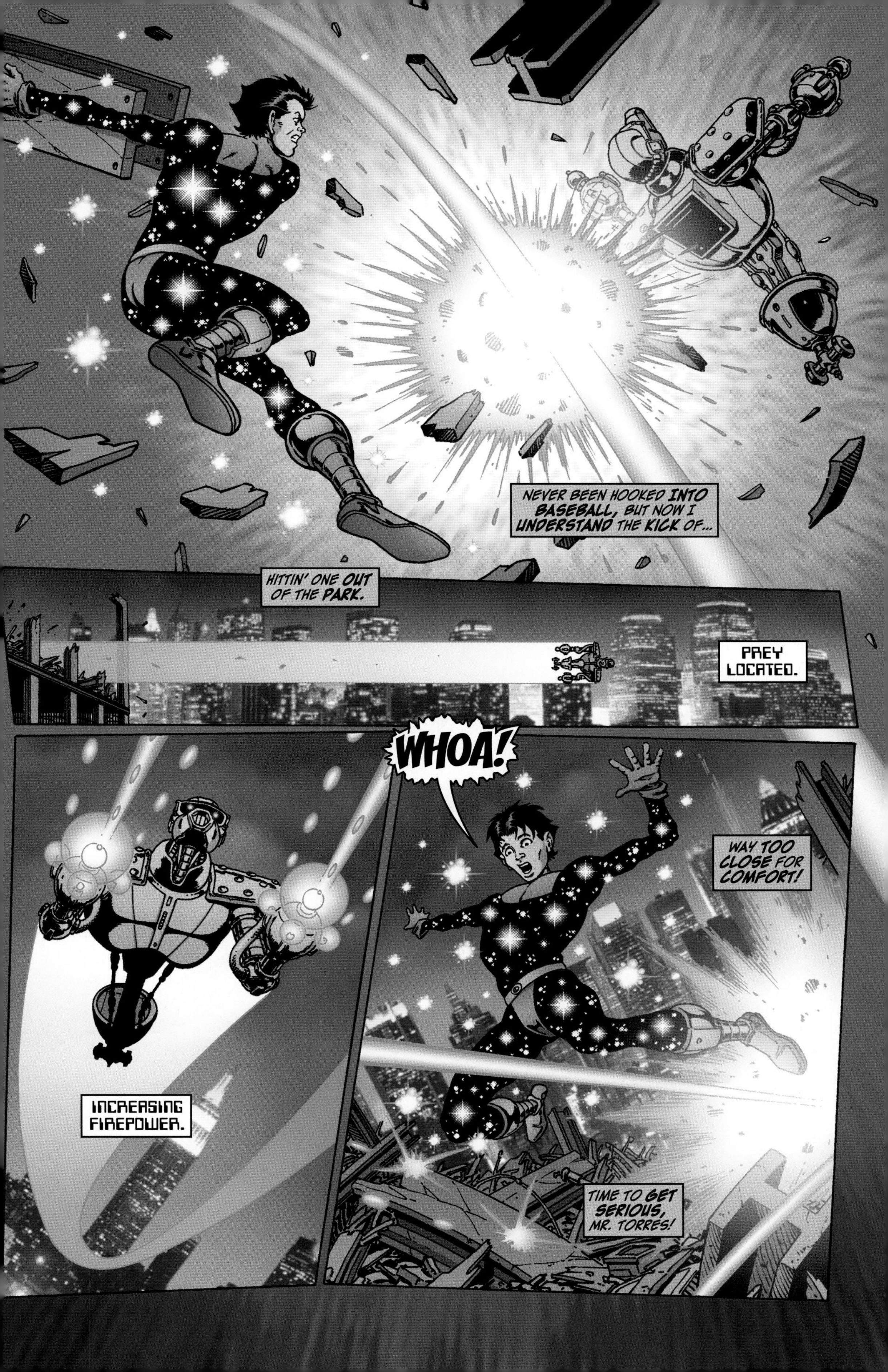
NEVER BEEN HOOKED INTO BASEBALL, BUT NOW I UNDERSTAND THE KICK OF...
HITTIN' ONE OUT OF THE PARK.
PREY LOCATED.
INCREASING FIREPOWER.
WHOA!
WAY TOO CLOSE FOR COMFORT!
TIME TO GET SERIOUS, MR. TORRES!

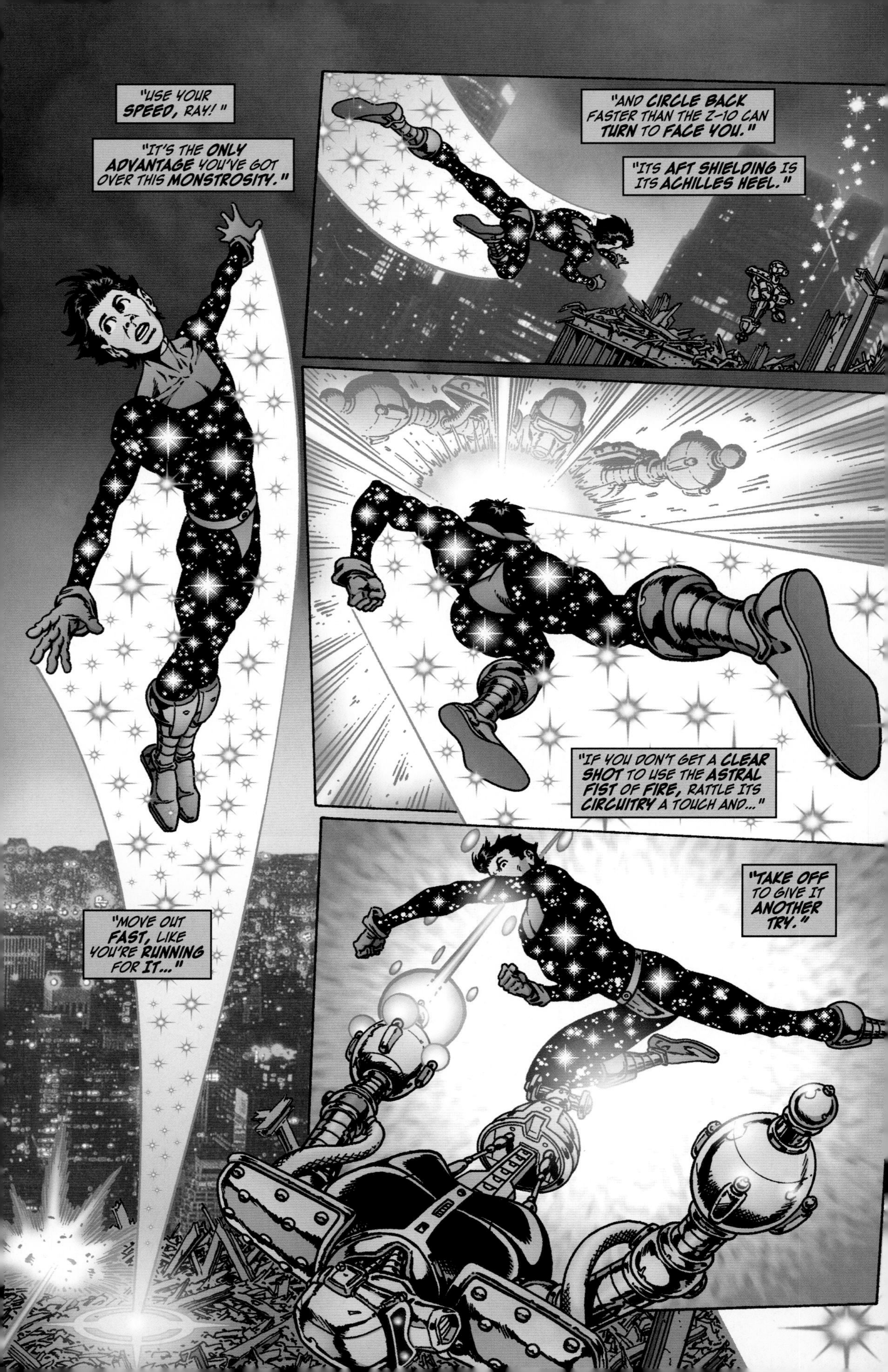
"USE YOUR SPEED, RAY!"
"IT'S THE ONLY ADVANTAGE YOU'VE GOT OVER THIS MONSTROSITY."
"MOVE OUT FAST, LIKE YOU'RE RUNNING FOR IT..."
"AND CIRCLE BACK FASTER THAN THE Z-10 CAN TURN TO FACE YOU."
"ITS AFT SHIELDING IS ITS ACHILLES HEEL."
"IF YOU DON'T GET A CLEAR SHOT TO USE THE ASTRAL FIST OF FIRE, RATTLE ITS CIRCUITRY A TOUCH AND..."
"TAKE OFF TO GIVE IT ANOTHER TRY."

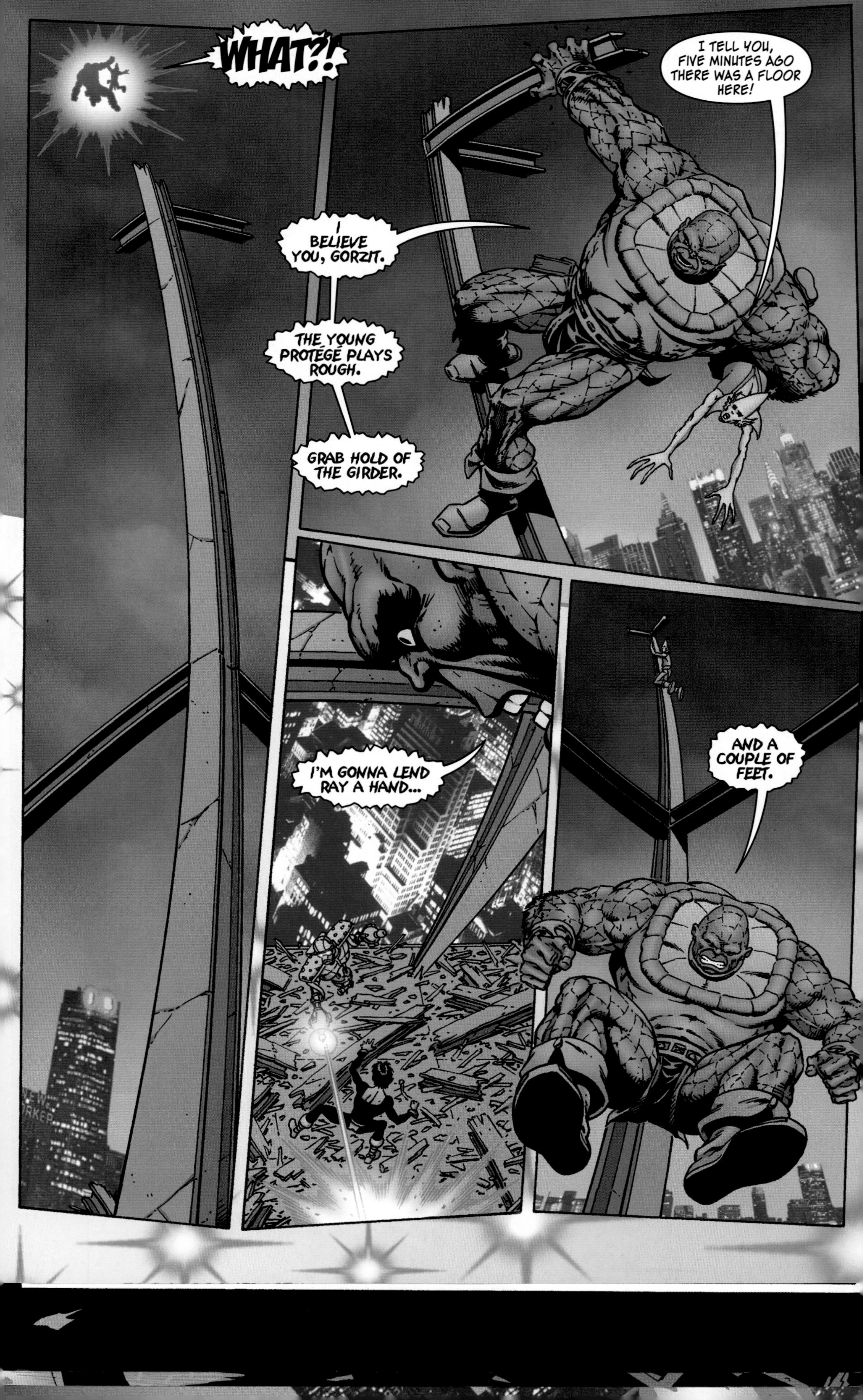
WHAT?!
I TELL YOU, FIVE MINUTES AGO THERE WAS A FLOOR HERE!
I BELIEVE YOU, GORZIT.
THE YOUNG PROTÉGÉ PLAYS ROUGH.
GRAB HOLD OF THE GIRDER.
I'M GONNA LEND RAY A HAND...
AND A COUPLE OF FEET.

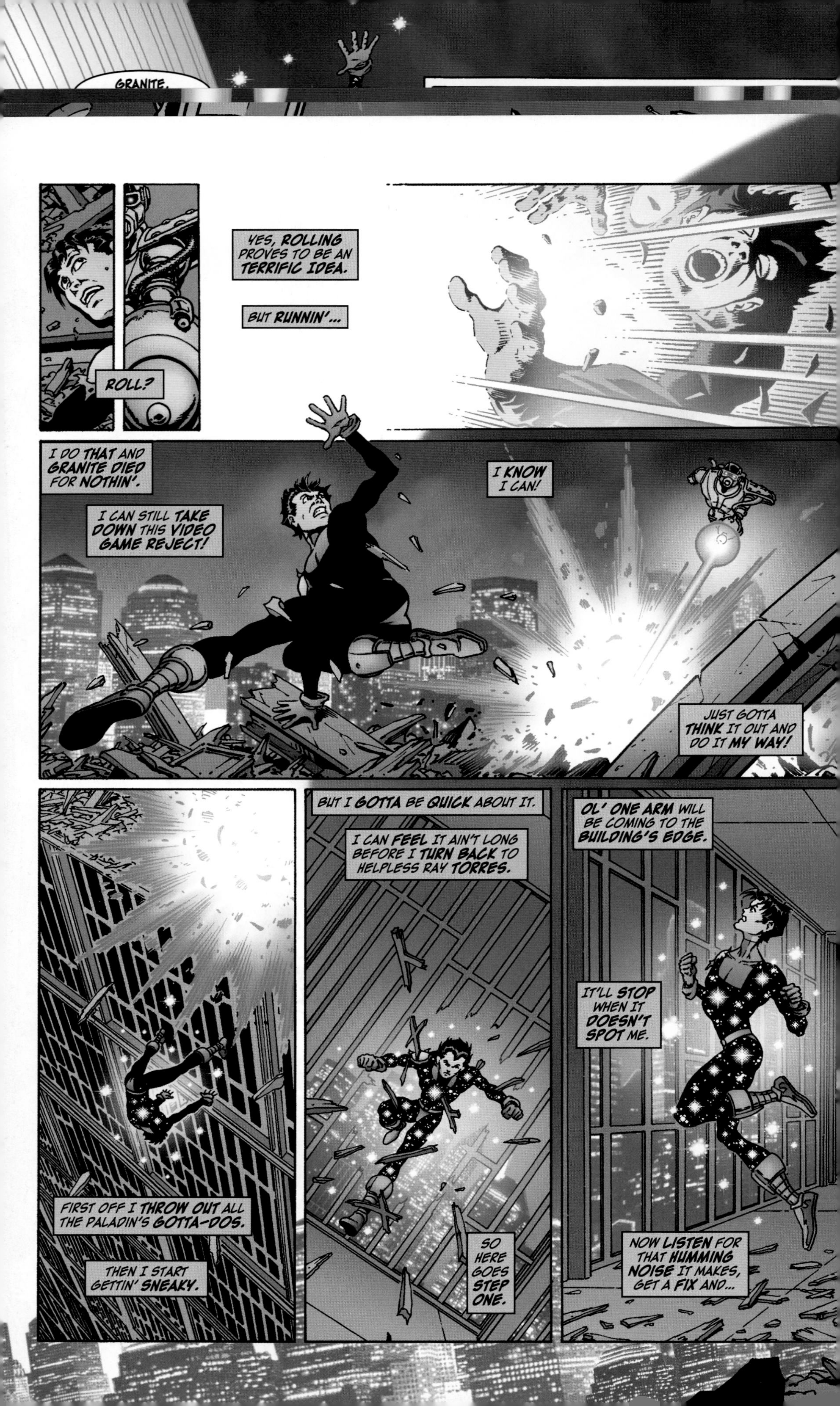
GRANITE.
ROLL?
YES, ROLLING PROVES TO BE AN TERRIFIC IDEA.
BUT RUNNIN'...
I DO THAT AND GRANITE DIED FOR NOTHIN'.
I CAN STILL TAKE DOWN THIS VIDEO GAME REJECT!
I KNOW I CAN!
JUST GOTTA THINK IT OUT AND DO IT MY WAY!
FIRST OFF I THROW OUT ALL THE PALADIN'S GOTTA-DOS.
THEN I START GETTIN' SNEAKY.
BUT I GOTTA BE QUICK ABOUT IT.
I CAN FEEL IT AIN'T LONG BEFORE I TURN BACK TO HELPLESS RAY TORRES.
SO HERE GOES STEP ONE.
OL' ONE ARM WILL BE COMING TO THE BUILDING'S EDGE.
IT'LL STOP WHEN IT DOESN'T SPOT ME.
NOW LISTEN FOR THAT HUMMING NOISE IT MAKES, GET A FIX AND...

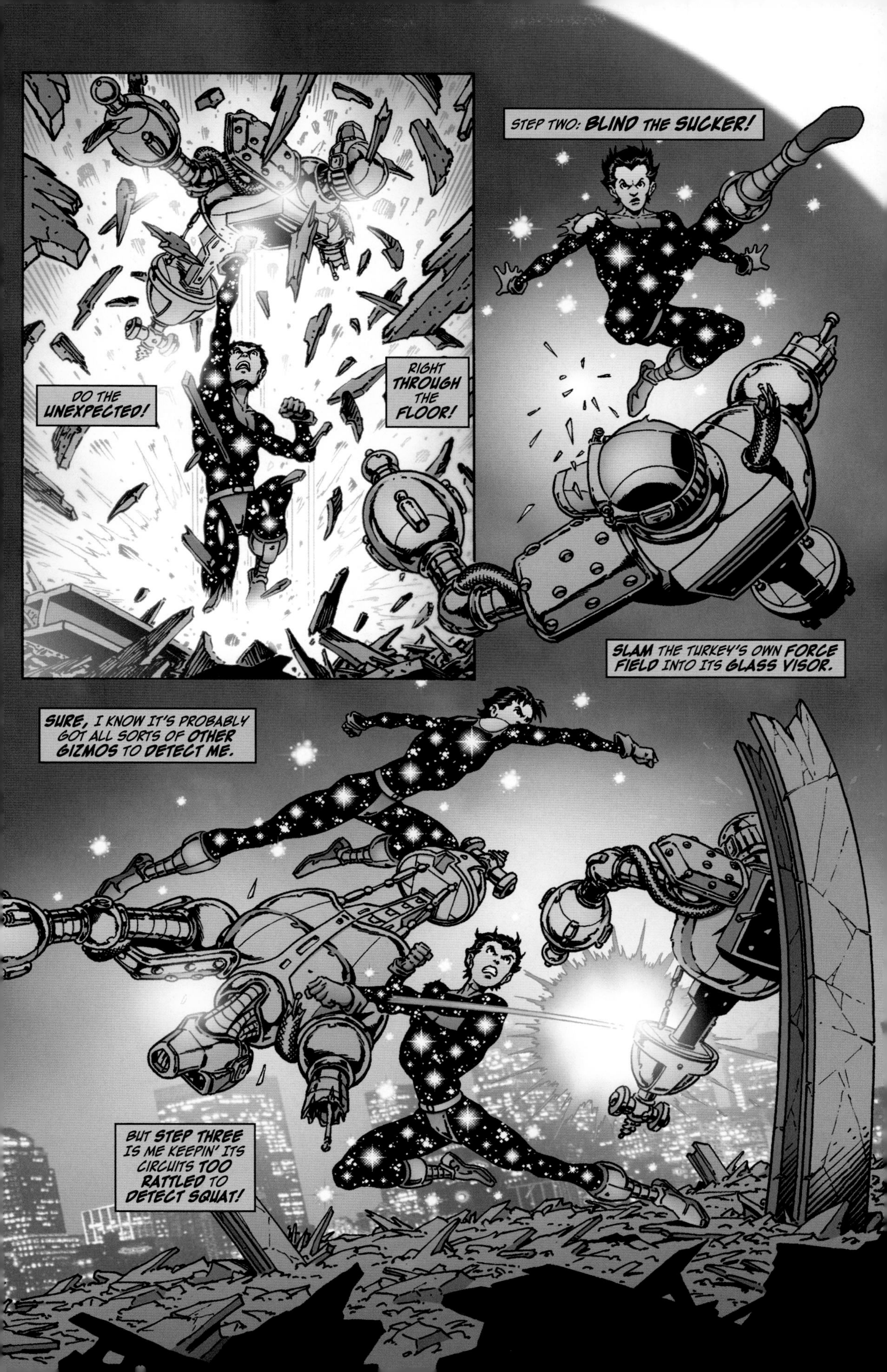
DO THE UNEXPECTED!
RIGHT THROUGH THE FLOOR!
STEP TWO: BLIND THE SUCKER!
SLAM THE TURKEY'S OWN FORCE FIELD INTO ITS GLASS VISOR.
SURE, I KNOW IT'S PROBABLY GOT ALL SORTS OF OTHER GIZMOS TO DETECT ME.
BUT STEP THREE IS ME KEEPIN' ITS CIRCUITS TOO RATTLED TO DETECT SQUAT!

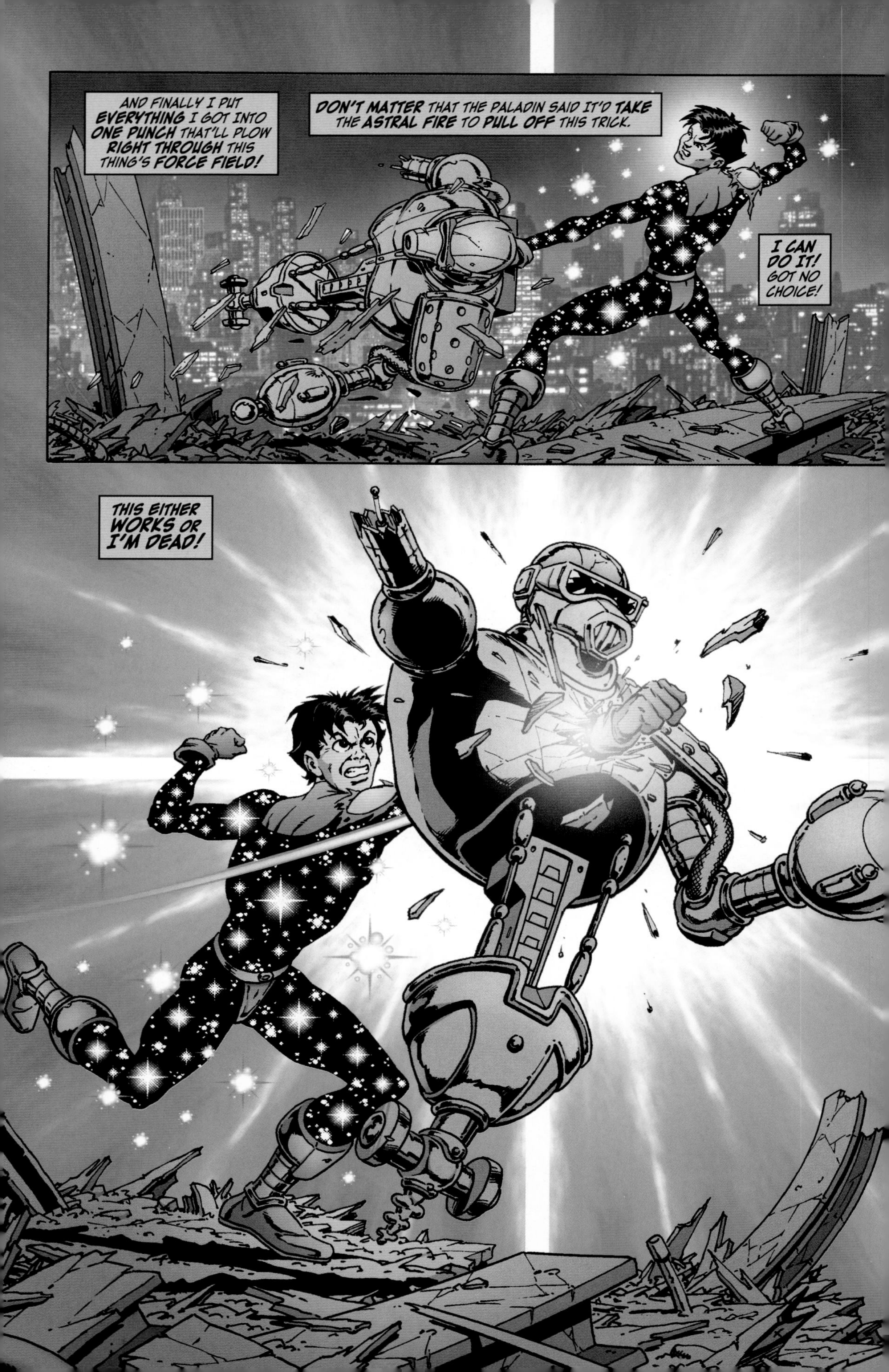
AND FINALLY I PUT EVERYTHING I GOT INTO ONE PUNCH THAT'LL PLOW RIGHT THROUGH THIS THING'S FORCE FIELD!
DON'T MATTER THAT THE PALADIN SAID IT'D TAKE THE ASTRAL FIRE TO PULL OFF THIS TRICK.
I CAN DO IT! GOT NO CHOICE!
THIS EITHER WORKS OR I'M DEAD!

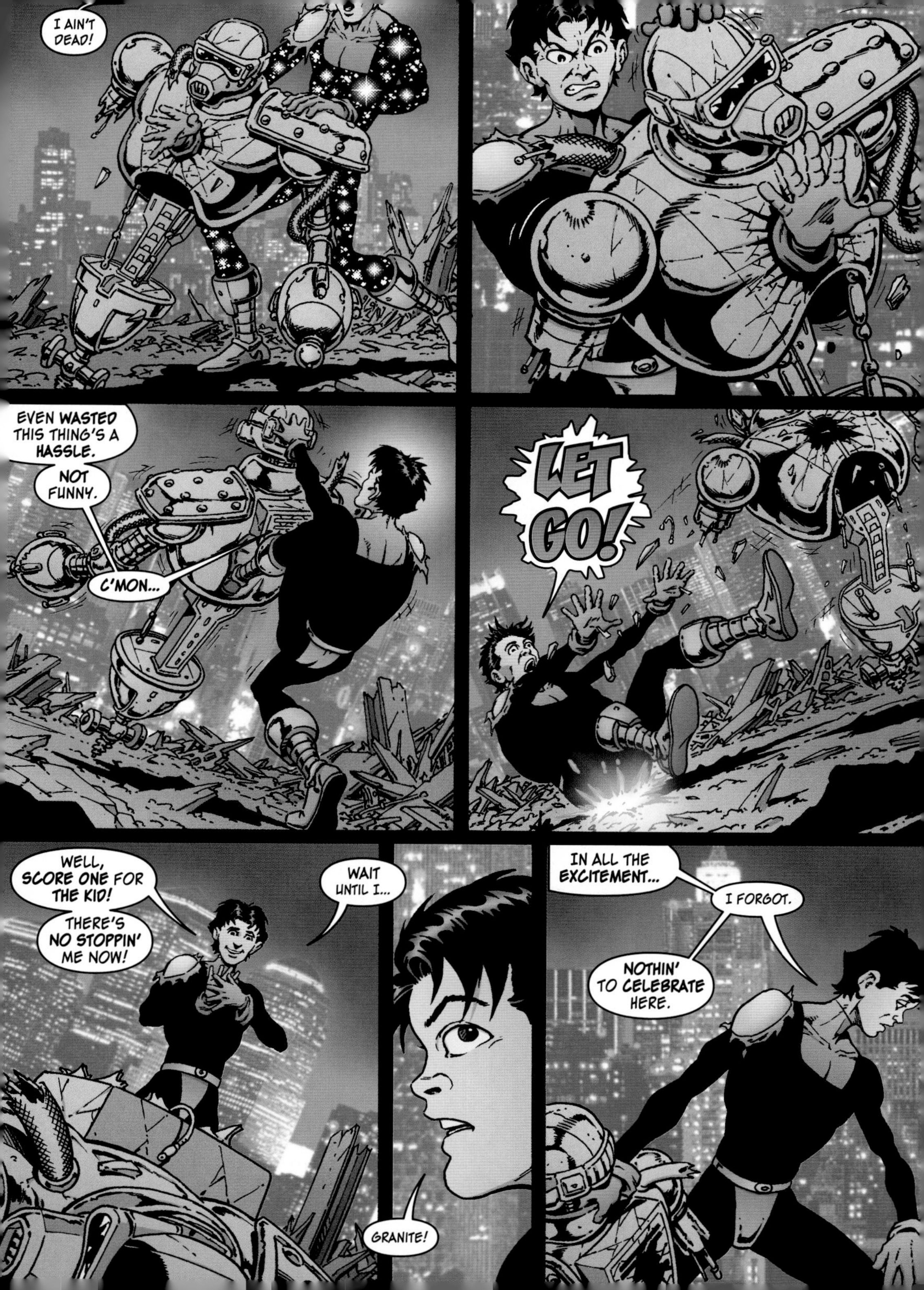
I AIN'T DEAD!
EVEN WASTED THIS THING'S A HASSLE.
NOT FUNNY.
C'MON...
LET GO!
WELL, SCORE ONE FOR THE KID!
THERE'S NO STOPPIN' ME NOW!
WAIT UNTIL I...
GRANITE!
IN ALL THE EXCITEMENT...
I FORGOT.
NOTHIN' TO CELEBRATE HERE.

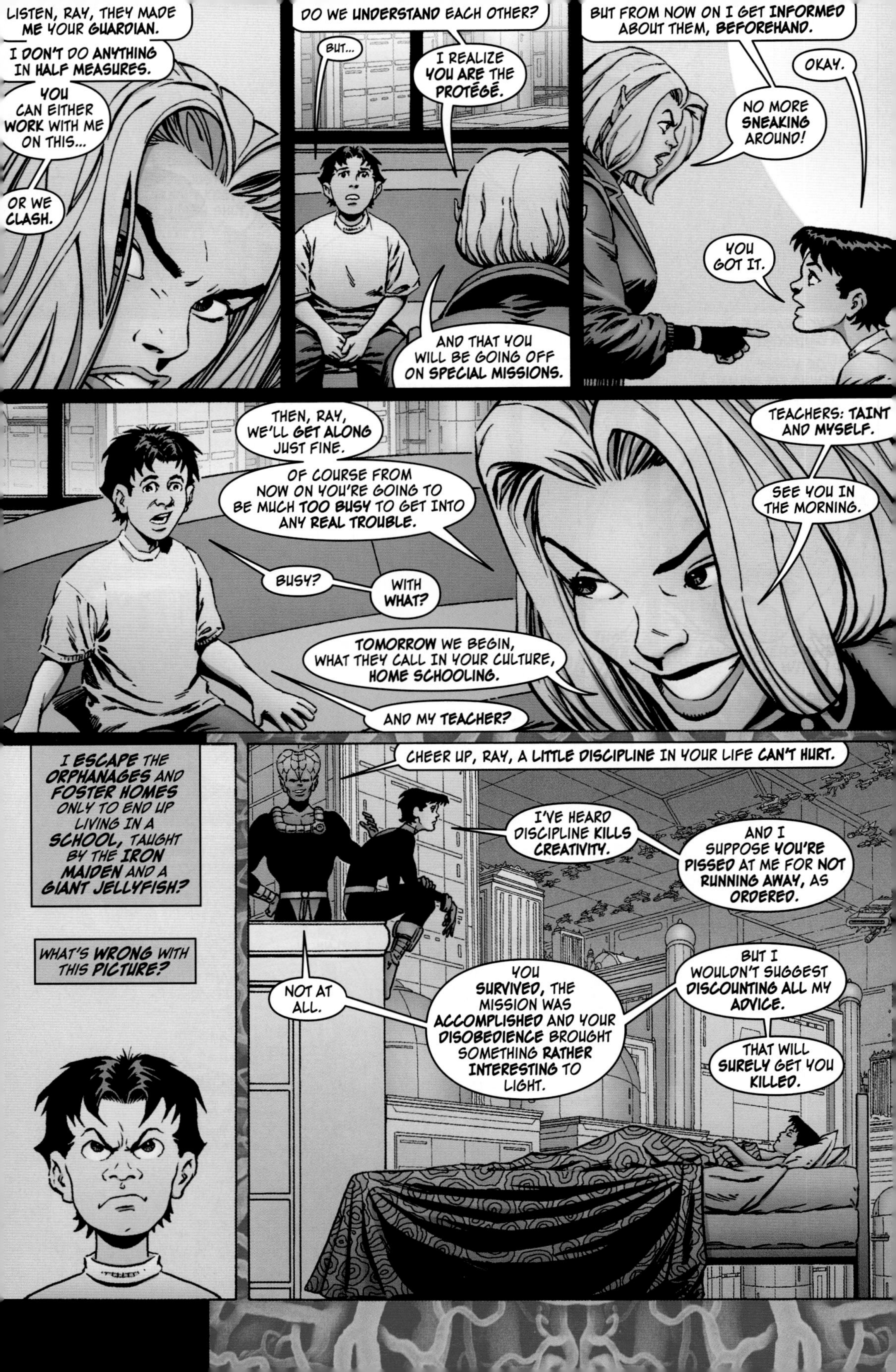
LISTEN, RAY, THEY MADE ME YOUR GUARDIAN.
I DON'T DO ANYTHING IN HALF MEASURES.
YOU CAN EITHER WORK WITH ME ON THIS...
OR WE CLASH.
DO WE UNDERSTAND EACH OTHER?
BUT...
I REALIZE YOU ARE THE PROTÉGÉ.
AND THAT YOU WILL BE GOING OFF ON SPECIAL MISSIONS.
BUT FROM NOW ON I GET INFORMED ABOUT THEM, BEFOREHAND.
NO MORE SNEAKING AROUND!
OKAY.
YOU GOT IT.
THEN, RAY, WE'LL GET ALONG JUST FINE.
OF COURSE FROM NOW ON YOU'RE GOING TO BE MUCH TOO BUSY TO GET INTO ANY REAL TROUBLE.
BUSY?
WITH WHAT?
TOMORROW WE BEGIN, WHAT THEY CALL IN YOUR CULTURE, HOME SCHOOLING.
AND MY TEACHER?
TEACHERS: TAINT AND MYSELF.
SEE YOU IN THE MORNING.
I ESCAPE THE ORPHANAGES AND FOSTER HOMES ONLY TO END UP LIVING IN A SCHOOL, TAUGHT BY THE IRON MAIDEN AND A GIANT JELLYFISH?
WHAT'S WRONG WITH THIS PICTURE?
CHEER UP, RAY, A LITTLE DISCIPLINE IN YOUR LIFE CAN'T HURT.
I'VE HEARD DISCIPLINE KILLS CREATIVITY.
AND I SUPPOSE YOU'RE PISSED AT ME FOR NOT RUNNING AWAY, AS ORDERED.
NOT AT ALL.
YOU SURVIVED, THE MISSION WAS ACCOMPLISHED AND YOUR DISOBEDIENCE BROUGHT SOMETHING RATHER INTERESTING TO LIGHT.
BUT I WOULDN'T SUGGEST DISCOUNTING ALL MY ADVICE.
THAT WILL SURELY GET YOU KILLED.

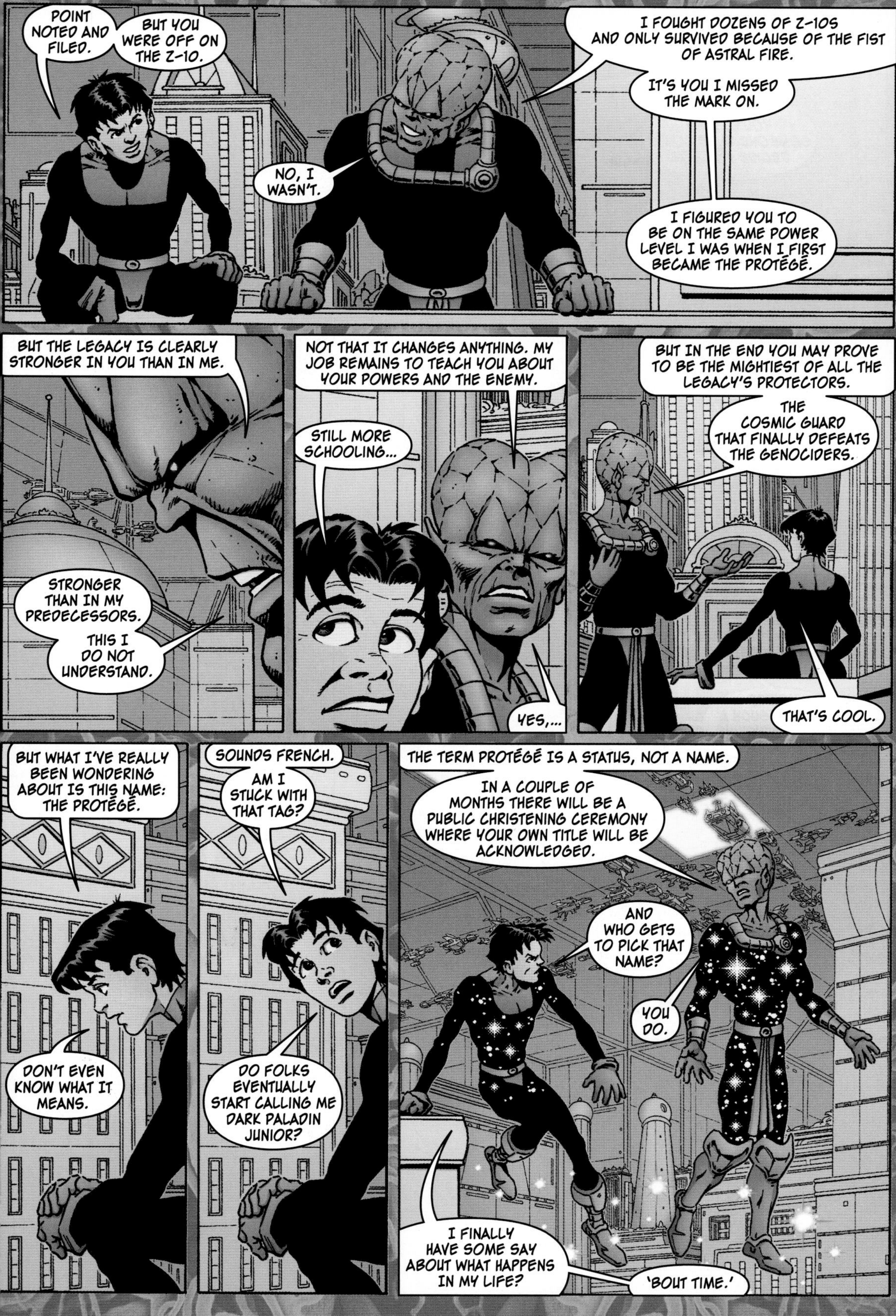
POINT NOTED AND FILED.
BUT YOU WERE OFF ON THE Z-10.
NO, I WASN'T.
I FOUGHT DOZENS OF Z-10S AND ONLY SURVIVED BECAUSE OF THE FIST OF ASTRAL FIRE.
IT'S YOU I MISSED THE MARK ON.
I FIGURED YOU TO BE ON THE SAME POWER LEVEL I WAS WHEN I FIRST BECAME THE PROTÉGÉ.
BUT THE LEGACY IS CLEARLY STRONGER IN YOU THAN IN ME.
STRONGER THAN IN MY PREDECESSORS.
THIS I DO NOT UNDERSTAND.
NOT THAT IT CHANGES ANYTHING. MY JOB REMAINS TO TEACH YOU ABOUT YOUR POWERS AND THE ENEMY.
STILL MORE SCHOOLING...
YES,...
BUT IN THE END YOU MAY PROVE TO BE THE MIGHTIEST OF ALL THE LEGACY'S PROTECTORS.
THE COSMIC GUARD THAT FINALLY DEFEATS THE GENOCIDERS.
THAT'S COOL.
BUT WHAT I'VE REALLY BEEN WONDERING ABOUT IS THIS NAME: THE PROTÉGÉ.
DON'T EVEN KNOW WHAT IT MEANS.
SOUNDS FRENCH.
AM I STUCK WITH THAT TAG?
DO FOLKS EVENTUALLY START CALLING ME DARK PALADIN JUNIOR?
THE TERM PROTÉGÉ IS A STATUS, NOT A NAME.
IN A COUPLE OF MONTHS THERE WILL BE A PUBLIC CHRISTENING CEREMONY WHERE YOUR OWN TITLE WILL BE ACKNOWLEDGED.
AND WHO GETS TO PICK THAT NAME?
YOU DO.
I FINALLY HAVE SOME SAY ABOUT WHAT HAPPENS IN MY LIFE?
'BOUT TIME.'

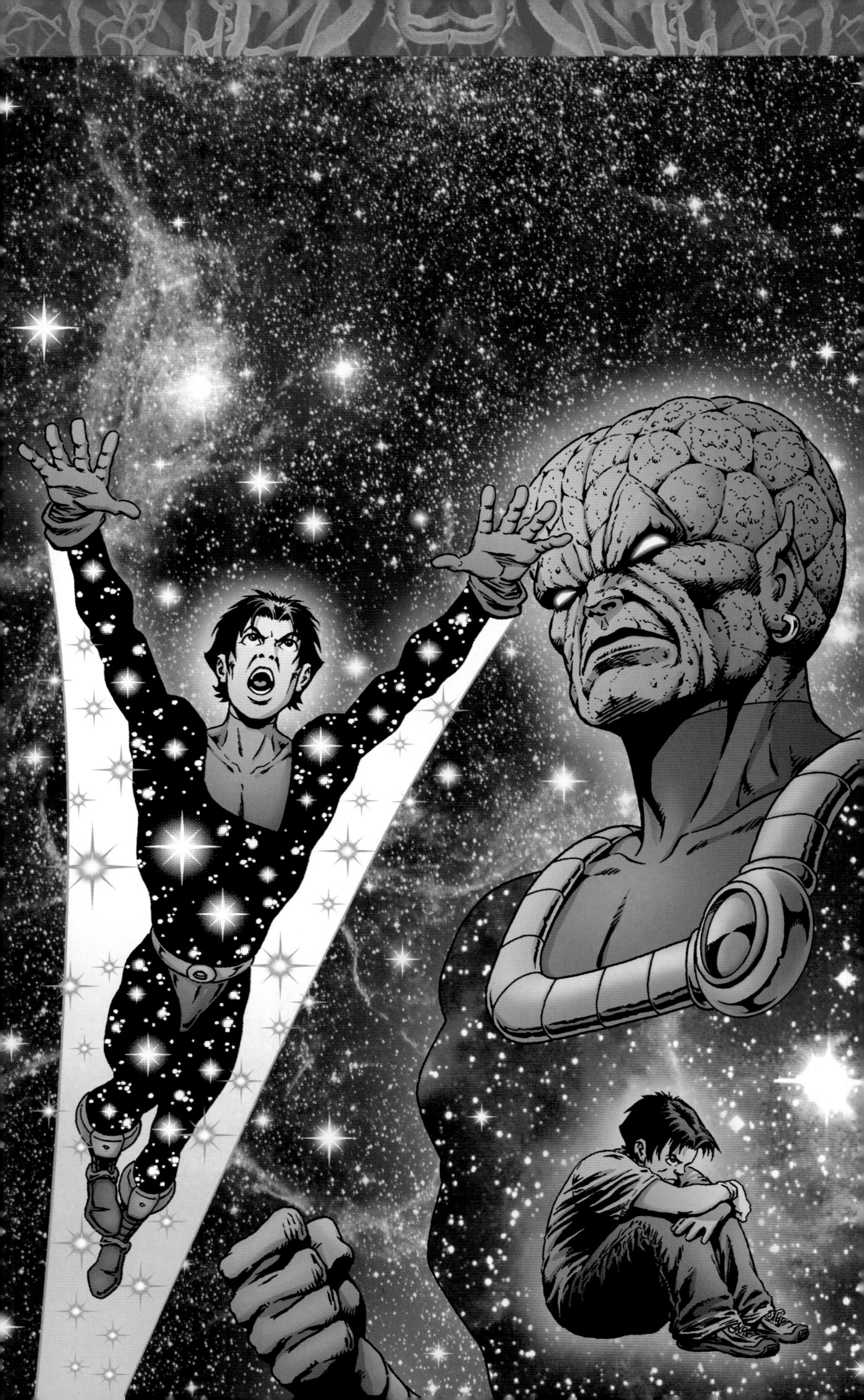

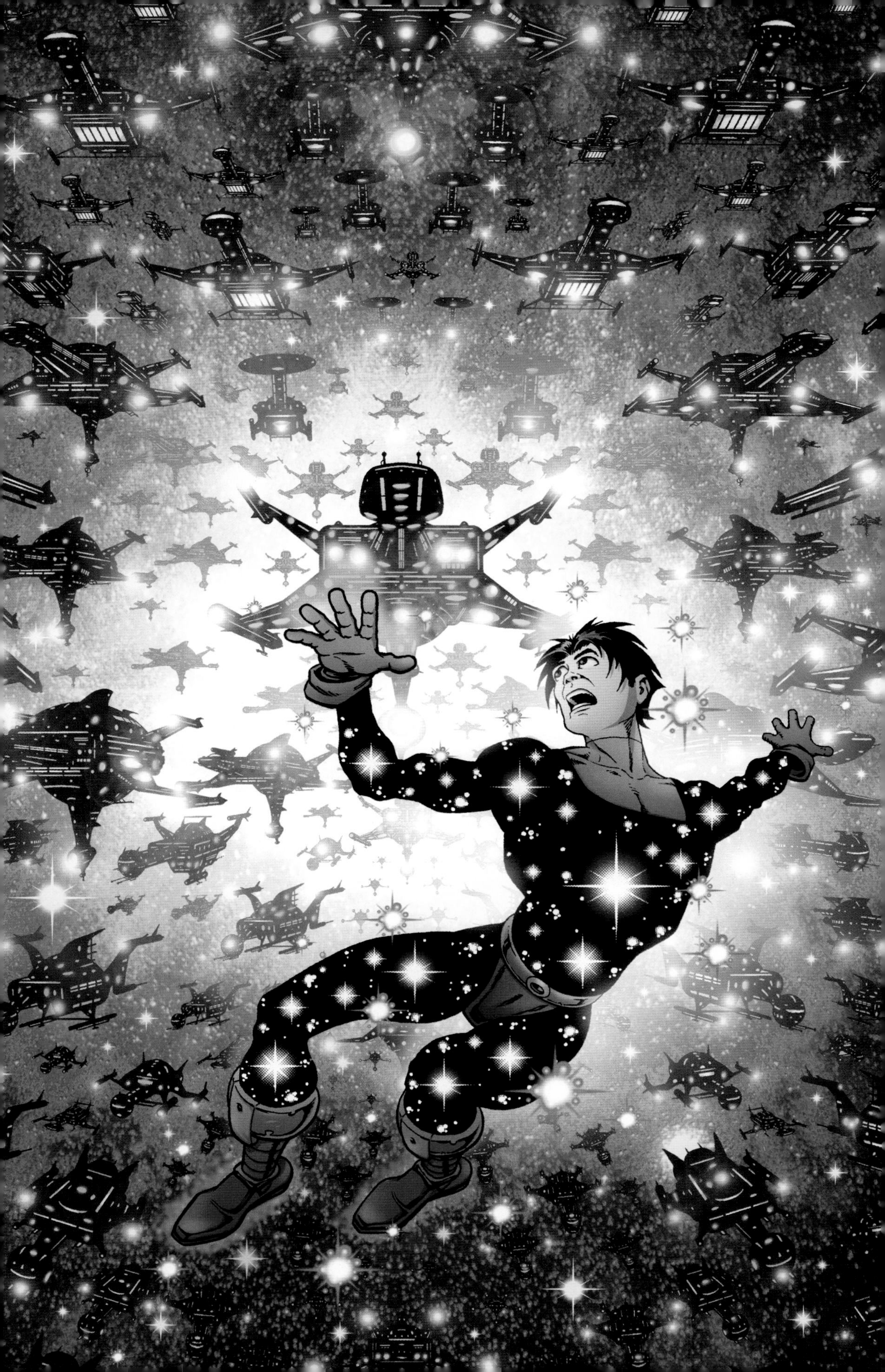

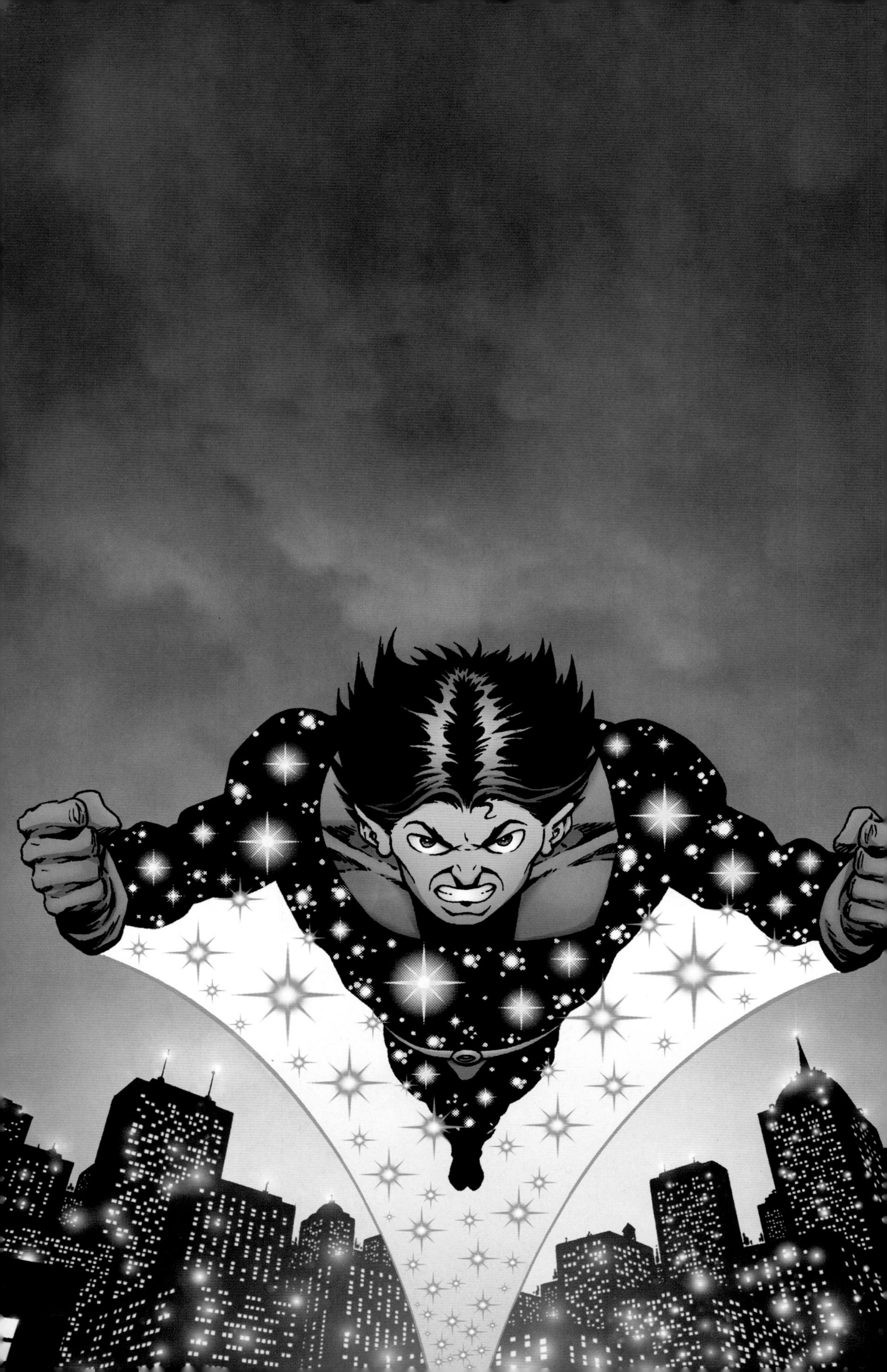

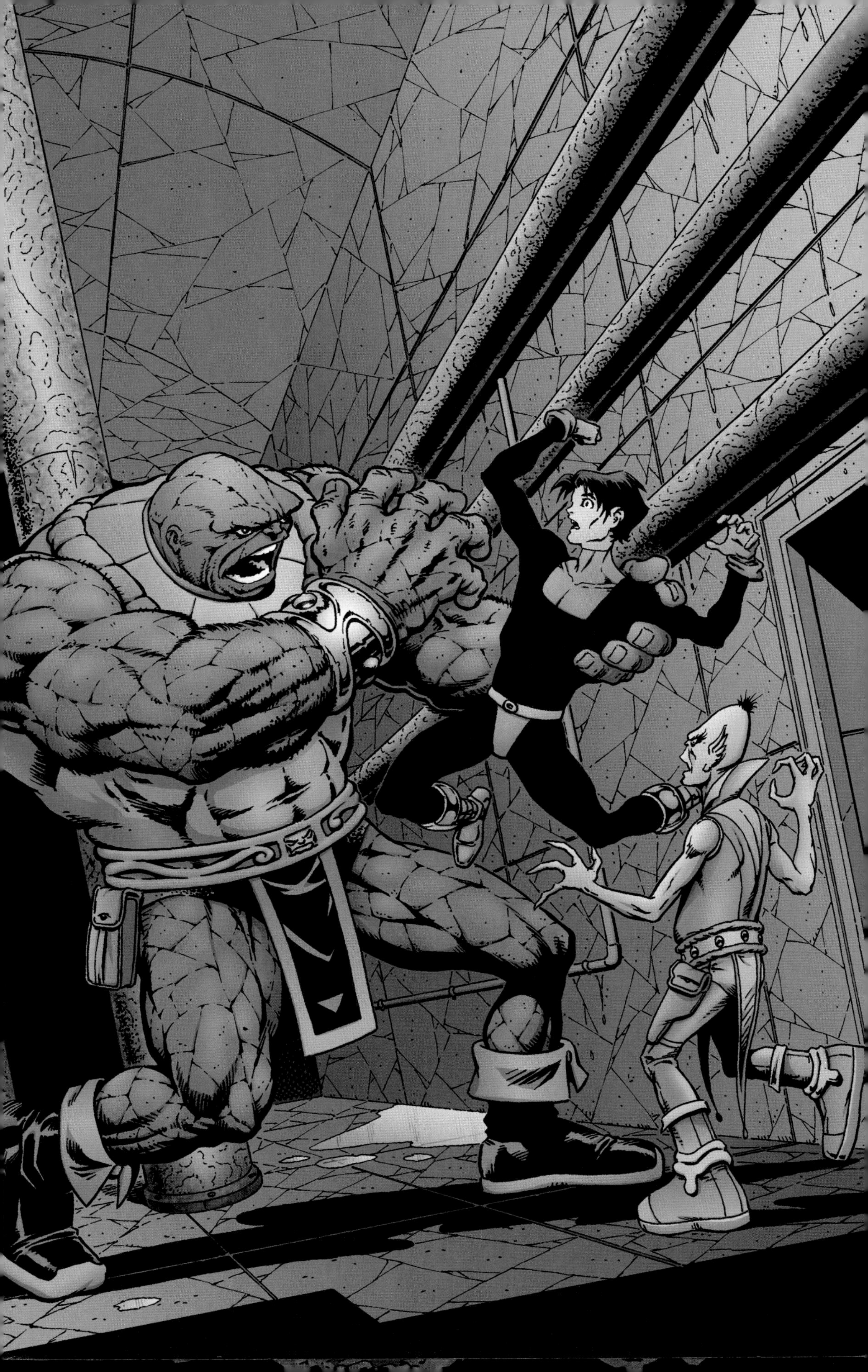

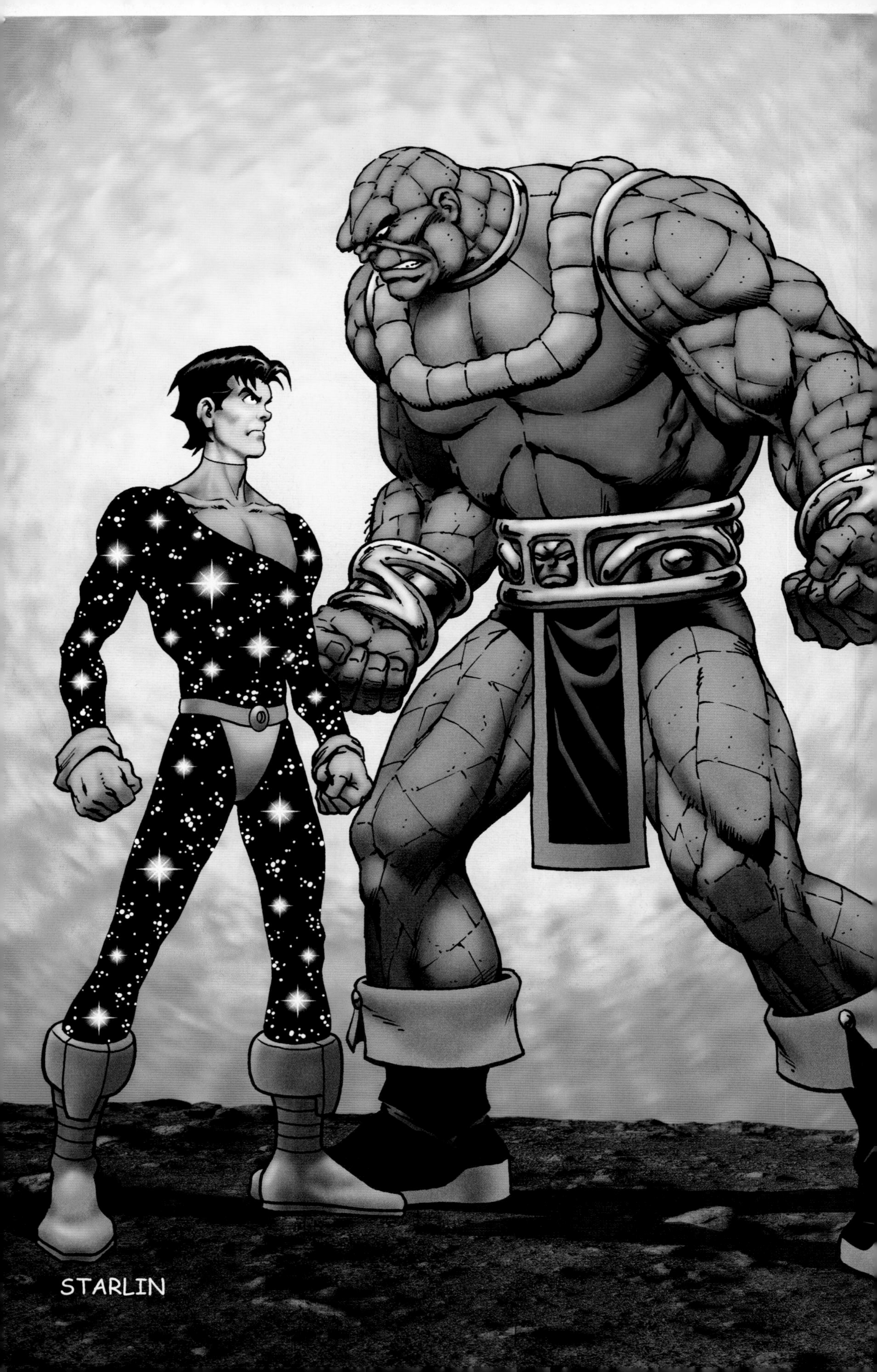
STARLIN

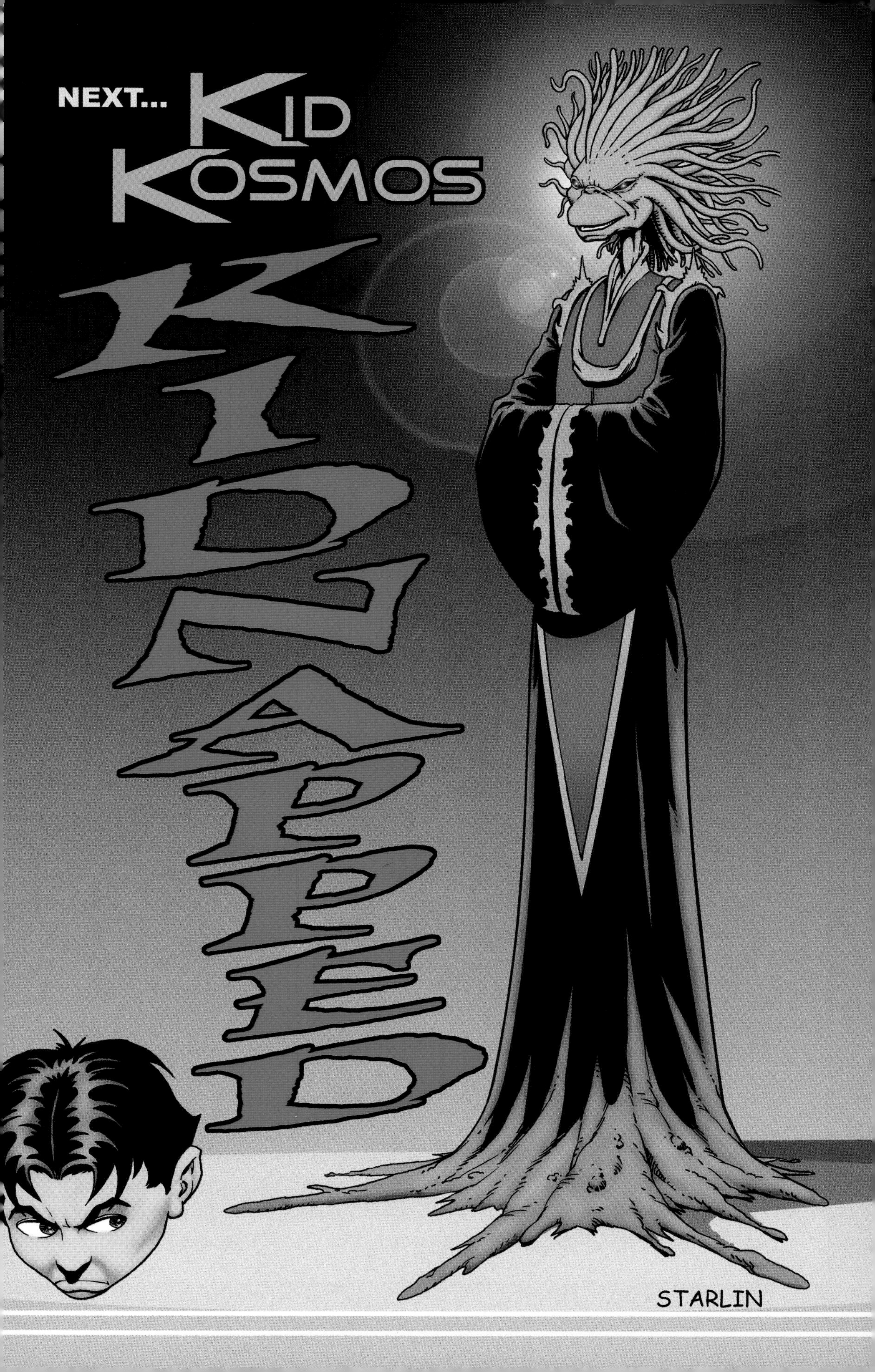
NEXT... KID KOSMOS
KIDNAPPED
STARLIN

Born James P. Starlin, on October 9th, 1949 in Detroit Michigan, Jim was educated in a Parochial (Catholic) grade school and public high school. He served in the U.S. Navy, 1968-71, as a photographer's mate and then started at Marvel Comics in 1972, and has been working on and off with comics ever since. His credits include Amazing Spider-Man, Avengers, Batman, Batman: The Cult, Batman Family, 'Breed, Brute, Captain Marvel, Cosmic Guard, Cosmic Odyssey, Creepy, Daredevil, Daredevil/Black Widow: Abattoir, Darklon The Mystic, DC Comics Presents, Death of Captain Marvel, Detective, Doctor Strange, Dreadstar, Eerie, Epic Illustrated, Fear, Fighting American, Gilgamesh II, Hardcore Station, Heavy Metal, Heroes Against Hunger, Heroes for Hope, Hellboy's Weird Tales, House of Secrets, Incredible Hulk, Infinity Abyss, Infinity Crusade, Infinity Gauntlet, Infinity War, Iron Man, Legion of Superheroes, Marvel Spotlight, Marvel Team-Up, Marvel Two-in-One, Master of Kung Fu, Omac, The Price, Punisher, Rampaging Hulk, Silver Surfer, Silver Surfer/Warlock: Resurrection, Spaceknights, Special Marvel Edition, Star*Reach, Strange Tales, Supreme, Sword of Sorcery, Thanos Quest, Thor, Unity 2000, Warlock, Warlock and the Infinity Watch, Warlord, The Weird, and Wyrd: The Reluctant Warrior, The End, Thanos, "Luna Moth" in Michael Chabon Presents: The Amazing Adventures of the Escapist, and most recently DC Comics' Mystery in Space. Jim also co-wrote four novels with Daina Graziunas: Among Madmen, Lady El, Pawns (serialized in Dreadstar) and Thinning the Predators (released in paperback as Predators). He remains a co-founder of Electric Prism, a software design, new media company in Woodstock, NY.   For more information on Jim Starlin go to **www.starlin.com.**